THE RAF
AIR SEA RESCUE
SERVICE
1918–1986

THE RAF AIR SEA RESCUE SERVICE 1918–1986

Jonathan Sutherland and Diane Canwell

Pen & Sword
AVIATION

First published in Great Britain in 2005 by
Pen & Sword Aviation
an imprint of
Pen & Sword Books Ltd
47 Church Street
Barnsley
South Yorkshire
S70 2AS
England

ISBN 1 84415 155 7

British Library Cataloguing-in-Publication Data
A CIP catalogue record for this book is
available from the British Library

Typeset in Palatino by
Phoenix Typesetting, Auldgirth, Dumfriesshire

Printed and bound in England by
CPI UK

Pen & Sword Books Ltd incorporates the Imprints of Pen & Sword Aviation,
Pen & Sword Maritime, Pen & Sword Military, Wharncliffe Local History,
Pen & Sword Select, Pen & Sword Military Classics and Leo Cooper.

For a complete list of Pen & Sword titles please contact
PEN & SWORD BOOKS LIMITED
47 Church Street, Barnsley, South Yorkshire, S70 2AS, England
E-mail: enquiries@pen-and-sword.co.uk
Website: www.pen-and-sword.co.uk

Dedication

Thanks Dad

Contents

Introduction

The authors are indebted to the RAF Marine Branch and in particular HMAFV *Bridport*. Had it not been for the decision to allocate the *Bridport* to the RAF in the post-war years, Corporal Coxswain 'Johnnie' Sutherland would never have met a local girl, Vera Stoodley.

More seriously, this history of the RAF marine craft, their exploits, crews and personalities, spans the years 1918 to its closure in 1986. It was a period that saw bouts of expansion and contraction of the armed services that bedevilled planners and personnel alike.

The history of the Marine Craft Section and the Air Sea Rescue Service, which in the post-war years were merged as a unified Marine Branch, encompasses periods of war and peace, punctuated by innumerable alarums and excursions. The tales of the supremely independent, individualistic, spit-and-polish-hating, webfooted RAF sailors are a testimony to their indomitable spirit. The men often risked all in their flimsy craft to save ditched crews and countless others. In wartime the crews never discriminated in their rescues; friend or foe, they always endeavoured to bring the men safely home to dry land.

The Marine Craft crews were masters of 'make do and mend'. Even in peacetime they often put to sea in craft that should have long been mothballed. In wartime, often lacking the basic ability to defend themselves, they ventured into enemy-held waters. They survived poundings from shore batteries, the unwanted attention of enemy aircraft and the ever-present fear of enemy motorboats. Regardless of weather conditions the Marine Craft Section tended to the every need of their charges: the flying boats. The Air Sea Rescue Service also continued to risk life and limb to ensure that 'the sea should not have them'.

The authors are particularly indebted to former Marine Craft Section, Air Sea Rescue and Marine Branch veterans from several decades. John Sutherland, whose service spanned the Second World War and the 1950s was the catalyst behind this book. Our thanks also go to Don Thurston, who has virtually single-handedly set up and run the excellent Marine Craft and Air Sea Rescue Museum at the Norfolk and Suffolk Aviation Museum, Flixton, Suffolk. Don served in the Far East during the war and provided much-needed assistance and photographs. Ted Shute, veteran of the Malta siege, selflessly provided us with assistance, as well as photographs from his personal collection. Owen Newlands, a post-war Marine Craft veteran who served with 1103 MCU and with the Marine Craft Section at Kormaskar provided valuable information and photographs. Thanks also go to 1950 Marine Branch veteran Rick Mortby, who managed to fill in many of the post-war holes in our research and to Jack Culham, wartime engineer on board HSL 2557. Additional assistance and encouragement were also received from Tony Overill, son of Deckhand A. G. Overill, who was captured after the German attack on HSL 108 in 1941. We would also like to thank Tony Campling for his encouragement and support through the many months of research.

Above all the authors would like to thank the thousands of unsung members of the service for their inspirational stories and deeds over the years. Whether wartime or peacetime, Marine Craft or Air Sea Rescue, this book hopefully records your sacrifices and service.

This extract from the Malta RAF newsletter *Island Wings,* 1942, sums up the spirit of the men:

The Horse and the Mule live 30 years and nothing known
of Wines and Beers;

The Goat and Sheep at 20 die and never taste of Scotch or
Rye;

The Cow drinks Water by the ton but at 18 years is mostly
done;

The Dog at 15 cashes in without the aid of Rum or Gin;

The Cat in Milk and Water soaks and then in 12 short
    years it croaks;

The modest sober bone dry Hen lays eggs for nogs and
    dies at 10;

All animals are strictly dry, they Sinless live and swiftly
    die;

But Ginful, Sinful Rum-soaked Marine Craft Section men

Survive to three score years and ten

And some of us, those mighty few,

Stay pickled till we're well passed ninety-two.

THE RAF
AIR SEA RESCUE
SERVICE
1918–1986

CHAPTER ONE

The Origins of
RAF Air Sea Rescue

At a meeting of the War Cabinet on 11 July 1917, the Prime
Minister, David Lloyd George, instructed General Jan
Christiaan Smuts (1870–1950) to investigate, report and
recommend the organisation of air units and operations. The
report and recommendations, dated 17 August 1917, was to
bring about the creation of the Royal Air Force, an independent
fighting arm, and with it the beginnings of the air sea rescue
service and the marine craft section. The proposals were to bring
down the wrath of the Admiralty and the army, who would both
have units stripped from their control. What had rankled and
alarmed the two senior services was a specific statement made
by Smuts in the report:

> The day may not be far off, when aerial operations with
> their devastation of enemy lands and destruction of indus-
> trial and populous centres on a vast scale become the
> principal operations of a war to which the older forms of
> military and naval operations may become secondary and
> subordinate.

The first use of aircraft in the British military had come with the
formation of No. 2 Company (Air Battalion) Royal Engineers on
1 April 1911. 1 April, as we will see, was to be an auspicious date
for the Royal Air Force. Shortly after the creation of No. 2
Company, a sub-committee of the Imperial Defence Committee
was formed, chaired by Lord Richard Bardon Haldane
(1856–1928), Asquith's former Lord Chancellor. Haldane was

considered to be one of the greatest war cabinet ministers, but was to be hounded out of office in 1915 after a sustained series of attacks in the media, suggesting that he had pro-German sympathies. His sub-committee looked at the provision of aviation assets and recommended the creation of a flying corps with an integral offensive arm, a naval contingent and a flying school. His proposals were to cause enormous friction between the army and the navy.

In the guise of the Air Battalion, which was authorised on 28 February 1911, the army, as we have seen, had already established an air operation, headquartered at South Farnborough. No. 1 (Airship Company) was based at South Farnborough and No. 2 (Aeroplane Company) was based at Larkhill. The bulk of the flying personnel either had flying experience or were holders of aviation certificates.

The navy had been involved with aircraft since 1908 and had their own flight-training facilities at Eastchurch, Hampshire. They would continue to operate the flying school and referred to their own air wing as the Royal Naval Air Service (RNAS). It was to be the RNAS that would prove to be the greatest stumbling block in terms of integration.

On 13 May 1912, as a direct result of Haldane's technical sub-committee recommendations, the army's Air Battalion was elevated to corps status by royal warrant. The Royal Flying Corps, Army Wing was thus created and with it a sister organisation, the Royal Flying Corps, Naval Wing. It was this duplication of the naval service that was to create immense problems between the army and the navy. The navy had absolutely no intention of relinquishing its air wing. The first head of the RFC, acting Major Fred Sykes, was faced with an uphill battle against the power of the Admiralty.

The immediate concern, from the point of view of the RFC, was the establishment of a joint army and navy school of aviation. It was situated on Salisbury Plain at Upavon, and began operations on 19 June 1912, with an establishment of 180 officers and other ranks. Understandably the situation was somewhat chaotic. The army wing of the RFC was purchasing its aircraft directly from the Royal Aircraft Factory, whilst the naval branch ordered their own aircraft from a variety of sources. Meanwhile, the navy itself was establishing a network for their own RNAS, in almost direct contravention of the principles set down by the foundation of the RFC.

By January 1914 the naval wing of the RFC had seven airships, forty land aircraft, and thirty-one seaplanes manned by 130 officers and 700 petty officers. By this stage they had established operational seaplane bases on the Isle of Grain in Kent, Felixstowe in Suffolk, Cromarty on the Moray Firth and Calshot on the Solent. The establishment of Calshot was significant as this would become the future home of the Royal Air Force sailors.

The Admiralty was still agitating and lobbying for approval to make the RNAS a separate service. The intense pressure paid off and on 26 June 1914, just over a month before the outbreak of the First World War, approval was given. On 1 July 1914 all the personnel and assets of the RFC (Naval Wing) were transferred to the RNAS. At a stroke the RNAS had now acquired over seventy aircraft (with a further forty on order), naval air stations, seven airships and a seaplane carrier.

Operationally, the RFC and the RNAS at the beginning of the First World War had two major roles. The RFC was primarily tasked with the support of the army's land operations. To this extent they would be involved in reconnaissance and artillery spotting. As far as the RNAS was concerned, they were to provide coastal defence from either land- or sea-based aircraft. The RNAS in particular required attendant marine craft and personnel to support this role. Already the two services were diverging. The RFC created squadrons that were both mobile and self-supporting, each with its own ground staff. The RNAS, covering the British Isles in terms of air defence, created wings and operated them as separate units of land- and sea-based aircraft.

When the First World War came in August 1914 the RNAS deployed the Eastchurch Wing. The former RFC (Naval Wing) and navy procurement policies meant that seven different aircraft were part of the structure of the force. They would be supported by an assortment of ground staff, including carpenters, sail-makers, joiners and blacksmiths. The rest of the RNAS was responsible for fleet reconnaissance, coastal patrolling and, of course, air defence.

On 15 August 1914 Brigadier-General Sir David Henderson

assumed command of the RFC. His successor, Hugh Montague Trenchard, who took over on 19 August 1915, already had three years' experience with the corps and his vision and drive were to reap dividends, and ultimately bring about the creation of the Royal Air Force.

Trenchard had been an army captain in the Boer War and had been severely wounded. Later he caught a crippling fever in Nigeria and was posted to a seemingly quiet staff job at the Central Flying School at Upavon in July 1912. One condition of the appointment was the ability to fly an aircraft. He quietly obtained a certificate of competence and in his official position as Station Staff Officer he set an examination, passed himself and presented himself with his wings! By 1913 he had become Assistant Commandant, but by the following year, after the commencement of hostilities, the entire Central Flying School assets and personnel were shipped over to France (by this stage sixty-three aircraft, 105 officers and some 100 vehicles). Trenchard had to start again, rebuilding the school with reserves. In August 1915 he, too, was posted to France to take up command of No. 1 Wing RFC, whilst simultaneously becoming Commander of the RFC.

Throughout the war the competition between the RFC and the RNAS, as far as resources and production output were concerned, was intense. The RFC and Trenchard faced shortages of aircraft, personnel and equipment; quite simply what was available was being snatched by the Admiralty. The RNAS was greedily pressing into service as many flying boats, seaplanes and land aircraft as possible. In particular, it had an acute need for vessels to manoeuvre and attend to their water-based aircraft. Meanwhile, in Canada, the army was instituting an important new step. The RFC (Canada) had created a new training facility on Lake Ontario and had established a Marine Craft Service. It was far in advance of what the RFC in the British Isles had managed to accomplish. The Canadian operation had around ten vessels, including a couple of armoured target boats, an ambulance launch and other launches and dinghies.

As early as 1916 moves were afoot to bring an end to the competition between the army and the navy for resources. Lord Derby was given the difficult task of forcing the services to come to an accommodation about inter-service rivalry. The navy flatly refused to cooperate and after just six weeks Derby resigned. His closing remarks were to be prophetic; he believed that an agreement would be impossible and that the RFC and the RNAS should be merged.

This was the situation in 1917 when Smuts delivered his report to the War Cabinet in August. Just the previous month the War Cabinet had indicated its desire to double the strength of both the RFC and the RNAS. The catalyst for the review Smuts had undertaken had come from a rather unexpected quarter.

On the morning of 13 June 1917 some fourteen German Gotha bombers had dropped 4 tons of explosives on the London dockland area. They were back in force three weeks later, when twenty-two Gothas hit London once more. It had become patently obvious that neither the RFC nor the RNAS could launch retaliatory attacks on German cities, nor could they protect even the capital from German raids.

By the end of 1917 the Air Force Act had passed through parliament, fought all the way by the Admiralty and the War Office. To add to the discontent in the army, the navy and Whitehall, the Air Committee was scrapped and replaced by a dedicated Air Ministry. The fight continued to rage up to – and beyond – the royal assent on 7 March 1918. Whether the army and navy liked it or not, the RFC and the RNAS would become the Royal Air Force effective from 1 April 1918 – and like it they did not.

Trenchard was appointed as the first Chief of Air Staff (CAS), but as a result of his supposed inflexibility and the machinations (as he saw it) of the politicians, he resigned before the RAF officially came into being. He would, however, return.

Still fighting a rearguard action, the Admiralty lost control, at a stroke, of the vast resources it had built up in a few short years. The RNAS, at the time of the handover, amounted to around 67,000 personnel, 2,949 aircraft of varying types, 103 airships and some 126 air stations.

A significant event for the future exploits of the RAF at sea was the creation of the Marine Craft Section (MCS) on 12 April 1918. The first Senior Officer for Marine Equipment was Lieutenant Colonel G. R. A. Holmes. He was joined by four other officers, including Captain W. E. G. Beauforte-Greenwood (a former lieutenant in the Royal Navy Volunteer Reserve, RFC

captain and later a flight lieutenant in the RAF). The other three
senior officers at the time were Acting Majors A. W. Farrar, H.
Eves and W. B. Sinclair.

As far as the bulk of the former RFC and RNAS personnel was
concerned, little had changed. Officially a new rank structure
was introduced, but the old RFC and RNAS rank descriptions
were still used for at least another year. The RNAS had been
supplied with both navy blue and khaki uniforms, with
accompanying naval insignia. The RFC had their own khaki
uniforms, clearly of army heritage, with Sam Browne belts,
knee-length boots and epaulettes. The former Royal Engineers
were similarly attired and for some time, given the fact that the
war was not over, the issue of uniforms and adaptation to
existing uniforms remained haphazard.

The RAF eventually adopted the now familiar blue-grey
uniform (which was actually adopted as a result of the availability of a large cancelled export order of serge), but the largely
ex-naval MCS found it wholly inappropriate for their work. The
material made them hot, sticky and itchy in the summer and stiff
in the colder months. The serge soaked up seawater and the
brass buttons quickly acquired verdigris. The cheese-cutter cap
tended to disappear into the water when there was the slightest
of breezes and had to be held in place with a chinstrap. The
official cap badge of the RAF was an adaptation of the one used
by the RNAS, which officially (but not so described in as many
words until 1947) sported an eagle, but many referred to it as an
albatross.

At this stage the marine craft trades were listed as: deckhand,
driver (motor boat) and motorboat coxswain. During the last
months of the war strenuous efforts had begun to recruit volunteers to undertake training. In September 1918 the RAF listed
some eighteen captains, five lieutenants and two second
lieutenants as motorboat officers. By November 1919, there was
a reduced complement of two flight lieutenants, two pilot
officers and a solitary flying officer. In the meantime much had
changed, not least the cessation of hostilities and the return of
Trenchard.

Trenchard returned to the post of CAS on 11 January 1919.
The war was over, but the battle against the army and the navy
had never really ceased. The War Office and the Admiralty were

amongst the most vociferous in trying to return to pre-war norms and take back the control of the aircraft and personnel they had lost. They did not succeed, but, the fledgling RAF, in its peacetime role, dropped strength from 27,333 officers to just 1,246 and from 263,837 other ranks to 36,608.

Trenchard was determined to establish the separate identity of the RAF and began a root and branch transformation of the service. On 1 August 1919 the new rank structure came into force; it was distinctly RAF, with rank names liberally lifted from both the army and the navy. 'Warrant officer' was of naval origin, whilst 'sergeant' and 'corporal' were taken straight from the army. A significant difference saw the army rank of private being replaced by aircraftman.

Trenchard, Holmes, and ultimately Beauforte-Greenwood, were faced with the very fundamental question of knowing what assets they now controlled. Whilst the process of converting men and equipment into their RAF personae was underway (including a vast renumbering exercise), a full inventory was required. Holmes needed to know the type, state and number of the craft he had under his command and, above all, whether or not he had the personnel to man them. He had estimated that the MCS had anything from between 300 and 500 vessels of varying types, both powered and non-powered. Beauforte-Greenwood's inventory, after having visited all the marine craft bases, suggested the figure was 323. Of these around 50 per cent were serviceable, but some bases had barely 10 per cent of their craft capable of being put to sea. Neglect during the latter stages of the RNAS's existence was a major contributory factor, but equally there was a distinct lack of trained personnel. Holmes suggested that of the 323 craft only 150 should remain in service and the remainder should be scrapped as surplus to requirements (and indeed the Marine Craft Section's ability to man them). However, the Air Ministry's information indicated that they had closer to 423 craft available.

Holmes was also required to make an estimate of the peacetime requirements of the MCS. Officially the wartime establishment had been estimated at 551 marine craft. Holmes suggested that 367 craft would be needed and just fewer than 2,500 men. He wanted seventy-three craft to deal with flying boats, thirty-two capable of putting out to sea, ninety-two docking lighters, eighteen aircraft ferries and half a dozen of both kite balloon vessels and compass barges.

To add to the confusion, it became clear that around fifty sundry vessels had been loaned to the RNAS by the Admiralty. Most of them were motorboats (variously 20–40 ft (6–12m) long) and the RAF returned around twenty-five of them. The navy itself had in its possession a number of motorboats that, on paper, now belonged to the RAF. These craft were being carried on larger vessels. The navy suggested that they remain there but be manned by RAF personnel. The simple expedient was to transfer them to the navy.

When Beauforte-Greenwood's inventory arrived on Holmes's desk in the autumn of 1920, a peacetime establishment compromise had finally been reached. It was suggested that 191 powered craft, plus seventy-one non-powered craft, would serve for the time being as the preferred strength of the MCS.

Gradually,during 1920, the exact nature and duties of the MCS had begun to become clear. The Air Ministry required it to handle seaplanes when afloat and to take responsibility for their landing areas. The vast majority of seaplanes at this time were converted land aircraft, simply fitted with hollow floats. There were also some flying boats (essentially designed so that the lower part of the fuselage operated like the hull of a vessel). Both the seaplanes and the flying boats were difficult to manoeuvre in water close to the shore, as they were apt to be blown this way and that in the wind, as a result of their lightweight construction. The aircraft were also constructed of wood and fabric, making it essential that they were taken out of the water at the earliest opportunity, to prevent them from becoming waterlogged and difficult to fly.

The MCS was also made responsible for the creation and maintenance of seaplane and marine craft buoys and moorings. Servicing was needed at six-monthly intervals. Systems and accountability were also put in place to ensure that the section maintained a complete inventory and that the current state of each vessel was noted. Gradually, a further system was also introduced to create a more logical means by which each of the vessels could be identified, although it was to be some years before this systematic numbering system was applied to all the craft.

Of the greatest significance was another Air Ministry order of 1920. The MCS was given the role of ensuring that a vessel was available whenever aircraft were flying over the sea. A motorboat was required either to be on station or to be ready to get underway, in case an aircraft got into difficulties and had to ditch in the sea. The first references to what would become universally known as 'standby flying' (SBF) and 'crash kits' were detailed. The standby motorboats were required to carry saws for both wood and metal, wire-cutters, axes, crowbars and grappling irons. Clearly the intention was that they should be capable of performing air sea rescues, despite the fact that the Air Sea Rescue Service as such was not created until 1941.

The Air Ministry gave specific instructions, a standard that would provide the blueprint for air sea rescue operations during the Second World War and after:

At all units where a large boat or seaplane flying is carried out, or at any other unit which is provided with motorboats where overseas flying is carried out, a motorboat will be detailed to stand-by in case of any accident occurring while flying is in progress. This boat will either be under way in the flying area or standing by at the pier. If standing by at the pier, the engine will be run for a few minutes before flying starts and at least once every hour in the summer and every half-hour in the winter.

Sixty years later the basic principles of the availability of a motorboat and the equipment carried would remain familiar to RAF personnel in the service. As significant as detailing the additional role for the MCS was the instruction to make vital alterations to the service's 35–40 ft (11–12m) motorboats. Henceforth, motorboats detailed for standby duties would carry two 6 ft 1½ in (1.87 m) stretchers; the RAF launches were also to be seagoing ambulances for downed crews.

By the early 1920s the bulk of the work carried out by the RAF Marine Craft Section was confined to the relatively protected inshore areas. Many of the volunteers lacked sea experience and seasickness was common. Navigation skills were also rudimentary, which made the section reluctant to venture into the open seas. The primary concern, for the time being, was to get to grips with the inshore hazards, the shipping channels, tides and sandbanks. The section would rarely be called upon to deal with problems at night; night flying was initially unknown and the rudimentary aircraft used by the RAF only ever ventured into the skies on days when visibility was good and there were no strong winds. Some crews, a hard core of men, had come from the RNAS and provided an experienced nucleus, but the general level of competence was not high, and manpower was still well below the recommended levels suggested, some 2,086.

Training facilities were established at Smoogroo, Shetlands, Gosport, Hampshire and Marske, Yorkshire. Lee-on-Solent and Calshot were being used as cooperation bases by the RAF and naval units. Also at Gosport was the Torpedo Development Squadron, which was used by the MCS for training in torpedo recovery operations. The Marine Aircraft Experimental Establishment was based on the Isle of Grain, Kent, where four motorboats were stationed, in addition to several other vessels.

The section had also established a presence at several seaplane bases: Donibristle, Dover, Dundee, Felixstowe, Leuchars, Plymouth and Portland. Abroad, there were bases in Malta and Alexandria. There were also several detachments operating with naval vessels and a single Kelvin at the airship base at Pulham, Norfolk.

The men often found themselves working long and hard hours. The pay was not generous, but recruits were happy to accept the relative financial security of the service in the increasingly difficult economic climate. Many were former members of the merchant service; others were civilians with experience of and an aptitude for marine craft. The service attracted boatwrights, deckhands, fishermen and those who had operated on coasters and harbour ferry vessels.

MCS detachments now tended to consist of a coxswain and a fitter/driver/petrol (F/DP), both considered to be technical posts. The remainder of the crew were deckhands, classed as non-technical tradesmen. The working uniform was khaki with impractical leather buttons. During this time only the 'walking out' uniform was RAF blue. Most of the men were issued with heavy boots.

In 1921 the Marine Craft Training Section, based at Gosport, was shifted to Haslar. In the following year it was again moved to a spit of land at the junction of Southampton Water and the Solent, RAF Calshot. It remained here on and off until the winding up of the Marine Branch in 1986, and it became the main focus for all future recruits, no matter where they would subsequently be transferred to.

In the early days, this Section tended to deal with young men in the eighteen to nineteen age group. They would spend a period at Calshot then be transferred to an operational unit. At Calshot they would learn the ins and outs of the motorboats, and they might return there for additional training as required. MCS training was, of course, preceded by a stint at RAF Uxbridge. Here the recruits were introduced to the joys of parades, marching, inspections, physical training, weapons training and RAF procedures. When the recruit finally arrived at the Marine Craft Training School the focus was on how he was to carry out his duties, both aboard the vessel and onshore. Discipline was strict and recruits were required to sit a written examination at each stage of the training, in addition to displaying their practical abilities to do the job. Once they had managed to pass all the examinations, they became Aircraftmen First Class.

By 1924 a standard motorboat crew would consist of a corporal coxswain, a couple of deckhands and an F/DP. Standard duties would be to ensure that any flotsam or jetsam was cleaned away before an aircraft left and to be available should the aircraft run into difficulties. In time and subject to vacancies, the crew could expect promotion to corporal second class coxswain, then sergeant, flight sergeant, moving up to warrant officer first class coxswain.

Even at this early stage, officers would often complain about the apparent scruffiness of the men. This was an MCS tradition, not for contrary reasons, but borne out of the practicalities of the work. Quite simply, the uniforms never really stood up to the punishment they received. A combination of sea salt and sun, constant soakings and work in all weathers took a heavy toll of the uniforms. In no time at all, the colour was bleached out and the stitching in particular turned white.

By the mid-1920s the training course at Calshot had been extended to around three months. Signalling, using both sema-phore and lamps, was included (radios were not yet fitted to the vessels). All manner of paperwork was required, including an intimate knowledge of rope-breaking strains and knots. Rigging, serving canvas and dealing with moorings was also covered. The trainees were also instructed in boat construction to help them carry out emergency repairs. First aid was also essential, and this session was led by the station medical officer. Finally, of course, there was instruction in all manner of boat work, including rowing, sailing, sculling, handling vessels alongside a pier, towing aircraft, refuelling, the use of anchors, taking soundings with a lead line, the use of a compass and the art of mooring to buoys.

In 1924 the Marine Aircraft Experimental Establishment (MAEE) moved to Felixstowe from the Isle of Grain. Felixstowe had been an important RNAS aircraft base during the First World War. The MAEE had an enormous mobile crane, which was used to lift flying boats out of the water and deposit them on cradles railed on the jetty. The Titan crane, as it was known, was later used to lift and drop flying boats during impact tests. Naturally there was a need for an MCS presence there. As the aircraft became more sophisticated, the RAF and the MCS realised they would need faster vessels, capable of carrying more injured crew members. The impetus for change came from an unexpected source; the Schneider Trophy Trials. Back in 1912, Jacques Schneider, the French Under-Secretary for Air, suggested a competition that would develop the range and reliability of flying boats. His vision of the future saw flying boats connecting the world in a network of routes, primarily for passenger travel. In the sixteen years until his death in 1928, Schneider would see enormous technological advances in both engines and airframes, which would transform the lightweight biplanes into sleek and fast monoplanes. Far from fulfilling his vision of reliability and range, however, the trophy was won and lost on speed. This factor directly influenced the development of the MCS's launches and emphasised the need for the RAF to develop high-speed rescue launches and services.

In 1927, Squadron Leader L. Slater, AFC, and his RAF high-speed flight team, which were to compete in the 1927 race in Venice, spent a fruitful two months operating out of Calshot. The MCS provided facilities, vessels and crews from Calshot, Cattewater, Felixstowe and Lee-on-Solent. Whilst its seaplane lighters and other vessels were useful, it became abundantly clear that the ex-naval seaplane tenders, Kelvins and other vessels detailed for rescue standby were woefully inadequate. Their speed and capacity to deal with the injured crew members was limited, and an interim solution was quickly needed. In the event, they decided that they needed to borrow three Thorneycroft 54 ft (17 m) coastal motorboats (CMB) from the navy. These had originally been designed as fast attack boats and they were capable of reaching 35 knots in calm conditions. They were not ideal, however, as their Y 12 petrol engines did have the unhappy habit of catching fire when they were started up; indeed one of the CMBs was lost in this way. They also lacked an astern gearbox, making them not only difficult to manoeuvre, but also difficult to slow down.

After an eventful two months, Slater and his pilots, Flight Lieutenant S. M. Kinkhead, Flight Lieutenant S. N. Webster and Flight Lieutenant E. O. Worsley, headed off to Venice. Webster won the event with a speed of 281 mph (452 kph) and Worsley came second with 275 mph (442 kph); they had both flown the Supermarine (S5). It was then decided that Calshot should host the Schneider Trophy race in 1929.

Not only did the British win the Schneider Trophy again at Calshot, this time with R. J. Mitchell's Supermarine S6 (1,920 hp, achieving an average speed of 328 mph (528 kph)), but it also saw the influence of a man who had made his name during the First World War. In 1922 an architect's clerk with no previous military service, by the name of J. H. Ross, had presented himself to the RAF recruiting office at Covent Garden in London. During his medical examination he had great trouble explaining the presence of severe scars on his buttocks. He claimed he was twenty-eight, and failed the medical examination. Winston Churchill and the Secretary of State for Air, Hugh Trenchard, pulled strings, mainly because Trenchard was aware of the man and knew that he was actually thirty-three.

Ross began his basic training at RAF Uxbridge, where he found the physical side of the training course extremely difficult. None the less he passed his examination at the end of the course and was posted to RAF Farnborough. Here he managed to draw attention to himself by not fitting in very well and being accused of mocking and abusing his officers. In 1923, after the *Daily*

Express revealed his true name, he had to leave the RAF. Trenchard offered him a commission, but he turned it down. In truth, now his name was known, no officer would accept the man, such was his prestige and reputation.

Ross became T. E. Shaw, enlisted as a private in the Tank Corps and trained at Bovington Camp. He soon rented Clouds Hill Cottage to avoid having to live in the barracks; his visitors included Thomas Hardy and George Bernard Shaw.

In 1925 he met Trenchard and in the August of that year, at the age of thirty-seven, he became an aircraftman second class and proceeded to RAF Uxbridge for his induction course. Training was waived and Shaw was transferred to the Cranwell Cadet College, Lincolnshire. He settled in well and made no real attempt to disguise his true identity. In 1927 he was posted to Karachi. The media was intrigued when he travelled to the North-west Frontier and in September 1928 another series of speculating headlines in the *London Evening News* and the *Sunday Express* suggested he was on a secret spying mission, speculation which prompted the RAF to recall him from India.

By now, of course, everyone was aware that Ross/Shaw was in fact none other than T. E. Lawrence, Lawrence of Arabia, the man who had arguably single-handedly wrested the bulk of the Middle East from the Ottoman Turks during the First World War. He was an Oxford graduate, a diplomat and the holder of the DSO.

Lawrence boarded the SS *Rajputana* in January 1929 and was met at Plymouth by Wing Commander Sydney Smith, the commanding officer of RAF Cattewater. Lawrence had met him in Cairo and he managed to persuade Smith to appoint him as the Cattewater Orderly Room Clerk.

Lawrence corresponded directly with Trenchard on a number of issues regarding the service. The RAF ultimately adopted all his suggestions for improvement. These included: changes to weekend passes, which elapsed at midnight on Fridays instead of when the men would be expected to report for duty on the Monday morning; officers wearing caps in the men's mess; the frequency of kit inspections; the requirement for officers to carry walking-out canes and for the men to wear bayonets at church parades; and the haphazard rules about wearing civilian clothing off duty. Another suggestion was to change the name of

RAF Cattewater to RAF Mount Batten, as he felt that Cattewater was an ugly name.

Lawrence found himself detached to RAF Calshot during the period of the Schneider Trophy Challenge in 1929. One of the tenders at Calshot was a US-constructed speedboat, a Biscayne Baby, which Major Colin Cooper had lent to Smith and Lawrence. After giving it an overhaul, they christened it *Biscuit*. Work continued on the little craft until April 1930 and Lawrence was often seen patrolling around the Plymouth Sound area. Smith and Lawrence were therefore at hand at Calshot not only to see Britain win the Schneider Trophy in April 1929, but also to experience the limitations of the launches being used by the MCS.

Lawrence's insights into the daily routines of an MCS crew member continued and he was part of the duty crew that attended a tragic crash of the R101, which caused the deaths of forty-seven people in October 1930. He also witnessed another air sea rescue mission on 4 February 1931 when a Blackburn Iris seaplane crashed into Plymouth Sound a short distance from RAF Mount Batten. Lawrence was amongst the first of the MCS to reach the crash site, diving into the water and helping to pull out six people; six others had been killed. Both of these incidents had proved that the motorboats (Brooke built), the Kelvins and the other rescue launches were not up to the task. They were simply slow, it was difficult to get sea-laden survivors into them and the stretcher adaptations were insufficient. In addition to these problems it was also difficult to administer first aid on the craft.

The lobbying of Smith, Lawrence and Beauforte-Greenwood at the Air Ministry and the Admiralty was about to pay off. The decision was reluctantly taken to engage the services of the British Powerboat Company, specifically Hubert Scott-Paine, to come up with a solution to the launch problems.

On 19 February 1931, at Stokes Bay, seaplane tender RAF 200 was put through its trials. The design was revolutionary and the vessel came through with flying colours.

CHAPTER TWO

The Arrival of the Launches

By the late 1920s many of the launches being used by the RAF were former RNAS craft and upwards of ten years old. The vast majority were 35 ft (11 m) launches that had been built by Brooke Marine of Lowestoft (65 hp engines). There were also many Kelvins, the 50 ft (15 m) 45 hp craft that ran on paraffin (but needed a petrol start). In 1928 the Admiralty began casting about for replacements on behalf of the RAF.

The British Powerboat Company's (BPBC) seaplane tender RAF 200, which was given its first sea trials on 19 February 1931, was the first craft specifically designed for the RAF. For the trial it was fitted with a pair of Brooke 100 hp, six-cylinder engines and managed to make nearly 23 knots. The results of the trials were very promising and it was decided to carry out a further range of trials and subsequent modifications at RAF Mount Batten. Mount Batten was a good choice; not only did its location help to allay the fears of Hubert Scott-Paine that his competitors would be able to watch the developments, but also Smith and Lawrence were there. Beauforte-Greenwood was well aware of the support and suggestions that they could offer: they were as convinced as he was that the new design would ultimately be exactly what the RAF needed. Also present at Mount Batten was another advocate of the new design, Flight Lieutenant Jinman. He had been at the Solent trials of the RAF 200 and was an engineering officer with the 209th Flying Boat Squadron.

The trials team at Mount Batten consisted of Lawrence (although officially an aircraftman, he was clearly in charge of activities), Corporal Coxswains Heward and Staines and a fitter,

Corporal Bradbury. Initially the four men were an attachment to the BPBC guards at Hythe for the orientation on the RAF 200. Lawrence was clearly in his element; he drove himself, the other three men and the seaplane tender very hard, and by the end of April the first 50 hours' running time had been clocked up. Lawrence wrote in his report:

> The boat has been found to behave extremely well in all weathers including broken 19 ft [5.8 m] seas. In one run up-channel from Falmouth to Plymouth against a strong south-east wind and in breaking water she only shipped solid sea once; an average of 12 mph [19 kph] was achieved.

Lawrence was delighted with the overall performance. He had discovered that the slope of the vessel below the wheelhouse meant that it could glide through the water, unlike most speed-boats. In short, he believed that the RAF 200 was ideal and would definitely do the job required of it by the MCS. One issue remained to be resolved: the question of the engines. It was considered that the Brooke 100 hp (petrol) units were past their best in terms of design. Hubert Scott-Paine contacted Henry Meadows, who was based in the Midlands and was already producing 100 hp engines for Vickers tanks. This meant more and more trials and Lawrence and Bradbury remained on attached duty at Hythe to help oversee the installation of the new engines. The trials of the new version of the seaplane tender were completed in June 1931. The RAF immediately ordered a further eight of the craft and the RAF 200, together with Lawrence, transferred to Mount Batten for further tests, then on to Calshot so the Marine Craft Training Section (MCTS) could use it.

The new trials and tests incorporated another use: as a towing vehicle for practice bombing targets. The RAF 200 excelled at this job. In the past the MCS launches had proved to be too slow to simulate attacks on real vessels. Lawrence continued to run practice bombing trials using his own vessel, *Biscuit*, after the RAF 200 had been sent to Calshot. Again he was instrumental in establishing the standard practice for target moving, known as the 'splash targets', a system that would be used by the RAF for some years to come.

Around October 1931 Lawrence went back to Hythe to help oversee the production and trials of the next eight seaplane tenders. Unfortunately a fire at the yard destroyed all but one of the craft, the ST 201, whilst they were in production. None the less, the ST 201 was completed and sent with Lawrence to Mount Batten, with the purpose of training crews there in its performance and handling. The following month saw another development, this time in planing dinghies. Lawrence was sent back to Hythe to help with the testing of a new engine, designed to be used for the RAF's 16 ft (4.9 m) vessel. The engine, a Power-Meadows 8/28 would prove to be a considerable improvement.

Essentially the new vessel, known as an inboard planing dinghy, was designed to replace the wide variety of pulling dinghies used by the MCS. The pulling dinghies were used between moored aircraft and other vessels, essentially rowing boats. The MCS was also using old 35 ft (11 m) launches for similar jobs. The new inboard planing dinghy could do all of these jobs. The RAF tended to use a variety of different boat engines, largely converted truck engines, but the new vessel, with the Power-Meadows 8/28, was capable of just over 18 knots by May 1932. Lawrence attended its trials that month. In January 1932 Lawrence had thrown his attention into the ST 202, which had just been completed. It had a new throttle and gearshift system and over the space of a few weeks many prob-lems had to be attended to, by both Lawrence and the BPBC specialists. Lawrence wrote an instruction booklet, which was printed in March 1932, *The 200 Class Royal Air Force Seaplane Tender*. Although it was written in his usual literary style, it was to prove an invaluable instruction manual for crew members. Newspaper reports (*The Times*, April 1932) also told of Lawrence's voyage in the ST 201 from Calshot to RAF Donibristle in the Firth of Forth.

The summer of 1932 saw the testing of a flying boat refuelling version of the 16 ft (4.9 m) planing dinghy. The test craft, with Lawrence at the helm, almost sunk in the Solent *en route* from Dover. The vessel struggled in difficult waters, and ultimately gave up the ghost after being holed in the mouth of Newhaven harbour. Luckily a pinnace was escorting Lawrence and she managed to tow her to safety.

With work on the armoured target boat (ATB) well underway

in 1932, it was an exciting time for the MCS, which seemed to have turned a corner and was now on the verge of having a range of purpose-built boats for the majority of its work. The ATB, under the guidance of Lawrence, Beauforte-Greenwood, Scott-Paine and a Captain Nicholson for the Hadfield's Armour Plating Company, had been developed into two prototypes that undertook trials in the Solent. The vessels could do around 30 knots and were capable of withstanding the smoke bombs dropped by RAF aircraft (the crew had steel helmets and gas masks for additional protection).

The two prototypes were sent with Lawrence to RAF Bridlington for further trials. By the beginning of 1933 Lawrence was again thinking of his future. He wanted to return to anonymity, particularly after the lurid media headlines regarding his involvement in the ATBs had proclaimed: 'Colonel Lawrence is a Human Target'. Lawrence applied to buy his release from the RAF on 28 February 1933 and sadly began his preparations for a return to civilian life. However, he still very much wanted to be involved in the evolution of MCS vessels, so Beauforte-Greenwood organised a transfer to RAF Felixstowe. Here he would be able to work with Jinman at the MAEE. His new role would be the development of high-speed rescue boats and salvage vessels.

The next two years were as eventful as ever. Lawrence was relentless in his pursuit of the modernisation of the MCS and the acquisition of new vessels that could actually do the job and were capable of what he believed were the challenges ahead. He helped Scott-Paine to convince the Admiralty of the need for high-speed patrol craft and, most notably, the development of the high speed launch, HSL 100, which would become the very first high-speed, offshore rescue vessel. He was also deeply involved in the development of a high-speed planing craft that was subsequently patented by Edward Spur in 1938. He had meetings with Spur at the BPBC yard and the resulting craft, the *Empire Day*, bore the inscription 'To L of A à compte' (to Lawrence of Arabia on account). Unfortunately, by the time it was made public, Lawrence had already been dead for three years.

On 2 February 1935 Lawrence finally left the RAF for the last time. On 13 May, riding from Bovington Camp to Clouds Hill

Cottage, he swerved to avoid two boys on bicycles. He was badly injured and after lying in a coma for six days died at the age of 46, on 19 May. One of his pallbearers was Corporal Bradby of the MCS. As it transpired, it may have been the end of an era for the MCS generally, but a new one was dawning that would springboard the service into the public eye in a few short years.

The mid- to late 1930s proved to be an important time for the section. On 18 August 1933, the B1 (671), an 18 ft (5.5 m) bomb loading dinghy, was given its sea trials. Lawrence had been there and the craft had achieved an unladen speed of nearly 16 knots. The specification for this vessel required it to be capable of carrying two 500 lb and two 250 lb bombs. When the crew was added, the vessel could make a reasonable 7.5 knots. When it had delivered its load it could then make nearly 17 knots.

On 10 May 1932 a refuelling scow was tested, built by the Cowes firm of Saunders-Roe Ltd. The craft was some 34 ft (10.4 m) long, probably powered by a pair of 5 hp engines. It was not a great success and only trialled in good weather, with empty tanks. Prior to that, J. S. White provided thirteen refuelling boats between 1930 and 1931. These had two 40 hp engines and were 40 ft (12 m) long. The refuelling vessels were made by a variety of manufacturers and upwards of 139 45 ft (13.7 m) vessels were used, either with two Scammel petrol engines (56 hp) or 49 hp Ford engines.

Much of the development of the MCS's vessels and procedures were driven by need. As the 1920s passed and the service entered the 1930s, it became increasingly apparent that the floatplanes they had been dealing with in the past were just that, a thing of the past. Increasingly flying boats and amphibians replaced them. In truth they were easier to deal with, as their higher wings made it simpler to get alongside. Not only were they fitted with better mooring equipment, but the metal skins meant that there was no longer any rush to get them out of the water. Whilst the floatplanes had been light and susceptible to winds and currents, the newer flying boats were heavier and much more cumbersome. They had a far greater range and because of their size, weight and technical superiority they could be flown at night.

This meant that the MCS had to modify its standby procedures. Night flying meant that they had to prepare landing and take-off areas in the dark. This required the motorboat crews to set flare paths in the direction of the wind; the floating flames would be set on dan buoys. This gave way to setting out 'pram dinghies' with oil lamps and later a trial of battery-powered lights. In high winds they would steam upwind and hold the lights in place with a string.

The new flying boats, with increased crew numbers, fuel needs and bomb-carrying capacity, also meant that the MCS needed better bomb scows and refuelling vessels. The space needed for landing and take-off was extended, requiring the MCS to check and clear larger spaces of water for flotsam and jetsam.

Prior to 1937 the largest flying boat in the RAF inventory was the Blackburn Iris, which had a crew of five and carried up to eight passengers. This set a definite limit on what would be the worst-case scenario in the event of an accident. The introduction of the Short Sunderland, however, meant a crew of thirteen and the capacity to carry around sixteen passengers. Clearly the MCS reserve provision would be woefully inadequate. The introduction of the RAF 200 class bridged the gap well. It was such a success that not only did the last one not roll off the production line until 1940 (ST 324), but its construction lived on until at least the 1960s.

The Scott-Paine RAF 200 series carried a four-man crew and was capable of achieving speeds of up to 25 knots. It was 37 ft 6 in (11.4 m) long, with an 8 ft 8 in (2.6 m) beam, managing an average speed of 22 knots, and could operate for around five hours. What was remarkable about this vessel was the fact that it was not only robust, but was also constructed using the hard-chine method. This meant that the keel, the stern and the primary fore and aft members were made of solid pine (Columbia). The main frames and the outer skin were constructed from African mahogany, whilst Canadian rock elm was used for the deck and the chine strakes. The side planking was equally unique as it meant that the mahogany planks were fitted diagonally to the keel and chine, with oiled and doped calico sandwiched between the planks. The overall construction, particularly the diagonal planking, borrowed much of the pioneering work that had been carried out by the designer Linton Hope back in 1916.

The Kelvins had also proved to be unsuitable in the long run. The MCS needed a purpose-built boat that combined the jobs of the Kelvin (mainly towing and the handling seaplanes) with other tasks, including torpedo recovery and the retrieval of moored targets. It was clear that flying boats were perfectly capable of air sea bombing, torpedo use and gunnery targeting. The answer seemed to lie with the pinnace. Indeed the RAF had already had experience with these since 1918, when the RNAS had handed over three steam pinnaces. The result was the general purpose (GP) pinnace, which was introduced in 1926. It was some 56 ft (17 m) long, with a beam of 11 ft 9 in (3.6 m) and a draft of just 4 ft (1.2 m). It had a Gardner 4 TS semi-diesel engine (96 hp) capable of around 10 knots. It was not ideal, as the helmsman was exposed, with only a canvas dodger for protection, and received the full blast of the engine exhaust in his face from the large funnel in front of the helm.

Some of the GP pinnaces were later fitted with McLaren 90 hp or Gardner 6L2 diesel engines. The original craft could not go astern as they only had ahead and neutral gearboxes. The fitter had to stop the engine and use a bar to ease one of the cylinders to dead centre, then restart the engine so it went in the reverse rotation direction.

In 1935, GP pinnaces P31 and P32 came into service. These were Thorneycroft-built 56 ft (17 m) vessels, with two Gardner engines capable of 12 knots. These shared the double diagonal planking of the RAF 200. They not only had an officer's cabin, but also crew quarters that incorporated a galley and a toilet. Overall the vessels could carry up to eighty passengers in the large aft hold (or floating flame paths, mooring buoys or torpedoes).

In 1938 came the development of the P33. This vessel was 60 ft (18.3 m) long and its third engine meant that it was capable of 15 knots. The officer's cabin had been shifted from near the wheelhouse to below deck and a larger wheelhouse had been constructed. Whilst all this was being developed, tested and put to use, the Marine Craft Policy Committee had radically new ideas. In 1936 they announced that new 64 ft (19.5m) HSLs were to be introduced and that motorboat officers would command them. Despite hopes that warrant officers and senior coxswains would be promoted to command them, these ranks were barred from applying and the committee began a national recruitment campaign.

Beauforte-Greenwood and Scott-Paine had worked with Lawrence on a launch of around 60–70 ft (18–21 m). The idea was that the crew could live and work on board and it would be ideal for handling seaplanes as well as rescues. In June 1935 the Admiralty, on behalf of the RAF, put out the tender. Scott-Paine had invested considerable time and money in developing the new highspeed launches and he now faced the very real prospect of his major competitors snatching the tender from under his nose. Amongst those that did compete – and ultimately fail – were Saunders-Roe, Thorneycroft, Vosper and J. S. White. They all tried to match the specification, but in truth Scott-Paine always had the advantage as he had been the main instigator in the development and, above all, he could offer better engines. He had already enlisted the business partnership of Henry Meadows and had begun adapting Napier Lion aircraft and racing boat engines to give them a better marine gearbox. The new adaptation would be sold as the Power Napier Sea Lion engine. While the RAF dithered, the Admiralty ordered two of the 60 ft (18.2 m) vessels and perhaps for the first time they had in their possession a true motor torpedo boat (MTB).

As it transpired, the RAF 100 was a basic adaptation of the 60 ft (18.2 m) motor torpedo boat. It was 64 ft (19.5 m), with a range of 500 miles (800 km) and a top speed of 35 knots, powered by three Power Napier Sea Lion engines. The engines were configured so that the centre one provided a cruise mode for the vessel, whilst the two outer ones drove the outboard propeller shafts. Using either one or all three of the engines, the RAF 100 was extremely manoeuvrable. The vessel incorporated bunks for the eight crew members and an officer's wardroom, which also doubled as a sick bay.

In May 1936, with the Royal Navy in possession of their first motor torpedo boat, the RAF's prototype highspeed launch slipped into the water at Hythe. On 23 May the RAF 100 left Southampton, bound for Grimsby via the English Channel and the North Sea. Beauforte-Greenwood was one of the men onboard and amongst those who accompanied him was a civilian substitution officer (CSO), the captain of the RAF trawler, *Cawley*, L. R. Butters, who would become the first officer to be commissioned to command an HSL. The RAF 100, with Scott-Paine at the helm, made an average speed of around 30 knots. There were no serious difficulties and the trip to and from Grimsby took a little less than twenty-five hours. Further trials were carried out on 14 July 1936 and again Scott-Paine and Beauforte-Greenwood were onboard, along with Bradbury, senior officers from RAF Manston, officials representing the War Department, a Napier representative, Squadron Leader Norrington and a representative from the Patent Log Company. At trial the vessel managed just over 36 knots, equivalent to 41 mph (66 kph). Later in the day it was retried and a speed of 45 mph (72 kph) was logged.

The Air Ministry was clearly impressed and immediately ordered Nos 101–114 to be delivered in 1937. Two additional vessels, 115 and 116 were ordered in 1938 and 117–132 in 1939. As it transpired, in its original form the RAF 100 ceased production at 121, as the remaining eleven vessels, which were due for delivery in 1941, were respecified for a later design.

The RAF set high standards for the officers who would command these new high speed launches. They needed to have Master Mariner Certificates. As a result the majority of the men were either Royal Naval Reserves or Royal Naval Volunteer Reserves. The status of the direct-entry officers was confused and, at first, unfair. Officially the new skippers were part of the Reserve of Air Force Officers (RAFO). This meant that they were not technically classed as career officers and that their commissions were not permanent. Understandably many felt aggrieved and by 1938 some of the new launch masters transferred back into either the Royal Navy or the Merchant Navy. This left the RAF with something of a dilemma and somewhat reluctantly the Air Ministry finally allowed warrant officers and senior coxswains to apply for launch master commissions.

In December 1938 Air Chief Marshall Sir E. R. Ludlow Hewitt, the Air Officer Commanding in Chief of Bomber Command, held a conference. He was perfectly aware that his force would be launching raids across the North Sea in the event of war breaking out, and he believed that his men's preparation for this task was being severely hampered by the lack of adequate air sea rescue facilities. At that time the MCS had a single high-speed launch at Donibristle, which was transferred to Blyth in 1939, one each at Felixstowe, Manston, Pembroke Dock and Tayport, and two at Calshot. The inadequacy of this provision was readily apparent. Between Tayport and Felixstowe, some 400 miles (640 km) of coast, there was not a single HSL. Nor was there cover for the west coast, Northern Ireland, Yorkshire and large parts of Scotland, from which Bomber Command was converting auxiliary squadrons for use.

In 1939 Air Vice Marshall W. Sholto-Douglas decided that thirteen high-speed launches would be needed in the Middle East. When war was declared in September 1939, there were just four overseas; the 105 was in Singapore, at RAF Seletar, the 109 in Aden, the 110 in Basra, and the 107 was sent to Kalafrana in Malta. Two more had been earmarked for Penang and Ceylon, but ultimately they were transferred to Grimsby and Great Yarmouth. In fact it would be three years before the number of launches stationed abroad was in any way adequate to deal with the demands. In the last few months before September 1939, with a useful number of former Merchant Navy officers being recruited to the RAFO, other experienced Merchant Navy deckhands were helping to fill the high-speed launch crew ranks.

In early May 1939, Flight Lieutenant Manning took 400 airmen, a stock of 250 lb bombs, two pinnaces, two refuellers and four seaplane tenders from King George V Dock in London to Alexandria, via Malta. Half of the airmen were offloaded at Malta, to join the aircraft carrier HMS *Eagle.* When the RAF depot ship *Dumana,* arrived at Alexandria the MCS established a presence that would last for another five years. Pinnaces 21 and 37 patrolled Aboukir Bay, each covering the area for a period of two weeks.

The *Dumana* was to have an eventful war. By September 1941 she was at Bathurst in West Africa. She was in Durban on 25 September 1942, where she took officers, men and marine craft to Madagascar and then she sailed, via Diego Suarez, to the Maldives, offloading equipment and supplies at Addu Atoll. She disembarked 42 Squadron personnel at Colombo on 14 October 1942 and then sailed to Bombay and then to Karachi, where she became a depot ship for 212 Squadron. She remained based under the control of 225 Group until 19 March 1943, when she was ordered to head for Bombay for a refit. By 27 April 1943 she was back in West Africa and it was planned that she would be used to accommodate flying boat personnel. In fact she operated as a transport between Bathurst and Lagos, but *en route* to Freetown on 24 December 1943 she was torpedoed and many of the MCS contingent, along with others, were lost. Later a memorial was erected near Abidjan in the Ivory Coast, where many of the bodies had been washed ashore.

On 10 May 1940 Winston Churchill, a long-time supporter of the RAF, became Prime Minister and on the very same day the Germans broke through the Ardennes, assaulting western Europe with fifty-four divisions. The Allies' situation rapidly deteriorated and despite many courageous rearguard actions, the Germans swiftly overran France. By 20 May it was clear that the British Expeditionary Force (BEF) and other Allied personnel in the vicinity of the Channel ports would need to be evacuated. It was agreed by the War Office that non-essential personnel should be evacuated immediately in order to safeguard supplies for frontline troops. With effect from 20 May, 2,000 men would need to be evacuated each day and on 22 May a further 15,000 should be made ready. Early in May 1940 the Royal Navy had begun its requisitioning of cross-channel ferries, steamers, trawlers and other vessels. Some had been converted into hospital ships, minesweepers or escorts. A list had also been drawn up of all privately owned vessels. The intention was to be able to use various harbour craft and other vessels for non-essential work, freeing up the naval vessels. Although these early preparations probably did not have anything to do with the subsequent Dunkirk evacuation, foundations were in place that would prove invaluable.

The Dunkirk evacuation, known as Operation Dynamo, began in earnest at 1857 hours on Sunday, 26 May 1940. The *Luftwaffe* had pounded Dunkirk harbour and the town; storage tanks were in flames, the quays were wrecked and only the west mole was capable of taking berthed vessels. As luck would have it, the BEF and their French allies managed to disengage from the advancing German divisions and the subsequent two-day pause in German land operations proved to be vital in evacuating many thousands of men. The speed at which the Germans had overrun France and had scattered the BEF and the

French had taken Hitler by surprise, he faced complete victory and at the crucial moment was unsure how – or even whether – to press home his advantage.

Before 26 May 1940 some 28,000 men had already been evacuated from the Channel ports of Boulogne, Dunkirk and Ostend. On the first full day of Operation Dynamo (27 May), 8,000 men made it back to Dover. Despite having been severely damaged, the east mole was put into service on 28 May. Other vessels were coming in close to the shore and taking men straight off the beaches at Malo-les-Bains, Bray Dunes and La Panne. Indeed 6,000 of the 18,000 men rescued that day were taken from these beaches. A further 50,000 were evacuated the following day, but by now the Germans had resumed offensive land operations and La Panne was no longer safe. Elements of the BEF and the French doggedly held the shrinking perimeter around Dunkirk. Adverse wind conditions prevented men from being picked up from the beach and all the while there was the constant bombing and strafing from the *Luftwaffe*. None the less, 54,000 men were lifted from Dunkirk on 30 May.

On the night of Wednesday, 29 May the MCS was put on standby to assist in the evacuation. At Calshot, one pinnace and five seaplane tenders left their moorings at 0430. HSL 120 would proceed to Dover on June 3 and return to Calshot the following day. In all some six launches, Pinnace 32, seaplane tenders 243, 254, 276, 291 and AMC 3 (which belonged to the Civil Aviation Authority) began making for Dunkirk. Pinnace 32 headed for Ramsgate, but a fouled propeller meant that she would play no part in Operation Dynamo. The five seaplane tenders were towed out of Dover shortly after dawn on 31 May, but strong winds and rough seas meant that they had to proceed under their own power. They approached to within 12 miles (19 km) of the French coast and they then were engaged in ferrying troops off the beach to larger vessels out to sea. Throughout the entire operation they were under continued attack from German aircraft. It was estimated that the five seaplane tenders managed to save around 500 men.

Tender 254, with four crew members, was the first to be lost when she got in too close and was virtually capsized by the number of men attempting to clamber aboard. She was incapable of movement and had to be abandoned. AMC 3, with three crew members, including Corporal C. Webster, suffered a different fate. An army officer's clothing got caught in the propellers and Webster was forced to cut the engines. The waves swept the boat around and it hit the beach and was holed.

Despite the fact that the seaplane tenders were unsuitable for work so close to the beach because of their underwater fittings (propellers, rudders, etc), they still made for the lines of men patiently waiting, sometimes up to their necks in the sea. Despite having lost ST 254 and AMC 3, the three remaining craft, which had all suffered underwater damage, continued to ferry men backwards and forwards. ST 276 and 291, after suffering signifi-cant damage, began to be towed back to Dover by a French vessel. ST 243 remained in the vicinity of Dunkirk for so long that it was only just able to return to Dover with the fuel it still had.

On 1 June, with the crews feverishly trying to repair and cannibalise their vessels, they were told that they would no longer be required. But by the early morning of the following day, two of the vessels had been made serviceable and in the event it was just as well because they were told to take a naval berthing party into Dunkirk harbour. The crews quickly collected extra fuel and requisitioned two Lewis guns, which were lashed to the boats with broken tow bars and an engine's starting handle. With two boats and three crews, volunteers were asked for. Corporal Flower, Leading Aircraftmen Clarke and Wooton and Aircraftman White manned ST 276, whilst Corporal Lawson and Leading Aircraftmen Hunt and Lockwood and Aircraftman Kernohan crewed ST 243. Their passengers were twelve Royal Navy personnel, including a senior officer, who was accompanied by Pilot Officer Collins in command of the MCS party aboard ST 243.

According to the account given by Flower (who later became a Group Captain), the two vessels got underway at 1430 hours on 2 June. By 1700 hours they were around 8 miles (13 km) off Gravelines. No sooner had they come within hailing distance of one another in order to finalise how they would proceed into Dunkirk harbour than three Junkers 88 Stuka dive-bombers attacked them. Whilst Flower and Lawson took evasive action, three sticks of bombs and heavy machine-gun fire was unleashed against the two vessels. Wooton and Lockwood, the two crafts' fitters, began to return fire with the Lewis guns. They both blazed away at the German aircraft as they circled for another attack. When it came a near miss on ST 243 split the vessel from stem to stern along the keel. It was only a matter of minutes before the seawater engulfed the engine and even as the launch sank, Lockwood continued to fire back. ST 276 swerved and turned in order to avoid the attacks.

The Germans made five more attacks on the little vessel, which was weaving at 18 knots. Wooton continued to return fire, but one of the attacks damaged the starboard engine and knocked out some of the controls in the wheelhouse. Amazingly nobody was hurt and as the German aircraft disappeared into the distance, ST 276 spun round to try to help the survivors of 243. None of the crew or passengers had been wounded, but they were suffering from skin burns from the petrol in the water and were finding it difficult to breathe because of the fumes. ST 276 had to make the difficult decision to abandon the survivors, otherwise there would have been no chance that the naval berthing party would have reached their destination at Dunkirk harbour. Indeed, according to Flower, the senior Royal Navy Officer, who was floating in the water with the other survivors, adamantly ordered them to head for Dunkirk. Flower promised to return to pick them up.

ST 276 was only capable of around 7 knots and as a result did not reach Dunkirk harbour until 1900 hours. She pulled alongside a Royal Navy motor torpedo boat and a senior naval officer, under German artillery fire, told Flower that he should scuttle the ST 276 and return to Dover aboard a destroyer. Flower refused; he had promised the survivors of ST 243 that he would come back to pick them up. A compromise was quickly reached and at sunset, with a Royal Naval Volunteer Reserve lieutenant on board, they headed back along the coast to try to find the position where they had last seen the men floundering in the water. Darkness was closing in, but Flower and his crew continued their fruitless search until they were forced to give up. At 0730 on Monday, 3 June ST 276 moored in the inner submarine basin in Dover harbour. Of the people aboard ST 243, only Aircraftman Kernohan survived; the others were all lost.

By 2 June the situation around Dunkirk had deteriorated to

such an extent that operations were now restricted to the hours of darkness. Throughout the 2 and 3 June evacuations continued, plucking another 52,000 men from certain capture. On 3 June, HSL 120, commanded by Pilot Officer R. G. Spencer, arrived in Dover. After just two hours to refuel and rest she was underway again at 1900 hours, headed for Dunkirk. Bizarrely they were accompanying an Admiral's launch, which was under the command of Lieutenant C. W. S. Dreyer. Dreyer's vessel, MTB 102, was on its eighth return trip to Dunkirk. Two days before she had come alongside the sinking HMS *Keith* and rescued Admiral Wake-Walker. The following day they had saved General Alexander. HSL 120 and MTB 102 were to escort Admiral Wake-Walker back to Dunkirk, where he was to supervise the embarkation of the last French troops.

When they approached Dunkirk harbour the water was littered with all manner of floating hazards. The crew also discovered that they had two stowaways on board, a pair of wireless operators from the Sunderland flying boats that had been moored at Calshot. They had been refused permission to accompany the vessel and after suffering from severe sea-sickness finally showed themselves. HSL 120 managed to make it back to Dover and on the morning of 4 June the last British vessel, a 40 ft (12 m) MTB commanded by Lieutenant J. Cameron, left Dunkirk harbour. By that stage, some 338,226 men had been extricated from either death or captivity. The immense effort to save these men was to prove decisive in the future and would ensure Britain's ability to continue to wage war against Germany.

Meanwhile, in Malta, HSL 107's crew had taken over the former Italian Airways office and very shortly after the Italian declaration of war, was almost destroyed by an acoustic mine. Incendiary bombs later hit the vessel, but fortunately spares were on hand from torpedo boats stationed in Malta. HSL 107 was often required to rendezvous with Hurricanes flying in from aircraft carriers. The rendezvous point was just off the Italian island of Linosa. On one occasion 107 was spotted by an Italian aircraft and shot up (the Italians later claimed that they had sunk a British torpedo boat). On another occasion she was guiding in a flight of Hurricanes when five failed to find Malta at all. One of them crashed into the sea and the pilot was killed. Also around this time they plucked an Italian pilot from the sea.

HSL 107's first official rescue whilst based in Malta is said to have been on 12 June 1940, when they picked up Petty Officer Sabey and Lieutenant Manning.

In the immediate aftermath and chaos of the evacuation from Dunkirk, Britain faced seemingly overwhelming aerial assaults from the *Luftwaffe*. It had not been envisaged that Britain would be the front line against the Germans; it was assumed that the bulk of the troops and airfields would be based in France. Therefore, when the Allies were driven from the continent it became obvious that air operations would now need to cross the sea, but the preparations for dealing with ditched crews was rudimentary at best.

Air Chief Marshal Sir Hugh Dowding had jealously held many of his Fighter Command squadrons out of the fight in France. He had realised that there was every possibility that his airmen would have to fight a defensive war over Britain and around her shores. As a result, by July 1940, he could muster around 800 aircraft. Two hundred of these were Spitfires and a further 400 Hurricanes. At the height of what would become known as the Battle of Britain, between mid-July and the end of October 1940, some 537 of his aircrew were lost. Of this number 215 were killed or missing after having ditched in either the English Channel or the North Sea. At this stage Britain's ability to find and rescue ditched aircrew was underdeveloped. Civilian fishing vessels, merchant ships, the RAF, the Royal Navy and the regular lifeboat service (the RNLI) all retrieved downed aircrew. At this stage, however, the chances of being found and surviving in the water were slim.

The fighter crews were issued with Mae West lifejackets, but they lacked dinghies and survival kits. Their heavy engines meant that the aircraft sank extremely quickly. In some cases the pilots had a matter of seconds to get out and very little chance to indicate their position in order to aid their search and rescue.

During the Battle of Britain thirteen high-speed launches were available. Just ten covered the North Sea and the English Channel, and at any one time at least three were non-operational. The engines had to be changed or refitted after just 360 hours of running. If nothing else this alerted the RAF to the fact that although the 100 Class launches were a vast improvement over what had been available before, the engines at the very least were not the easiest to maintain in peak condition.

Losses mounted and on several days casualties on either side were such that the chances of being rescued were reduced to virtually zero. Between 20 and 21 July 1940, twenty-one British and German aircraft were shot down and crashed into the sea. Of the forty men involved, just six were recovered and one of these was picked up by the German rescue service. Most crews that were nursing a damaged aircraft would attempt to make it back to a friendly coastline. Crash landing or baling out over territory held by their own forces immeasurably increased their chances of survival. During the Battle of Britain, however, crews from both air forces, who were forced to ditch over the sea had approximately a 20 per cent chance of returning to their squadron.

The most successful air sea rescue day during the Battle of Britain was 26 August 1940. Two Spitfires were shot down near Dover, another off the Sussex coast; two Hurricanes and two Defiants were lost over Herne Bay. Of these, all but one Spitfire pilot and two Defiant gunners were saved.

The chances of being picked out of the water were increased if the pilot could ditch in the Thames estuary. By September this was where the main action was taking place; massed RAF squadrons intercepted German aircraft as they made their turn, using the estuary as a navigational aid. It has been estimated that RAF craft, including the HSLs, picked up around forty British aircrew over the course of the Battle of Britain. To this figure needs to be added all the crew picked up by the other civilian and military services. It is certain that the total number of pick-ups proved to be a small, but decisive factor in returning experienced pilots to their squadrons to continue the fight.

During the last twenty-one days of July 1940, the RAF lost 220 aircrew killed or missing over the seas. The high fatality figures shocked everyone, but by October a further 260 had been lost. In August the Sea Rescue Organisation was set up to coordinate the picking up of aircrews that had baled out or ditched in the North Sea or the English Channel. Most of the responsibility for this fell to Coastal Command.

By comparison, the German rescue service was far better equipped; it had also been integrated into the *Luftwaffe* at an early stage in the war. German aircraft were fitted with one-man dinghies and the bomber crews had portable radios. The Germans tended to rely on He 59 floatplanes for sea pick-ups, although a large number of crew were picked up by E-boats of the German navy.

The Germans also set up a string of sea rescue floats from around October 1940. These peculiar-looking craft were moored virtually in the middle of the English Channel and consisted of a floating refuge that had no power of its own and had a 250 ft (75 m) line trailing in the current to help people clamber aboard. The float had a central tower; the craft was painted yellow and there were red crosses on the tower. Having clambered down the steps from the tower, the downed crew would find four bunks, food, clothing, water, blankets, lamps, a bucket and distress flares. Later the British designed their own rescue float of a broadly similar pattern.

The British cast about for a way to increase the life expectancy of downed crews in the water. Standard dinghies were really only capable of protecting them for a matter of hours, yet in many instances men were afloat in them for days. Two solutions were the Thornaby bag and the Bircham barrel. The Thornaby bag was invented and first used in 1940 by RAF Thornaby. It consisted of a bag constructed out of parachute fabric, with kapok pads from Mae West jackets. Inside was a survival kit consisting of first-aid equipment, tins of food, drink and cigarettes. It could be dropped close to downed aircrew but, except in calm conditions, it tended to burst open.

An alternative came from RAF Bircham Newton and was, in effect, a cylindrical container, often the tail container of a 250 lb bomb. It had a reinforced frame and a canvas bag inside to make it watertight. As with the Thornaby bag, the exact contents differed from station to station. Generally, however, it would have a first-aid kit, food, water and distress flares. The main purpose of both devices was to help the aircrew sustain themselves until a vessel could pick them up.

The next development came from Group Captain Waring, the Station Commander at RAF Lindholme. He and his colleagues invented a device to drop an inflatable dinghy, clothing, food and a first-aid kit in a series of containers. The original invention consisted of five, the largest of which contained the dinghy, which were dropped in the tail unit of a 500 lb bomb case. The dinghy inflated automatically when it hit the water. The four smaller containers, in 250 lb bomb cases, held clothing, water and food. The five containers were strung together with ropes so that once the crew had got into the dinghy they could pull the other containers towards them.

RAF bomber crews at least had dinghies, but fighter pilots' only means of staying afloat were their Mae Wests. The Ministry of Aircraft Production looked at ways in which a single-seat dinghy could be attached to a fighter pilot's harness. Initially they rejected the idea, but when a German single-seat dinghy was examined it was decided to copy this model and put it into production.

The experience of the Battle of Britain proved beyond doubt that the sea rescue service needed to be both improved and expanded. It was generally agreed by all the services that something needed to be done. The retrieval of RAF aircrew was of paramount importance and it was suggested that an air commodore be given responsibility as the Director of Air Sea Rescue Services.

An expansion of the service was one thing, but what was of equal importance was a considerable improvement in communication and coordination between the services. Any effective air sea rescue service needed to know, with a certain degree of precision, where they needed to search and for what. Simply having HSLs on standby or on station was not going to be sufficient to improve the survival rate of downed aircrew in the sea. A radical re-examination was required of how information was passed from Fighter Command, Bomber Command, or indeed any other service operating aircraft.

Provisional approval for the appointment of a new director was given on 24 January 1941. Initially he would operate for six months and then a review would be undertaken. At that point it would be decided whether it was working and whether it still needed to maintain a separate identity. The responsibility for the new directorate would be given to both the RAF and the Royal Navy. Subsequently Group Captain Croke was appointed as the first Director of Air Sea Rescue Services and his deputy was a

Royal Navy Captain, C. L. Howe. It was decided that the directorate would be called Air Sea Rescues (ASR) Services, in order
to avoid confusion with the already existing Naval Sea Rescue
Services. The new directorate would be set up at Coastal
Command headquarters.

CHAPTER THREE

The RAF Air Sea
Rescue Service

The new directorate began its work on 6 February 1941. From this point on it would be known as RAF Air Sea Rescue Service, and its adopted motto was 'The sea shall not have them'.

The service's responsibilities were three-fold:

1. to coordinate all sea rescue operations for aircraft and aircraft crews
2. to provide equipment that could be dropped by aircraft at crash scenes in order to improve the air crews' chances of survival until the arrival of rescue craft
3. to provide adequate marine craft, moored buoys and other aids to rescue.

From the outset it was going to be a feverish race against time. It was clear from the Battle of Britain experience that air sea rescue provision was inadequate. There was a great deal for Group Captain Croke and his team to accomplish.

The directorate was attached to the Area Combined Headquarters of Nos 15, 16, 18 and 19 Groups. This was essential in order to control and coordinate any air sea rescue operation. Liaison officers were appointed who could work alongside the four groups. The first step was to divide the rescue areas into four, following the areas of operation of the four Coastal Command groups. It was proposed that any RAF flying stations within these areas would contribute, or ultimately provide, some form of air sea rescue provision within those areas. At the time Lysanders of Fighter Command were responsible for searching coastal areas up to 20 miles (32 km) out to sea. This extended from the Wash, around the east coast and the English Channel, past the Bristol Channel to South Wales as far as Milford Haven.

In addition to the four liaison officers, a marine craft officer was appointed, as well as staff to liaise with the Royal Navy, and others to procure supplies, organise training and liaise with the aircraft production and medical authorities. Officially the directorate would answer to the Deputy Chief of Air Staff.

Before it started, in December 1940, thirty-eight additional high-speed launches had been ordered. Around eighteen of the twenty-eight that had been ordered prior to this were already in service. By the time the directorate was established, twenty-two high-speed launches were in service. This was still a hopelessly inadequate number, however; many more aircraft and launches were needed. Temporary provisions, such as the one-man triangular dinghy and British-made floats similar to those used by the Germans, were pressed into service.

In relation to its three primary responsibilities, the directorate had five major problems that needed solving. First, it wanted to influence the way in which aircraft were constructed so that crew that had ditched had a reasonable chance of being able to get out before the aircraft sank. The second problem was to teach the aircrew *how* to ditch and how to abandon their aircraft if they were forced to land in the sea. The third was how they could practically extend the life expectancy of the aircrew. The fourth was even more fundamental: once the aircraft had ditched and the crew had safely exited, how would the rescue craft be able to find them? Finally, assuming that they had been found, how could they be brought to shore in the fastest and safest manner?

The most logical solution to the problem of improved construction was to work with the research and development branch of the Ministry of Aircraft Production. They were already concerned with safety and were keen to develop aircraft that were strong enough to withstand the inevitable impact of ditching in the sea. Ways were investigated of improving the buoyancy of the aircraft, ways of making them more watertight and fitting flotation devices. Attention was also paid to the exit hatches. They needed to be positioned not only so that they were easy to open, but also so that they were not under water when the aircraft was floating. Adaptations could be made to existing production aircraft in the short term, but in the longer term ideas such as these had to be incorporated into future designs.

The Ministry of Aircraft Production was particularly interested in where to fit pneumatic dinghies and they had interviewed a number of downed aircrew to obtain vital information about their experiences when they had had to ditch. Based on their findings new emergency ditching drills were brought into effect.

All the other problems were meaningless if the crew could neither get out of the stricken aircraft, nor get themselves into dinghies to await pickup. Very little training had been given on ditching safety and the handling of dinghies. One of the new directorate's first instructions was that all commands should begin training on rescues. They requested that pilots and aircrew receive dinghy drill and that the Training Command include these features in their syllabus and in their lectures. By June 1941 the Ministry of Aircraft Production had produced a series of diagrams showing the main features of ditching drills and these were distributed to aircrew. The major problem, however, was that many of the crews believed that they were unlikely to have to ditch into the sea and time after time over the course of the war the directorate had to reinforce its message.

Two early successes seemed to indicate that the message was getting through. In April 1941 a Whitley ditched in the sea and it was seventy-two hours before they were picked up. They were sustained throughout by a Lindholme dinghy and a Thornaby bag. Then on 15 August 1941 a Wellington, with a training crew onboard, ditched 50 miles (80 km) east of Wick. Their instructor and wireless operator were both knocked out, but the trainees, following the new procedures, managed to extricate the two unconscious men and were picked up after just thirty minutes by the Royal Navy.

On the morning of 1 July 1941 a Hampden on search and rescue service spotted the crew of another Hampden in a dinghy some 60 miles (100 km) off Great Yarmouth. The crew of four had been on a bombing mission to Düsseldorf. They had been forced to ditch in the North Sea. They had managed to make it into the dinghy, but they could not find any paddles.

They just drifted, and by the eighth day had no more water; they were also drifting towards a minefield. On the morning of 1 July the Hampden spotted them and dropped a Lindholme dinghy, which they managed to reach. Shortly after midday on their ninth day they were finally picked up by an RAF launch. Whilst this incident proved the worth of the Lindholme device and the ability of the RAF launches to pick up crews, the inadequate search patterns were highlighted as a further major concern.

In August 1941, with two squadrons of Lysanders from the Army Cooperation Command already covering the south-east coast, the directorate still needed more search aircraft. They had repeatedly asked the Royal Navy to let them have some of their Walruses and six were finally transferred. By September 1941, therefore with a complement of thirty-six Lysanders and eight Walruses, Nos 275, 276, 277 and 278 Air Sea Rescue (ASR) Squadrons were formed.

The Lysander, which had originally been designed for reconnaissance, became the first RAF Air Sea Rescue search aircraft, but it was not large enough to carry the Lindholme equipment. Instead it carried four small dinghies, each containing food, water and distress signals, which were dropped from its wings.

In January 1941, the Air Ministry had decided to take a leaf out of the Germans' book and build sixteen experimental air sea rescue floats. They were painted red and orange and had, in addition to food, clothing, blankets and a cooking stove, distress signals, a signalling torch and an automatic wireless telegraphy set. Both naval and RAF vessels routinely visited them but during this period no rescues were ever made from them.

Former ASR member Ted Shute recalls a story about these experimental floats in 1941. He was on board an ASR vessel detailed to deliver RAF and Air Ministry officials who were to spend part of a day on a float to evaluate it. The vessel pulled alongside the float and the men clambered aboard, with their flasks and sandwiches, opened the float's hatch and disappeared down the staircase. The launch powered away to take up its position a few miles away on station, with instructions to return to collect the men after about five hours. Meanwhile, the two officials discovered to their horror that the float was already occupied and three *Luftwaffe* crew promptly surrendered to them. An uncomfortable five hours was spent in the cramped float before the launch returned.

Following a meeting on 14 January 1941, the Royal Navy was asked in February to identify navigational buoys that could be fitted with ladders and ropes to provide a temporary refuge for downed aircrew. The buoys would be equipped with water, food, first-aid equipment, a lamp, a knife, a yellow flag and a Very pistol. By mid-1941 the scheme was extended to include the waters off Cardiff, the Tyne and Milford Haven.

Stationary floats or buoys were comparatively easy to check, but the majority of downed men would not be in a position to get themselves to either. Finding men who were in a dinghy and were almost certainly drifting still remained a considerable problem. In some cases they may have managed to send an SOS seconds before ditching, but even this was not always helpful, since direction-finding equipment was relatively rudimentary and there was no way of knowing how much time had elapsed between the sending of the SOS and the actual ditching. This problem was compounded by the fact that the longer the time between receiving the SOS and the search getting underway, the greater the likelihood that the weather and drifting would affect their position. The ultimate solution would be the installation of a radio in the dinghy, but this development was some way off. The Germans released a fluorescent dye into the water and the aircrew wore yellow caps, but this still did not get around the problem of finding the general location of the crew in the first place. A suggestion was to provide a homing pigeon which could be released by the crew, detailing their position. But in many cases the crew themselves were not entirely sure of their position. Floating signal torches, flares, kites, inflatable balloons and other devices were all investigated.

The lack of launches and the shortage of trained crew were still considerable problems. By the end of 1941 only thirty-nine high-speed launches were available, less than half the figure that had been recommended as the bare minimum. The construction programme had not yet been geared up to the transformation between peace and war. There was a dearth of skilled labour, and competition for materials was fierce. As a result only twenty-two launches were available by February 1941. Contemporary estimates suggest that only two were being completed each month. Both the early types, 64 ft (19.5 m) and 63 ft (19.2 m) had a high rate of mechanical failure. It is estimated that on 6 February 1941 just four high-speed launches were available for duty on the whole of the east coast between Dover and the Shetlands. Despite pre-war orders to bring the complement up to strength it was not anticipated that reasonable numbers would be available until the end of 1941.

In February 1941 the RAF had fourteen 60 ft (18.3 m) diesel-engined pinnaces based at Sullom Voe, Invergordon, Gosport and Calshot. They were primarily used for carrying supplies and personnel, and for torpedo recovery. They were relatively good boats, but woefully inadequate in rough seas. There was a large number of 40 ft (12 m) seaplane tenders of various types, primarily based at Sullom Voe, Helensburgh, Invergordon, Bridlington, Wells-on-Sea, Gosport and Calshot. These craft were primarily used for close work with seaplanes and flying boats. They were not ideal for rescue work, except when the pick-ups were very close to the shore. The Royal Navy was providing a number of motor launches, usually around 110 ft (35 m) long and able to travel at around 20 knots. These were available for rescues when they were not being used in their normal role as coastal patrol boats, but many of them had too deep a draught to cross mine barriers. In February 1941 around twenty were available for rescue work on a daily basis, based primarily at Portland, Dover, Newhaven, Dartmouth, Milford Haven and Falmouth.

There were other miscellaneous naval coastal craft, including some converted motor yachts, but their rescue capacity was severely limited, particularly in poor weather. Other naval vessels such as torpedo boats, minesweepers, launches and patrol craft were also theoretically available for rescue, but they had many other duties to perform. As far as the North Sea and the east of the English Channel were concerned, therefore, the availability of rescue craft was severely limited. Moreover, the area between the Isle of Man and Land's End, was virtually the preserve of the Royal Navy in February 1941.

The new British Power Boat Company Type 2 high-speed launch, which became known as the Whaleback, was an adaptation of a motor anti-submarine boat. It was the first high-speed launch to be fitted with gun turrets. It was powered by twin

Rolls-Royce Merlin engines and sixty-nine were built. Twenty-one were delivered before October 1941. Indeed the first completed Whaleback, HSL 141, entered service in February 1941. It was brightly painted, with a yellow deck and upper works, slate grey superstructure and a gloss black hull. The colour was intended to indicate to the Germans that it was a rescue boat, but this did not deter them from attacking the boats.

In July 1941 HSL 108, operating out of Gorleston, received a report that a Blenheim of No. 139 Squadron, operating out of Horsham St Faith, had been damaged during a daylight raid over Oldenburg. She was preparing to ditch in the North Sea, to the north-west of Terscheling Island. The crew of seven left Gorleston at approximately 1600 hours on 1 July and steered a course north-east for around four hours. We are indebted to Tony Overill, whose father was among the crew, for the account of what happened.

Meanwhile, having been finished off by an Me 109, the three crew of the Blenheim had ditched and managed to get into their dinghy. For a time the dinghy was shadowed by a Short Stirling of No. 7 Squadron, but this was driven off when it was attacked by two Arado Ar 196 floatplanes. The Stirling was later shot down by another Me 109 and there were no survivors. A Heinkel HE 59 was despatched to pick up the crew of the Blenheim, and took them back to the German air sea rescue base at Schellingwoude, to the north of Amsterdam.

HSL 108 had discovered what they believed was a yellow dinghy, but it turned out to be a Dutch navigational buoy. As they left it they were attacked by the two German Arado Ar 196 floatplanes, which smashed up the boat and set the engines on fire. The crew used their fire extinguishers and the engine died. Being of the earlier type, HSL 108 had no defensive capability, and the crew had to hoist a seaman's sweater in lieu of a white flag. The coxswain, Sergeant Hales, had been slightly injured and the wireless operator, Leading Aircraftman Guilfoyle, had been seriously injured with a bullet wound in his chest. One of the German aircraft landed whilst the other circled. The Germans were prepared to evacuate any of the wounded, but the crew failed to understand them and after a while the Germans flew off once more. Running repairs were carried out on HSL 108, but it was still shipping water.

By dawn the following day the boat was very low in the water and at that point a Heinkel HE 59 floatplane and the two Arados returned. The crew of HSL 108 was ferried over to the HE 59 one at a time and taken to Schellingwoude and subsequently transferred to a prisoner-of-war camp. The launch was recovered by the Germans and used by the *Luftwaffe* until 2 August 1943, when it was sunk, as *Vorpostenboot* VP 1108, by a British aircraft.

Guilfoyle died of his wounds and was given a burial at sea by the Germans. The skipper, Flying Officer Jackman, was sent off for hospital treatment, whilst Coxswain Hales, the engineer Raybould and Deckhands Drayson, Overill and Daggert remained for the rest of the war in Stalag Luft III.

HSL 143 suffered a similar fate in 1941 when seven Me 109s set upon it. The vessel was badly shot up and the crew was captured. It was soon realised that yellow paint only served as a homing beacon for enemy aircraft, and it was not long before everything was painted slate grey, leaving only a small part at the top of the wheelhouse yellow. By August 1941 it was further decreed that all ASR launches should be fitted with defensive armament, at the very least, two twin Browning .303 turrets. Henceforth all craft being built would have this armament and it would be added to all existing vessels. It was still to be at least a year before the majority of the launches were fitted with machine guns, however, partly owing to the shortage of weapons and partly to the reluctance of many of the HSL skippers to have them fitted.

The Marine Craft Policy Committee, meeting in March 1941, had appreciated the fact that they needed vessels that were capable of cruising at relatively low speeds in areas where air operations were being launched, but also of travelling at at least 25 knots for short periods of time in an emergency. The vessels also needed to be able to put out from harbours in rough seas and to be able to maintain reasonable progress in adverse weather conditions. The Admiralty was already constructing a number of Fairmile naval motor launches. They made it clear from the very beginning that whilst these vessels would be available to help in air sea rescue operations, this function would be subsidiary to their main naval operations. The Marine Craft Policy Committee, in cooperation with Coastal Command, the Air Sea Rescue Service, the Directorate of Operational

Requirements and the Ministry of Aircraft Production, decided that a new hull and engine type needed to be investigated at the earliest possible opportunity. This did not deal with the immediate problem, however; the country was at war and increased production was proving to be almost impossible, but the Air Sea Rescue Service needed launches immediately.

It was agreed on 1 April 1941 that each coastal group would have four flotillas of high-speed launches. A flight lieutenant would command each one and the number of vessels in each flotilla would depend upon the specific requirements of the operational area. A squadron leader would command each flotilla. It was a major step forward, but it did not deal with the dual problem of the lack of high-speed launches and the shortage of suitable officers.

It was estimated that 134 RAF craft were needed to cover the British Isles and that a further forty-four were needed for overseas commands. On 30 May 1941 the deficiencies were estimated at twenty-nine seaplane tenders and forty-nine high-speed launches. At that stage there were only four high-speed launches overseas, in addition to the single vessel that was with Coastal Command at Gibraltar. Despite this shortage, between February and May 1941, 213 aircrew of the 607 ditched in the sea had been saved. As several ASR veterans later attested, they had been told on innumerable occasions that the loss of a high-speed launch was a perfectly acceptable cost, provided they had managed to save an aircraft's crew. It was purely a matter of economics: the saving of experienced aircraft crew far outweighed the cost of purchasing a new launch.

The pressure was still on the Admiralty to release motor launches to the RAF to be used as rescue craft. In June 1941 the case was once again put to the Royal Navy. They refused, stating that they had insufficient craft for coastal services and that they could not possibly release any vessels until at least 1942. As an interim measure, general-service pinnaces were converted for air sea rescue purposes. It was estimated that forty more could be built by December 1941, so on 23 June, the Deputy Chief of Air Staff decided that the forty 64 ft (18.3 m) pinnaces would be allocated for rescue work.

Meanwhile, in June 1941, the British Air Commission reported to the Ministry of Aircraft Production on the availability of rescue aircraft in the United States. The Miami Ship Building Corporation was already constructing vessels for the Admiralty. An application was made to divert two vessels a month from Miami's contract of thirty vessels to the RAF. Nine high-speed launches were also due for delivery to South Africa and the South African government agreed to defer the delivery and allow the RAF to take them instead.

In July 1941 approval was given for twenty-one seaplane tenders to be allocated to calm weather sea rescue work. They were to be based at Coastal Command stations on the Isle of Man, on the coast of Wales and in eastern Scotland. At that stage, however, there were still only twenty-seven high-speed launches available.

On 28 July 28 1941 the Air Ministry announced the immediate expansion of the Air Sea Rescue Service. It was suggested that forty-eight high-speed launches, thirty-five seaplane tenders and forty pinnaces would provide the initial complement. The second stage would require sixty-four high-speed launches, with ten in reserve, fifty seaplane tenders, with ten in reserve and the forty pinnaces. It was optimistically believed that the initial strength could be attained by December 1941. In addition to these high-speed launches, more would be allocated to Coastal Command stations, notably at Dover, Rosyth and Nore. Pinnaces would similarly be available around the Shetlands and in the Irish Sea and seaplane tenders would be based with Coastal Command to cover Dover and the Western Approaches.

Before the creation of the Air Sea Rescue Service, a pilot's chance of being picked up if he had downed in the sea was little more than one in five. In the four months after February 1941 successful rescues had increased to 35 per cent and some or all of the crew had been picked up in 46 per cent of all cases. None the less the rescue service was still not expanding at the same rate as offensive air operations. Bomber Command was particularly concerned that it was not keeping up with their needs.

Around this time the Admiralty was discussing how their light coastal forces, which included vessels that were used for sea rescue, could be more efficiently organised. They appointed Captain C. L. Howe as Deputy Director of Air Sea Rescue. Meanwhile the Deputy Chief of Air Staff made a recommendation that air sea rescue services should be more closely coordinated with other RAF operations. It was proposed that Flying Control and Air Sea Rescue be amalgamated under a newly appointed Director of Aircraft and Aircrew Safety. A senior officer with a sound knowledge and experience was needed and on 20 August 1941 Marshal of the Royal Air Force Sir John Salmond, was offered the post, which he took up on 23 September 1941. His new organisation included the Directorate of Air Sea Rescue, the Assistant Directorate of Regional Control (which dealt with guiding aircraft to their bases) and the Directorate of Fighter Operations, which dealt with navigational warnings and airfield lighting. On the Air Sea Rescue side, a group captain would become a Deputy Director and a commander from the Royal Navy would support him.

A conference was called on 11 September 1941 to discuss the general organisation of rescue services. It was attended by the Deputy Chief of Air Staff, the Assistant Chief of Naval Staff and representatives from the Admiralty, Coastal Command, Bomber Command, Fighter Command, Army Cooperation Command and innumerable other administrative and operational directorates. The meeting learned that since the Air Sea Rescue Service had been created in 1941 it had rescued some 37 per cent of the 1,200 downed aircrews. The service was already enjoying the support of the Observer Corps, the Coastguard and the RNLI. Excellent progress had been made in providing aircrew with dinghies and lifesaving equipment and the proposal to fit navigational buoys as aircrew refuges along the east coast was nearly finished. The Admiralty had also loaned a number of operational vessels to help bridge the gap in rescue craft. The development of high-speed launches and their production was well underway, as was the production of additional pinnaces.

It was proposed that Lysanders and Walruses from Fighter Command would be used to search the coast up to 20 miles (32 km) out, but eventually it was agreed that this search area should be increased to 40 miles (64 km), covering the whole of the east coast to Flamborough Head, and then around the west coast and across to Northern Ireland. A very real problem, however, was that few aircraft were available, owing to operational requirements. The summer of 1941 had seen the loss of many experienced aircrews and each man lost reduced

Fighter Command's ability to send aircraft out for the next ditched crew. It was a vicious circle that needed to be broken.

Two squadrons of Hudsons, equipped with air-to-surface vessels (ASV or dinghies) equipment, were added to the Air Sea Rescue Services for deep searches. It was essential that men further out than 40 miles (64 km) should still have a chance of being picked up. Amazingly, the Admiralty even agreed to make good the deficit of fifty motor launchers. In March 1942 the Admiralty would hand them over, increasing the RAF's total to the ninety needed.

Despite the inadequate cover, there were a number of notable rescues in the first nine months of the ASR's existence. On 21 June 1941, three Me 109s attacked the highly experienced Squadron Leader Standford Tuck 40 miles (64 km) out from The Hague. He managed to shoot down two of them and damage the third, but his own aircraft was badly damaged and he was forced to bale out just 4 miles (6.5 km) short of the Suffolk coast. He managed to release his parachute harness just as he entered the water and swim over to his dinghy stowage and inflate it. Almost immediately a Lysander found him; a barge had also seen Tuck go down. Within ten minutes he was aboard the barge. A naval launch, alerted by the Lysander, then took him on board.

On the same day, whilst in air operations over Boulogne protecting bombers, a Hurricane pilot was separated from his squadron. He was making his way back across the Channel when he came under attack from several Me 109s. He manoeuvred and retaliated, but his ammunition was exhausted and he tried to outrun the German aircraft. He took several hits and his aircraft caught fire. He baled out and hit the water whilst still attached to his parachute. With great difficulty he managed to work himself free and inflate his dinghy. He was virtually in the middle of the English Channel and, using the sun as a bearing, he began to paddle. After about half an hour a Heinkel 59 floatplane, escorted by an Me 109, came overhead. The pilot baled out of the dinghy and hid in the water and luckily the German aircraft passed over-head. He climbed back on board and began paddling again; this time a Lysander passed overhead, escorted by several Spitfires. The pilot now saw a battle take place overhead as the Spitfires attacked a group of Me 109s. The British were reinforced by some

Hurricanes and during the dogfight a Spitfire and an Me 109 were shot down. The battle was soon over and the pilot paddled for another two hours until he could see the English coastline. As luck would have it some high-speed launches had been despatched to find the lost Spitfire pilot and the Hurricane pilot managed to attract their attention. He was taken safely home to Dover.

Yet another incident occurred on 21 June. Some Me 109s attacked an aircraft flown by a Czech pilot. The Czech's aircraft was hit about 8 miles (13 km) to the south of Folkestone. He desperately tried to reach the English coast, but it soon became apparent that he was not going to make it. He managed to make a good landing in the sea and for a time he floated in his Mae West. He then inflated the dinghy and had been in the small craft for barely half an hour when a Lysander and four Spitfires spotted him. They circled and then disappeared. Just fifteen minutes later a rescue launch arrived and took him to Dover.

The crew of a Whitley had a narrow escape on 18 April 1941. They were on a bombing mission to Berlin when several enemy night fighters bounced them over Hamburg. The Whitley's engines were hit and the pilot tried to nurse the aircraft back to England. It was steadily losing height and the crew threw out everything that was not screwed down. All the time the wireless operator broadcast distress signals. The aircraft was still 90 miles (145 km) out from the Humber at 0320 hours when the starboard engine caught fire. It now became apparent to the pilot that he would have to ditch. No sooner had they hit the water when the fuselage and starboard mainplane caught fire. The crew immediately baled out and they managed to get just 30 yards away when the aircraft blew up.

The dinghy had inverted when the crew had inflated it and everything except two marine distress flares had been lost. The crew struggled for two days in rough seas, unable to right the dinghy. On the third day they were so exhausted that they could not risk even getting off it to try to right it. They bailed with their shoes and two men took it in turns to paddle westward. They saw a number of aircraft trying to find them; another Whitley had indeed spotted them, but lost them in the high seas. The crew fired off their two precious distress signals to no avail.

They continued to paddle west and finally a Hudson found them and dropped supplies. It remained in orbit for the rest of the day and when it was forced to leave it dropped flame floats. A little later a Hampden dropped a Lindholme dinghy and the crew managed to clamber aboard. Just an hour later an RAF HSL made it to the scene, heading for the flame floats. The crew were picked up and taken to Grimsby; they had been adrift from 0320 hours on 18 April to 2200 hours on 20 April.

With the Admiralty's agreement to allocate fifty Fairmile launches, to be known as rescue motor launches (RMLs) from their production from March 1942, the temporary gap was filled by the loan of fourteen motor anti-submarine boats. However, as 1941 drew to a close, it became apparent that the forty RAF pinnaces they had been promised would not after all be available by December. There were delays in production and few if any additional pinnaces would be available by the end of the year. The RAF was forced to press their existing general service pinnaces into service as rescue craft. In fact, only one of these modified pinnaces was actually in service by December. So not only did the RAF lack high-speed launches, but the pinnaces that they had were unable to put out during the winter and in rough weather.

The new, enlarged ASR had therefore faltered at the first hurdle, but this was not the only problem; they also still lacked personnel. The Admiralty proposed a solution; they suggested pooling all Royal Navy and RAF surface rescue craft and placing the Admiralty in command. In December 1941, however, the Director General of Aircraft Safety was confident enough to respond that the service was beginning to be truly effective, and that any reorganisation would be detrimental. He suggested that economies could be made in design, maintenance and repair. The Admiralty agreed that this could be a way forward and an interchange of information regarding vessels, building capacity and engine supply would go some way towards avoiding duplication of effort.

The agreement with the United States in June 1941 for the supply of Miami vessels suffered a serious blow towards the end of the year, just at the time when the vessels were expected. The Japanese had attacked Pearl Harbor and the Americans were now concerned to divert all production to their own armed forces. The Miami boats would have helped to bring the RAF up to its initial establishment of ninety-six, but it was not to be.

Huge efforts were made during the winter of 1941–42 to ensure that the promised pinnaces were delivered at the earliest opportunity, but by April 1942 only seven of the forty had been delivered. However transfer of the naval rescue motor launches promised by the Admiralty was only two weeks' late; it took place on 1 April 1942.

Little progress had been made on fitting the twin Browning turrets to the high-speed launches. Indeed in December 1941 the Commander-in-Chief at Portsmouth made an official complaint about the delay. Despite his efforts, however, little progress was made and neither turrets nor guns were being made available. As late as April 1942 a naval rescue motor anti-submarine boat was attacked off Dover by German aircraft. It was almost powerless to defend itself and as a result several of the crew were injured and the captain was killed. An immediate investigation was launched and it was discovered that not one of the high-speed launches had yet been given its twin turrets. Indeed nothing happened until May 1942, when some Vickers guns were borrowed from the RAF and two guns were fitted on single pedestal mounts on launches operating in dangerous waters.

The Director General of Aircraft Safety was deeply concerned that the communication between aircraft and rescue boats was woefully inadequate. Operational aircraft, for example, often used different frequencies from those used by searching aircraft or vessels. It was therefore proposed that the existing aircraft and rescue vessels be fitted with VHF and HF radio equipment.

Meanwhile the proposals for the deployment of two Hudson squadrons had also suffered a setback. Aircraft were being provided to the Soviet Union and as a result Hudsons were being diverted for this purpose.

No. 279 Air Sea Rescue Squadron was formed on 24 October 1941, based at Bircham Newton, and was to be equipped with twenty Hudsons fitted with Lindholme rescue equipment. But it lacked aircraft; not only that, it lacked aircrew. A second squadron, No. 280, based at Thorney Island, began forming towards the end of November. It was also meant to be equipped with Hudsons, but had none. So by the end of 1941 ASR was still only supported by Fighter Command's Lysanders and Walruses.

The Director General of Aircraft Safety was informed in January 1942 that No. 280 Squadron could be allocated Ansons instead of Hudsons. It was decided that Ansons should also be allocated to No. 279. There was a major problem with this, however, as the Anson was unable to carry the Lindholme rescue equipment. So whilst accepting that it was a temporary measure, adaptations to the Lindholme equipment were made to enable the aircraft to carry it.

No. 279 Squadron therefore became operational in March 1942 and despite the difficulties proved to be of enormous value during the early summer. Some six crews were rescued in May and June, totalling thirty-five men. Five were picked up by rescue launches within five hours and the sixth was spotted and picked up in just over an hour. In addition to this nineteen other aircrew were rescued over the same period. In June No. 280 Squadron became operational and they managed to pick up a crew in their first month.

Because of the lack of longer-range search aircraft and the continued shortage of high-speed launches only 17 per cent of downed crews were picked up in February. Losses that month were 192 aircrew, of whom only thirty-three were rescued. This does not include those lost on 12 and 13 February. On the 12th reconnaissance aircraft spotted the German battleships *Scharnhorst* and *Gneisenau*, escorted by the *Prinz Eugen* and other vessels. There was also heavy air cover. It was readily apparent that a sea battle, accompanied by an aerial struggle, was imminent. Eight Royal Navy and five RAF rescue vessels were despatched to their rendezvous positions. Bomber Command and Coastal Command aircraft were scrambled to attack the German fleet. Indeed Bomber Command was to fly 242 sorties, Coastal Command forty-one sorties and Fighter Command 301. The Fleet Air Arm launched further aircraft. Once the German ships had passed through the area, the rescue craft, supported by aircraft from No. 11 Group, swept the area for downed fighter pilots. Eleven naval vessels were also despatched to the area. A motor anti-submarine boat and a motor torpedo boat picked up five Swordfish crew which had made torpedo attacks on the German vessels. Just two Hudsons of No. 279 Squadron, however, were available for deep rescue searches. Innumerable SOS signals had been received and at dawn on 13 February over fifty aircraft took part in the searches, approaching to within 30 miles (50 km) of the coast of Holland. Nothing was found. The overall engagement had cost Bomber Command fifteen aircraft, Coastal Command five and Fighter Command seventeen. The Fleet Air Arm had also lost crews, including the Swordfish pilots, the total amounted to around 120 men. The search and rescue had been a signal failure.

Although it was not possible to say why so few crew were visible, what became abundantly clear was that crews that had ditched in the sea needed to be assisted at the earliest possible opportunity. The problems were the same as they had always been: first finding the crew, then dropping dinghies and food and finally, and of most paramount importance, picking them up. A further worry was linked to bomber operations over this period. Bomber Command was launching more and more attacks on German cities and installations, and the likelihood was that if they were shot down or forced to ditch then they would be even further from the British Isles than before – indeed they would be too far away to be reached by marine craft.

Back in 1940, as Air Officer Commanding No. 5 Group, Air Vice-Marshal A. T. Harris had suggested dropping a glider boat, which could be towed by an aircraft. Upon landing, wings and a tailplane would be abandoned and a motorboat constructed, which would be powered by a 10 hp engine. At the time it was ruled out on the grounds that there were inadequate numbers of glider pilots. In September 1940 another idea had emerged, this time to produce a 32 ft (9.8 m) motor dinghy that could be dropped by a Hampden, but again it had been ruled out. Out of these failed attempts to come up with a suitable solution, however, the concept of a motor-driven lifeboat dropped by parachute developed.

Group Captain E. F. Waring at RAF Lindholme had arrived at the Air Ministry in September 1941. He made contact with Lieutenant Robb of the Royal Navy Volunteer Reserve. An experienced boatbuilder, Robb made drawings of a wooden vessel, approximately 20 ft (6 m) long, capable of carrying five to seven crew and fitted with a motor, sail and oars. To get over the problem of the parachute drifting, a release mechanism was

An armoured harbour defence launch of the 1940s. *Courtesy of Rick Mortby*

HSL 142 at Dover in May 1941 undergoing an engine change. *Courtesy of Ted Shute*

Crew of HSL 2557, January or February 1943, pictured in the front of the crew hut at Felixstowe dock, belonging to 26 ASRU. Jack Cullum is third from left. *Courtesy of Jack Cullum*

Thorneycroft 199 at Calshot with a Sunderland in the background. Note the barrage balloons. *Courtesy of Ted Shute*

Marine tender 3128 built in September 1944 and delivered to 238 MCU Calshot in October 1944. *Courtesy of Ted Shute*

1103 MCU using the Titan Crane at Felixstowe to lift a launch out of the water. *Courtesy of Owen Newlands*

1103 MCU refuelling a Sunderland at Felixstowe 1946. *Courtesy of Owen Newlands*

RAF 1328 and 1327 on the Norfolk Broads in 1945 to 1946. These were the last RAF launches built by Herbert Woods. *Courtesy of Owen Newlands*

Thorneycroft's HSL 2651 at Felixstowe in 1946. *Courtesy of Owen Newlands*

A 24ft Marine Tender at Felixstowe with 1103 MCU in 1946. *Courtesy of Owen Newlands*

Napier Sea Lion engines aboard a Hants and Dorset high-speed launch, taken in October 1944. *Courtesy of Don Thurston*

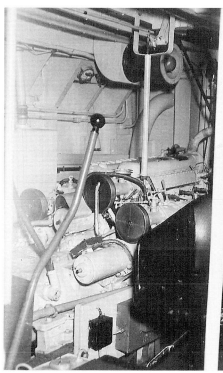
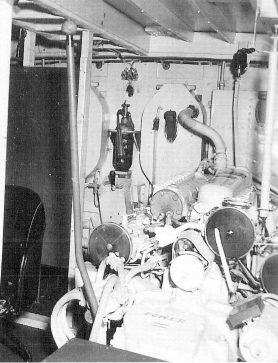

Seaplane tender 378 at Waltershofenhafen, Hamburg in 1948. *Courtesy of John Sutherland*

fitted so that it would not drag the boat away from the downed crew. A rocket-fired, weighted drogue was fitted to the bow to create a sea anchor. The boat could still capsize, however. Inflated buoyancy chambers could not be used because the craft had to fit in the belly of the aircraft that was carrying it. Consequently, a system was devised whereby carbon dioxide bottles would inflate the buoyancy chambers once the parachute had opened. To ensure that the downed crew saw the boat, two rockets were installed that would fire automatically when it impacted with the sea. They would fire out 200 ft (60 m) of buoyant line, one to port and one to starboard. Using these ropes the crew would be able to clamber onboard.

The contract to construct these craft was given to Uffa Fox, who was well known for constructing light sailing craft, and they were to become known as 'Uffa Fox boats'. Some changes were made to the design and minor modifications were needed to the Hudsons, but an acceptable compromise was reached by April 1942.

An example of how useful the Uffa Fox boat might be occurred in June 1942 when a Halifax crew ditched in the North Sea and found that their dinghy was drifting closer to the coast of Holland. They were in the sea for forty-eight hours and although they were rescued, they could have been taken out of danger far more quickly had the new invention already been available.

During July and August 1942 tests of the new airborne lifeboat met with general approval. On 19 September approval was given to begin construction of Mark I. A considerable problem arose in October 1942, however , when it was decided that Warwicks would be used for long-range searches, rather than Hudsons. The airborne lifeboat had not been tested on a Warwick so production was delayed. No. 279 Squadron was still using Hudsons, and had proved that the aircraft was successfully fulfilling its role. For the time being, therefore, they would retain them until at least March 1943. Limited production of twenty-four Mark Is was approved to cover the period before the boat could be redesigned for use on Warwicks. It was hoped that these twenty-four boats would be available by January 1943.

In March 1942 it was decided that each RAF airbase was

to appoint an air sea rescue officer, who would be directly responsible for ensuring that aircrew were given sufficient dinghy drill and taught the procedures when ditching and, above all, for making sure that all aircraft carried air sea rescue equipment. In the previous month there had been five cases of aircraft going down over the sea without any indication of their location and this new move sought to combat this problem.

New procedures to improve communication between aircraft and air sea rescue services were also put in place. In essence an aircraft in difficulties had to inform its own station of the problem and the fact that they intended to ditch. All relevant details would then be passed on, including course, air speed, height, position and time. Until the aircraft ditched it would continue to send out an SOS distress signal. The crew would need to ensure that all the lower escape hatches, bomb doors and communication doors were closed prior to ditching. The upper exits should be opened and the pilot should try to land into the wind, with his tail down. The rest of the crew would brace themselves. The crew would then evacuate the aircraft and climb aboard the emergency dinghy with any equipment they would need.

Improvements had been made to the dinghies during the spring of 1942; weather covers had been added to all the larger ones by April. The smaller K dinghies were fitted with a weather apron and hood. Marine distress signals were packed in a rubber waterproof cover, although this never proved to be very effective. Crews far preferred to take a Very pistol out of the aircraft and waterproofed red star Very cartridges became part of the dinghy pack. The smoke floats that had previously been carried were replaced by waterproofed distress signals and three of these were carried. There were continuing experiments to find highly nourishing food that would not take up a great deal of space. Drinks tended to be either tinned fruit juice or tomato juice, but by the end of the spring of 1942 canned water had all but replaced these.

Floating knives were now included, as were floating torches, a whistle, chocolate, water or fruit juice, first-aid equipment, skullcaps, paddles, a bailer, leakage stoppers, emergency rations, a telescopic mast and flag, distress signals, a dinghy cover and Very cartridges. Collectively they saved hundreds of lives.

It was also decided that the dinghies should have their own wireless transmitters. Experiments had begun back in 1941 and a prototype was finally available in September. However, with the capture of a German NS2 wireless the developers realised that their prototype was far inferior. Consequently, on 22 September 1941 the Ministry of Aircraft Production authorised the manufacture of 2,000 modified German sets. Approval for the prototype was given and it was proposed that a set should be made available for every dinghy. In addition to the 2,000 already on order, in January 1942 a further 8,000 were authorised. As an interim measure, a transmitter (T 1333), which could transmit SOS signals and therefore operate as a homing beacon, was developed. Despite technical problems the device, which was fitted with a gas-filled balloon to raise the aerial, was approved in December 1941, with the promise that it would be in service by May 1942. The device was dogged by delays, however. In April 1942 the balloon had been abandoned and a mast, or a rocket-launched kite, was proposed as a substitute. By July 1942 only sixteen had been delivered, with 100 promised the following month. Again the RAF had to make do and an order was placed for 1,000 copies of the German NS 2, produced by the Americans.

In October 1941 the Director General of Aircraft Safety had begun investigating a pigeon service that could be used for air sea rescue purposes. The RAF Pigeon Service was already established and was used by reconnaissance aircraft and bombers, particularly when communications otherwise could not work or were inadvisable. The major problem was that the pigeons would not fly when visibility was poor, at night nor when they were soaking wet. They were put in waterproof containers, but they seldom survived a crash or remained dry.

Having said that, the pigeon basket was replaced by a water-tight, floating pigeon container in January 1942. The next month there was an example of the use of a pigeon during a rescue. On 23 February a Beaufort flying out of Leuchars failed to return to base. At 2000 hours its last position was given as 150 miles (240 km) east of Aberdeen. When the aircraft ditched, one of the pigeons escaped, but the crew released the other with a message. The second bird was never seen again but the one that escaped made its way back to its loft. By estimating the time of the crash and the distance the pigeon could have covered given its condition, it was figured that the aircraft was around 100 miles (160 km) east of Aberdeen, not 150. A Catalina was despatched to search immediately, but could not find the dinghy. On the following morning a Hudson found it almost equidistant from the ASR bases at Blyth and Aberdeen, which were under the command of Rosyth. High-speed launches were despatched from both bases while a Walrus from the Fleet Air Arm base at Arbroath circled the dinghy. At around 1400 hours one of the Blyth launches got to the spot and picked up the four survivors; they were back on dry land by 1730 hours. From this point on aircraft ditching drills included the use of pigeons.

Investigations had also been under way to install a radar device in the dinghies. The idea was to provide them with an automatic distress signal that could act as a homing beacon to aircraft equipped with ASV. It was a form of oscillator and assuming that the high-speed launches could also be fitted with ASV, it should be possible to pick up crews in poor weather and at night. An officer created an experimental oscillator at No. 608 Squadron, Bircham Newton, and in February 1942 the Ministry of Aircraft Production authorised trials. Little progress was made, however, despite reminders in March and April. By May 1942, therefore, there were no transmitter sets, oscillators or in fact anything other than the pigeon service.

In March 1942, No. 13 Group, which covered the Scottish coast, requested air sea rescue cover. An ASR squadron of aircraft was desperately needed, but there were not enough Lysanders so Boulton Paul Defiants were earmarked as a possible replacement. They were obsolete as fighter aircraft, but trials proved that the Mark I was actually quite useful in the ASR role and accordingly, on 26 March 1942, No. 281 Squadron was formed. In fact the Defiant proved to be an improvement on the Lysander and the four existing Lysander squadrons, Nos 275, 276, 277 and 278, were switched over to Defiants at the beginning of May. This meant that the equipment that had been carried by the Lysanders needed to be redesigned. By June a modified dinghy container was designed for the Defiant, which like the Lysander could be dropped from the wings. The major drawback was that the Defiant could only carry two sets of dinghy packs instead of the Lysander's four.

By June 1942, with the RAF's increasing bomber offensive, the long-standing proposals for the expansion of high-speed launches appeared to be something of an underestimate. Moreover, increasing numbers of American aircraft were based in Britain, which added to the problem. It was therefore proposed that rather than just ninety-six launches, there should now be 126. The Treasury questioned these new demands, but it was pointed out that the initial establishment had not even been reached yet and that in any case it was only an initial establishment and not the final figure. The Treasury reluctantly gave their permission for the 25 per cent increase, provided that up to ten of the extra craft were pinnaces. Therefore by August 1942 the RAF was supposed to have 116 high-speed launches and eighty pinnaces. In actual fact, however, an audit of 1 August showed that they had just fifty-two high-speed launches, thirty-six seaplane tenders and twenty-two pinnaces, an increase of forty-eight craft in the first seven months of 1942.

The Irish government took possession of a 60 ft (18.3 m) RAF pinnace in August; manned by civilians, it would cover the Shannon area of the Irish Sea. It was loaned on the basis that any aircrew that it picked up would not be interned by neutral Ireland.

On the night of 11 August 1942 a Wellington was engaged in anti-submarine patrols in the Bay of Biscay. Early in the morning of the 12th the pilot informed his base that his starboard engine had failed and that he would be forced to ditch. This he did at around 0400 hours. The crew of six baled out, but the dinghy failed to blow out of the stowage. The crew managed to pull it out by hand whilst standing on the wing and clambered aboard. They spent the first three hours bailing. They used their only two marine signals when a Beaufighter and a Whitley passed overhead. Indeed nine more aircraft flew over them but the crew failed to attract the attention of any of them. They were finally spotted by a Whitley, which was being escorted by three Beaufighters. The Whitley dropped another dinghy and a Thornaby bag. The crew could not reach the dinghy, but in the Thornaby bag were a Very pistol and cartridges. Another Whitley came to circle the dinghy, but on its way back to base it was shot down and the whole crew was lost. A Sunderland was then despatched, escorted by Beaufighters. A German aircraft tried to engage them but soon sped off. The Sunderland put down on the sea, but the conditions were very rough and it was rolled over. A starboard engine burst into flames and the Sunderland sank. Now the Sunderland crew had to take to their own dinghy, which burst. One of the crew managed to swim to the spare dinghy that had been dropped for the Wellington crew, but by the time he reached it he was so exhausted he could not help his colleagues and the rest of the Sunderland crew drowned.

The next day two Whitleys circled the dinghies but they had to turn and flee when three Arados attacked them. There was no further help on 14 and 15 August owing to poor weather conditions. HMS *Tynedale* then left Falmouth to try to find them. There was a south-westerly wind and the Wellington's crew made a makeshift mast and sail, but they made little progress. On 16 August, two Beaufighters found them and signalled them to try and get closer to the man who had survived the Sunderland ditching. Two Hudsons appeared and one dropped Lindholme equipment; the dinghy landed upside down. The Wellington's crew clambered aboard with difficulty. They then lashed their own dinghy to the new one and paddled towards the Sunderland's survivor. After five hours they reached him and the three dinghies were lashed together.

Meanwhile, HMS *Tynedale* was still looking for them, escorted on and off by Beaufighters. A Junkers 88 was attacked by one of the Beaufighters and shot down and another Beaufighter fought off the attentions of two Fw 190s. Around this time a Sunderland passed over the three dinghies but, afraid of attracting the attention of enemy aircraft, the survivors did not attempt to signal her. On 17 August three Hudsons and two Beaufighters appeared over the dinghies; but there were still enemy aircraft in the vicinity. One of the Beaufighters spotted three Arados escorting a German motor launch and engaged them. Meanwhile there were other motor launches, motor anti-submarine boats, high-speed launches and Hudsons in the area. One of the Hudsons contacted the motor launches and gave them the position of the dinghies, but almost immediately it was attacked by two Fw 190s; luckily a Beaufighter managed to drive them off.

At 0730 hours two motor launches picked up the survivors.

Now, however, they were in danger from persistent German aircraft. They headed for home but were spotted by Fw 190s and later a Condor and a Junkers 88, before these could make their attack, however, some Beaufighters appeared. At 1720 hours the launches finally entered Newlyn harbour, 124 hours after the Wellington had ditched. Moreover, although the rescue was finally successful and seven men had been saved and two enemy aircraft damaged, a Sunderland, a Whitley and a Wellington had been lost, as well as seventeen crew.

CHAPTER FOUR

Dieppe to D-Day

O n 19 August 1942 Operation Jubilee was launched to capture Dieppe. There were a number of key objectives. The first was to test out the defences along the French coast, and the second to make an assessment of the Germans' ability to respond to landings. Thirdly the aim was to draw out the *Luftwaffe* into aerial combat over the sea. Aside from the British and Canadian units detailed for amphibious landings, the RAF were to deploy some sixty squadrons in order to provide cover and support. Fighter Command was to provide aircraft for air cover and close support, whilst Bomber Command was to target batteries, installations and concentrations of German troops. Coastal Command was available for reconnaissance and Army Cooperation aircraft would make other tactical attacks.

It was abundantly clear that the ASR would be required in significant numbers. Royal Navy forces would be responsible for sea rescues up to 3 miles (5 km) from Dieppe, whilst ASR units operating out of Dover, Ramsgate and Newhaven would cover the rest of the area. The first launches were put to sea shortly after 0430 hours to undertake their first rescue. In all thirty-one rescue vessels took part: fourteen high-speed launches, four from Ramsgate and five each from Dover and Newhaven; and seventeen naval vessels from Dover Command. From dawn, five Walruses, three Lysanders and twelve Defiants made continual patrols over the sea. The RAF was involved in the operation from dawn until the late afternoon, despite the fact that the land forces began withdrawing from Dieppe around midday. German opposition had increased as the day proceeded and RAF fighter cover over Dieppe ranged from three to nine squadrons, cover which was to continue during the ground forces' return trip.

In addition to the army's losses on the beaches and in Dieppe, 106 British aircraft were lost, eighty-eight of which were fighters, and around eighty aircrew were either killed or missing. German losses were crushing: they had lost between 150 and 200 aircraft. In theory the RAF's marine craft were under the protective umbrella of the fighter patrols, but in practice they often had to stray outside it in order to make a pick-up. They therefore also suffered losses: three were sunk, accounting for two officers and eighteen other ranks. Despite these casualties they continued to patrol and pick-up stricken aircrew. The ASR picked up twelve aircrew and the Royal Navy three. A fishing boat out of Rye picked up one more.

According to the official report, the RAF high-speed launches and the Royal Naval vessels responded to forty-seven SOS calls, most of which were near the French coast. No. 27 ASR/MCU Dover took the brunt of the casualties. HSL 123 was attacked by two Fw 190s and then again by four more. It then came under fire from shore batteries and was sunk. Two members of the crew were killed and the rest were wounded. HSL 123's partner, HSL 122 was bombed by Heinkel HE 111s; the captain and four of the crew were killed, and another later died of his wounds. The rest were wounded and two were taken prisoner. HSL 147 was attacked near the French coast by German aircraft and shot at by shore batteries. The captain and three of the crew were killed, two were posted missing and the others were taken prisoner. HSL 186 was attacked by Fw 190s and two of the crew were wounded.

Meanwhile, No. 28 ASR/MCU Newhaven had despatched HSLs 104, 106, 116, 117 and 177. The last two went to the aid of the two stricken HSLs from Dover and HSL 177 managed to rescue fourteen survivors. Among the craft despatched by No. 27 ASR/MCU (detachment) Ramsgate were HSLs 120 and 127.

There were a number of lessons to be learned from the Dieppe episode as far as ASR was concerned. Whilst it was standing orders for rescue motor launches and naval motor launches to engage both enemy aircraft and surface vessels if the opportunity arose, high-speed launches and anti-submarine boats were only to engage if fired upon first. Dieppe proved that the Germans considered any British vessel to be a target, so it was clear that additional protection was needed. The first step was to supply fifteen Oerlikon guns for the high-speed launches operating at Dover and Newhaven; work on this began in September 1942. Then craft in other areas of the south coast and the east coast south of the Humber, followed. Thirty-two vessels operating out of Dover, Felixstowe, Gorleston, Gosport, Grimsby, Newhaven and Newlyn were to be given an Oerlikon and four .303 Vickers machine-guns each. Armour plating would also be provided and additional protection given for turret gunners. In late October 1942, the Admiralty was asked to supply another seventeen Oerlikons and delivery began in December.

The aircraft allocated to ASR proved that the organisation was virtually at the bottom of the pecking order. They were almost all worn out or obsolete. Moreover the Defiant had not proved to be a useful substitute for the Lysander. The service badly needed another three close search squadrons and a further four squadrons from Coastal Command, which ideally would be Mosquitoes, Beaufighters or Havocs. With suitable aircraft the number of rescues could be increased, which would improve the efficiency of the service and improve the morale of aircrews.

It was agreed that Spitfires would replace the Defiants and Lysanders being used in high-risk areas and that Ansons would operate in the deep search role. This, of course, meant that the rescue equipment carried by Defiants had to be redesigned for the Spitfire, but the adaptation for the Anson proved to be fairly simple.

On 27 November 1942 the five Fighter Command squadrons earmarked for ASR were authorised to increase their strength by nine land aircraft and six amphibians. This still meant that the area between Montrose and Oban on the Scottish coast remained uncovered, even though there had been seventy ditching incidents in the area over the past twelve months. In December 1942 it was proposed that a squadron should be based at Castletown with detachments at Peterhead and Scatsta. This new squadron, No. 282 ASR Squadron, would come into operation on 1 January 1943 and it would have three Ansons and four Walruses.

In November 1942, after thirteen months of lobbying and work by Coastal Command and the Air Sea Rescue Service, an

RAF Marine Craft and Air Sea Rescue badge was finally approved. Requests had been made to the Under Secretary of State and the Director General of Aircraft Safety and various designs were put forward. The plea for a badge was fully supported by the media, who were becoming increasingly vociferous on the subject. The design that was submitted to the King for approval was a simple drawing of a launch, with the letters ASR. It was, however, decided that it would only be worn by aircraftmen. It was felt that to allow the masters of rescue aircraft to wear a special badge would be a serious breach of tradition and would simply open the floodgates for various other groups of specialist officers to demand their own badge.

In January 1943 Sir John Salmond retired and his post was abolished, to be replaced by a director of air safety. Air Commodore H. A. Haines was appointed as the first Director. Like Salmond he was responsible to the Deputy Chief of Air Staff and later to the Assistant Chief of Air Staff (Operations) when the Deputy Chief of Air Staff post was abolished. In August 1943 the responsibility was transferred to the Assistant Chief of Air Staff (General).

In February 1943 the air staff agreed to work towards what was called Target H. This was an ASR expansion programme, primarily related to aircraft, designed to take the service up to March 1944. The target was that by that date there would be eight and a half squadrons, each with twenty aircraft. The provisional programme, which was issued in March 1943, called for four squadrons in Coastal Command and one in Fighter Command, all equipped with Warwicks. The existing amphibian squadrons would continue to use their Walruses until the Sea Otter replaced them in 1944. The other squadrons would be equipped with Mosquitoes and Spitfires.

No. 280 Squadron was still using Ansons, Hudsons were not available. They had been given three Wellingtons in February 1943 so that they could orientate themselves for the switch to Warwicks. There was a dwindling number of Hudsons available and by April 1943, No. 279 Squadron had been reduced to twelve aircraft instead of their establishment of twenty.

The development of the Warwick was slow. A number had been produced that did not meet all the requirements of an ASR aircraft, but it was finally decided that the service would accept the incomplete version in lieu of the fully developed model. Ten were to be delivered in July and twenty more in August. Nos. 279 and 280 Squadrons both geared up for their arrival. They were ultimately to be given sixteen plus four as reserve, all equipped to carry an airborne lifeboat and Lindholme equipment. No. 280 Squadron was to receive its aircraft at the beginning of July and No. 279 Squadron in September. However, there were more production delays, and the Assistant Chief of Air Staff (Operations) wrote to the Secretary of State and told him that ASR was being severely hampered. Re-equipment took place over the summer and autumn of 1943 and No. 280 Squadron finally received its full complement at the beginning of October. They then had to be withdrawn from operational duties in order to carry out training.

Just as No. 279 Squadron was about to receive its Warwicks, Coastal Command decided that the squadron should retain their Hudsons and an entirely new squadron should be created with the Warwicks. On 11 November 1943 permission was given to create Nos 281 and 282 Squadrons. Fighter Command's new squadron, 282, would consist of ten Ansons and seven Walruses. No. 281, the squadron available to Coastal Command, would have an establishment of twenty Warwicks. Fighter Command now had five rescue squadrons and Coastal Command three.

Fighter Command now had responsibility for the seas running from Southwold to the Hook of Holland and from Land's End to Brest. Coastal Command was therefore responsible for all other areas, which would be covered by three squadrons of Warwicks and one squadron of Hudsons, operating out of Bircham Newton, Thornaby, Davidstow Moor and Tiree. No. 269 (Metropolitan) Squadron, which was based in the Azores, was re-formed in January 1944 and covered rescue operations in the Bay of Biscay.

During the last six months of 1942, 1,761 aircrew ditched in the seas around the British Isles and of these 66 per cent, or 1,166 men, lost their lives. The establishment of station air sea rescue officers had so far proved to be something of a failure; they lacked the necessary expertise. In February 1943, therefore, authority was given to create a School of Air Sea Rescue, and a new trade was created, that of safety equipment worker. Once these men had been trained they would be posted to squadrons and would be responsible for the packing, stowage and maintenance of emergency equipment. The school was established at Blackpool; it had three Ansons and made use of the ASR marine craft based at Fleetwood. Those attending the two-week training course would be drawn from Bomber Command, Coastal Command, Fighter Command, Flying Training Command, Transport Command and the US Air Force (USAF). The first course got under way at the end of May 1943.

Earlier in the month, on 14 May, a Lancaster bomber was hit at 17,000 ft (5,200 m) close to the coast of Holland. The pilot lost control but managed to regain it at around 8,000 ft (2,400 m). Although he jettisoned his bombs the aircraft continued to lose height. When he reached 4,000 ft (1,200 m) it was clear that he would have to ditch. By the time the wireless operator was aware that they were about to ditch, the aircraft was too low for a fix to be made on the SOS signal, in any case, he did not switch on the distress signal.

The aircraft managed to ditch successfully and the crew clambered into a dinghy with their emergency packs, pigeon container and radio transmitter. They cut two cords which they believed were holding the dinghy to the aircraft, but they were the cords holding an emergency pack with a signal pistol and other emergency equipment. One of the two pigeons had drowned because the lid of the container had not been closed properly and the other was soaking wet. When it was released it disappeared and was never seen again. The crew then spent twenty-four hours in the dinghy. Two Spitfires and two Bostons passed overhead but the crew were unable to attract their attention. Moreover, the radio did not work because the loading unit was missing.

For the next four days they drifted and got to a point where they could see both the French and English coasts. It was only on the fifth day that they were picked up 8 miles (13 km) north-east of Dungeness by a minesweeper.

By May 1943 ASR marine craft units around the British Isles had 130 high-speed launches, twenty-five pinnaces and twenty-seven seaplane tenders. In addition, the Royal Navy had fifty rescue motor launches and fourteen each of motor anti-submarine boats and air rescue boats.

In 1943 many of the new pieces of rescue equipment that had

been developed throughout 1942 finally began to be delivered. Arguably one of the most important was the airborne lifeboat. The first twenty-four were produced in January 1943; No. 279 Squadron's Hudsons had to be modified in order to carry them. The Mark I version was designed to carry a crew of seven and sustain them for seven days. It included a dinghy radio set, a Very pistol and cartridges, a waterproof torch, an Aldis lamp, smoke floats, waterproof outer suits, first-aid equipment, massage oil, chemical hot bottles, tinned water, drinking cups, condensed milk, emergency rations, cigarettes and matches. In addition to all this equipment there was also a compass, log and charts, repair materials, tools and bellows for inflating the self-righting compartments after leak stoppers had been used. All this equipment was stored in the boat's lockers, along with masts, rigging, oil, sails and petrol. The boat had to be dropped into the wind and when it neared the sea a cartridge was fired off that sent out a sea-anchored drogue to bring it with its bows to the wind. When the boat hit the water a second switch closed and two more rockets fired buoyant lines port and starboard to help the crew climb aboard.

On 5 May 1943 this life boat had its first opportunity to prove its worth. A Halifax bomber was hit by German flak and ditched in the sea just over 50 miles (80 km) east of Spurn Head. The bomb aimer was severely injured and at first the crew were unable to get the dinghy out. Eventually they managed to break into the stowage and pull it out. They clambered into it and soon afterwards a Hudson of No. 279 Squadron came to investigate the area, drawn to it by the SOS that had been sent before ditching. It circled for about an hour, at which time two more Hudsons arrived. The Halifax crew had no prior knowledge of the lifeboat and when one of the Hudsons dropped it they were amazed to see a vessel with propellers heading towards them. The lifeboat landed on the water, but the rocket drogue did not work. However, the automatic release for the parachutes functioned perfectly and the boat came to rest around 25 yards from the dinghy.

The injured bomb aimer was laid over the equipment hatch, which contained the instructions on how to operate the boat. Nevertheless the Halifax's engineer and navigator managed to get the engine started and they followed the course flashed to them by one of the Hudsons, using their Aldis lamp. They proceeded at 6 knots, towing the dinghy, but the rope broke and the dinghy drifted away. After a while the lifeboat's starboard engine failed but the Halifax crew still managed to make progress using the port engine and sail. Shortly afterwards the port engine also failed, but it was now daylight and by midday they were sighted and a high-speed launch and two rescue motor launches reached them and brought them home to Grimsby.

Experiments were under way to create a version of the airborne lifeboat that could be carried by Warwicks. The new version is variously known as Mark Ia and Mark II. These boats were 30 ft (9 m) long and designed to carry up to ten men at around 7 knots for about 300 miles (480 km). The reason for the confusion over the different marks was that as an interim measure there was an adaptation of the Mark I, which became known as the Mark Ia.

This new version did not become operational until the autumn of 1943. In November one was taken to America so that the USAF could begin work on adapting it for its own Flying Fortresses. It took the Americans just ten weeks to adapt and drop their version.

On 7 January 1944, at 1440 hours, four RAF Mosquitoes left Predannack to undertake an offensive patrol over the Bay of Biscay. At 1624 they spotted two Ju 88s. The Mosquitoes gave chase, overtaking one of the German aircraft and shooting it down. During the dogfight one of the Mosquitoes received hits to both its engines and it had to ditch. Operating at low level and over 170 miles (270 km) south of Land's End, they had little chance of sending a distress signal. The Mosquito landed safely in the water and within a few minutes the pilot and navigator had clambered out with both their K-type and L-type dinghies, both well equipped, with six red signals, leak stoppers, whistles, compass, map, sails, floating torches, emergency rations, ever-hot bags, paddles, drogues, aprons, bellows, rescue lines and floating knives.

The two men lashed the dinghies together and took it in turns to keep watch overnight. In the morning they hoisted a sail on the K dinghy and towed the other. They were making around 1 knot and heading in a north-easterly direction. At around midday four of their own squadron's Mosquitoes began circling them and a little later five Beaufighters arrived. They now knew that they had been spotted and shortly afterwards a Warwick from No. 280 Squadron dropped an airborne lifeboat around 100 yards from their position. The two men paddled the dinghies to the lifeboat and clambered aboard, where they found a message that said 'steer 350 degrees – good luck.' Unfortunately the parachute lines had fouled the propellers, so the pilot jumped over the side and used a knife to clear them.

They got under way using the starboard engine, but after an hour it stopped so they started up the port engine and continued along at around 3 knots, but shortly before dawn on 9 January this engine also stopped and they discovered that a rocket wire had fouled both of the propellers. They could not clear them so they erected the sails using the instruction booklet. They continued to make slow progress and in the afternoon a Mosquito began circling around them. The ditched men believed that they were somewhere to the south of the Scillies. In the evening a Liberator, flying out of St Eval, and high-speed launches and rescue motor launches from Penzance and the Scillies were despatched. The Liberator failed to spot the lifeboat and dropped flares and petrol beside one of the high-speed launches by mistake, while it was still 7 miles (11 km) from the lifeboat.

By midnight the wind had dropped and the men furled their sails and took it in turns to rest. Shortly afterwards they heard engines and to their delight they saw three rescue motor launches. It was a quarter to midnight on 11 January and they were about 40 miles (65 km) south-west of Land's End. They had been adrift in the water for over 100 hours, but they would probably have actually made it back to land under their own steam. Perhaps what saved them was the fact that the pilot was the squadron's air sea rescue officer.

Another successful drop of an airborne lifeboat took place on 14 July 1944. An operational training unit's Wellington was hit by flak around 20 miles (30 km) south of Caen. It was *en route* to drop pamphlets over Rennes. The pilot shrugged off the damage, but by the time he was 50 miles (80 km) from his target the oil pressure dropped to zero and he swung the aircraft around towards Bayeux to head for the sea. The crew began to prepare for ditching and signalled their base. At around 0210 hours they ditched 25 miles (40 km) west of Cap de la Heve.

They managed to clamber aboard their dinghy, all suffering from seasickness. By the morning they realised that they were drifting towards the French coast, which was still in enemy hands. They began to paddle feverishly away from the coastline and at around midday a group of Typhoons spotted them 15 miles (25 km) west of Le Havre. They continued to drift and by the following morning they were spotted by Typhoons 8 miles (13 km) off Cap d'Antifer. Hudsons of No. 279 Squadron were scrambled and they managed to drop an airborne lifeboat just 20 yards from them. The crew climbed onboard and jettisoned their dinghy.

Luckily two of the crew had experience with engines and within twenty minutes the boat was under way, heading north at around 7 knots. They had covered about 30 miles (50 km) when they were picked up by two high-speed launches about 37 miles (60 km) north-west of Cap d'Antifer. It was generally believed that even if the launches had not found them, they would have reached the Solent in around six hours.

Towards the end of 1943 the Q-type sailing dinghy was earmarked for use in a number of aircraft, including the Halifax, Lancaster, Warwick, Wellington and Whitley. A smaller version, known as the S-type, was also under development, but there were doubts about whether this would prove to be of any use. Early versions of the Q-type floundered as a result of the difficulty in assembling the sails and a simplified sail plan was sought. In January 1944 it was decided that the delays would be too great and that enough of the existing version should be made for the Halifaxes, Lancasters (with enlarged stowage – Marks II and IV), Warwicks and Windsors.

The Q-type had a chance to prove itself off the west coast of France on 17 May 1944. A Whitley, flying out of St Eval on anti-submarine patrols, suffered a starboard engine failure. The pilot managed to get an SOS signal off and prepared to ditch. The aircraft hit the water at considerable speed and the bomb aimer and rear gunner suffered fractures and other injuries. There was another mishap as the men evacuated the aircraft and clambered aboard their dinghy. The wireless operator threw the dinghy radio into the sea, but luckily they managed to retrieve it. The weather was extremely poor and two ASR aircraft that were sent out to find them had to be recalled.

The crew did spot a Whitley, but they were unable to contact it with their radio. At around 1000 hours the following morning they decided to try to rig up the mast and hoist the sails. The instructions proved to be somewhat beyond them, but they did manage to erect the mainsail. Towards late afternoon they were spotted by a Sunderland, but when it tried to make a landing close to them it stalled and its nose hit the water. The Sunderland was badly damaged and the captain killed, but the rest of the crew climbed aboard their J-type dinghy.

The two crews managed to lash their dinghies together. Shortly before dark a second Sunderland was seen and they managed to attract its attention with a Very pistol. Luckily a destroyer was on its way, having been appraised of the dinghy's position by the first Sunderland's crew. The next morning they saw yet another Sunderland and this time the floatplane managed to land successfully and take all the survivors on board. They were then transferred to the destroyer.

The original crew later stated that, despite their difficulties in erecting the sails, had it not been for them they would never have been spotted by the first Sunderland.

By February 1943 some 1,600 radio transmitter sets were ready for general issue. Two-thirds of this initial batch was given to home commands and the balance to overseas units. Possibly one of the first examples of their use occurred in May 1943 when nineteen merchant seamen were spotted in the Atlantic Ocean, some 450 miles (725 km) from the British coast. A Coastal Command's Sunderland managed to drop them a dinghy transmitter, but the weather was so poor that for the next four days they were not spotted. The seamen continued to transmit SOS signals and Coastal Command aircraft systematically searched the area. The signals continued for two further days and on the eighth day a destroyer managed to pinpoint their position and pick up the nineteen men.

Despite the issue of these dinghy radio transmitters, it was estimated that in only 5 per cent of cases were they ever taken into the dinghy. What was needed was a smaller set which could actually be stowed in a K-type dinghy. The first version was tested in February 1943 and became known as Walter. At the beginning of May 1943 it was decided to begin production.

A sacrifice would have to be made to accommodate it, however, and it was decided that it would replace the sailing gear. It was an interesting decision, particularly as the usefulness of the sail had been demonstrated in April. A Spitfire was shot down on the 11th around 135 miles (215 km) south of the Lizard. The pilot, in his K-type dinghy, was not seen until he was less than 50 miles (80 km) south of the Lizard on 17 April. A Lancaster spotted him and search aircraft were sent out to find him. An Anson saw him again in the evening of 18 April and guided in a Walrus by dropping flares. The floatplane managed to pick up the pilot. The pilot had covered over 100 miles (160 km) in seven days as a result of being able to deploy his sails.

It was not until October 1943 that Walter went into general production. It comprised a cylindrical battery container, a telescopic mast which could extend to 7 ft (2.1 m), and at the top an oscillator unit. The battery was capable of operating for twenty hours. The first units became available in January 1944 and they became general issue the following month.

Meanwhile, an American dinghy radio was being developed and it was finally agreed that around 12,000 of these sets would be delivered to the RAF during 1944. The British version of this set, known as the T 1333, had begun to be distributed in July 1943, but it proved to be inferior to the American version.

The use of pigeons as a tool for air sea rescue came under review in 1943. Indeed the Director of Aircraft Safety proposed that the pigeon service be abolished in November 1943. The birds had not been very effective up to this time and, considering that aircraft were operating further from the shores of the British Isles, it was doubtful that they could cover these extended distances.

On 11 October however, a pigeon did earn its keep. A Catalina left Sullom Voe, flying west of the Shetlands. Its wireless was out of commission and it was forced to ditch. The weather was poor and search aircraft could not take to the skies. A pigeon released from the Catalina, arrived at Sullom Voe that evening, and its message gave the aircraft's ditching location. A message was then transmitted to the Catalina's dinghy transmitter and shortly afterwards a signal was heard, very faint but strong enough to obtain a fix. Shortly after midnight the Catalina was spotted by a launch and the crew was taken on board.

Throughout 1943 there were constant arguments regarding the use of pinnaces and high-speed launches. It was certainly true that pinnaces were slower and more prone to mechanical defects. It was strongly believed that a smaller number of high-speed launches could do the job of the pinnaces. By August it was generally agreed that high-speed launches should replace pinnaces for most duties. In September it was agreed that the number of high-speed launches operating around the British Isles should be raised from an estimated ninety-six to 122, whilst the number of pinnaces be reduced from forty-five (plus nine in reserve) to eleven, with two in reserve.

In October 1943 the Browning gun turrets that had been promised two years' earlier finally began to be fitted to the high-speed launches. They had been dogged by technical difficulties and the lack of labour.

In 1943 there had been a huge increase in air operations, and some 1,188 aircraft had been lost at sea. This meant that 5,466 crew had been forced to ditch. The ASR had managed to pick up 31 per cent of them, or 1,684 men. Although the percentage was similar to that in 1942, the actual number of men picked up was double. The service had taken great strides. In its first seven months the Air Sea Rescue School had trained 526 officers and 3,000 safety equipment assistants. Training films had also been produced, including *Prepare for Ditching* and in December *Ditching Without Hedging*.

Huge numbers of USAF aircraft and personnel had also begun arriving in Britain from the spring of 1942. Initially the Americans trained and observed alongside their RAF counterparts, but this changed in the late summer of 1942 when the 8th Air Force arrived in great strength. It would have been wasteful for the Americans to establish their own air sea rescue service, so investigations were begun to see whether the RAF's existing Air Sea Rescue Service was capable of picking up many more ditched crews.

In May 1942, General Spaatz became commander of the 8th Air Force and transferred to the European theatre of operations in July, to prepare for the bombing of Germany. He and General Arnold, Commanding General of the United States Army Air

Forces, discussed the situation with the Assistant Chief of Air Staff (Operations), Air Vice-Marshal N. H. Bottomley. The Americans decided to look at the possibility of providing men and aircraft for a deep search squadron. On 8 September 1942 the 8th Air Force was officially informed that the RAF Air Sea Rescue Service was at their disposal.

As it happened two Flying Fortresses needed the service within just a month. On 9 October 1942, 108 Flying Fortresses, took part in their first large-scale mission to bomb targets at Lille at high level, and two had to ditch. One was shot down by an Fw 190, which crippled two of its engines. The radio operator sent out an SOS but the receiver was not correctly tuned. Two of the crew were injured when the pilot ditched the aircraft about ½ mile (800 m) off North Foreland. Nonetheless, they managed to clamber aboard their two rafts, one of which had been damaged by bullet holes. It took just ninety seconds for the Flying Fortress to sink. The crew was fortunate in that a Spitfire pilot had witnessed their crash. There were heavy seas but despite that an ASR craft arrived to pick them up within thirty minutes.

Meanwhile, arrangements had been made for RAF personnel to deliver lectures to American crews about ditching. One of the problems was the fact that for the first time American aircraft would be flying over large expanses of water. It was a natural tendency – and indeed part of the training of American crews – to bale out rather than ditch. Moreover, several of the American aircraft were not ideal for ditching. They lacked stowage space and, as a result, equipment that would be needed in a dinghy was stowed elsewhere on the aircraft.

What probably prompted the Americans to pay far more attention to air sea rescue was the loss of the 8th Air Force's own chief of staff, Brigadier A. N. Duncan. He was on board a B-17 belonging to the 97th Bombardment Group. He left Britain for North Africa, but about 90 miles (140 km) west of Brest, his aircraft caught fire and ditched. The other seven B-17s dropped emergency equipment and radioed Predannack, the base that they had just left, which in turn contacted No. 44 Group Headquarters at Gloucester. The message said that one man was on board a life raft and five or six others were in the water, just in their Mae Wests. One of the B-17s circled for over six hours, whilst two Hudsons, escorted by Beaufighters, came out to join in the search. Two Royal Navy destroyers also swept the area, but none of the men was seen.

An inquiry into the incident later showed that no members of the 97th Bomber Group had been apprised of air sea rescue drills. By January 1943 it was decided that all crews of the 8th Air Force should undertake ditching drills and be made aware of the right procedures. Their headquarters quoted two cases, which, had the crews been sufficiently trained, would have had radically different outcomes.

A United States crew returning from a flight over the sea sighted two men in a dinghy a few miles off the English coast. They obtained no fix when over the dinghy and only after landing passed the information onto the rescue services. A search plane was despatched on the general directions obtained from the United States crew but failed to return, resulting in the loss of the two men in the dinghy as well as the rescue plane and its crew.

One United States aircraft of a flight of fourteen, which departed from St Eval developed engine trouble. Instead of making use of emergency facilities the pilot became confused and proceeded out to sea where it was believed that the crew abandoned the plane. Proper knowledge and use of emergency facilities would probably have saved the lives of the crew, if not the aircraft.

On 7 March 1943 the first two US lieutenants of the 8th U.S. Army Air Force completed the RAF air sea rescue course. In the previous month nine US aircraft had been lost and of the sixty-five crew involved only one man was saved.

The RAF continued to pressurise the USA to work towards improving exits for crews in their aircraft, fitting flotation gear, using automatic dinghy inflation and improving stowage. It was clear that American crews were still not practising ditching drills and that they were still paying little attention to air sea rescue. In March, however, a unit equipment officer was appointed to every group and squadron. These men were responsible for making sure both that emergency equipment, particularly para-chutes and rescue equipment, were stowed aboard the aircraft and also that the crews knew how to use them.

On 4 March, despite only rudimentary dinghy drill (the crew remembered seeing a dinghy drill diagram for their B-17) there was a successful rescue of a Flying Fortress crew. On a bombing raid over Germany, the aircraft was badly hit. Three of its engines were put out of action, along with its radio. The pilot tried to nurse the aircraft home, but when he had reached 5,000 ft (1,500 m), he knew that ditching was his only option. The two pilots remained in their flying positions while the other eight members of the crew braced themselves in the radio room. Despite the fact that the aircraft broke up into four pieces when it hit the water, all the ten crew managed to escape. The dinghies had not been stowed properly – they were loose in the fuselage and bundled up with string – and it took the crew thirty minutes to inflate the first one. By then three of their number had drowned. With great difficulty the seven survivors clambered about the first dinghy and tried to inflate the second. They saw a floating object and it finally dawned upon them that it was a dinghy radio. They managed to grab it and launch a kite aerial, and begin transmitting an SOS. Six hours later a search aircraft spotted them and managed to drop a Lindholme to them. They reached it and two hours later a minesweeper picked them up. This was the first time that a Flying Fortress crew had been picked up as a result of using a dinghy radio.

A second incident involving a dinghy radio occurred on 21 May 1943. A Flying Fortress had ditched and high-speed launches were despatched to home in on the dinghy radio signal. Despite thick fog the ten men were picked up and brought home the following evening. Indeed, by the end of July, eight crews had been picked up using the radio.

The American crews used two life rafts, known as A3 types, in each of their heavy bombers. They were designed to carry five men each, were roughly boat-shaped and had oars. Because of a lack of stowage space, these life rafts could not be replaced by J-type dinghies. Initially, therefore, US fighter pilots did not have dinghies and until an American version was available they were issued with RAF K-type dinghy packs. They also had RAF parachute harnesses, as the American version did not have a quick-release mechanism. The American Mae West was also slightly different from the British version; it did not have a supporting collar, which meant that an unconscious man in the sea simply drowned. Modifications were underway, but as an interim measure the Americans began using the British version. US emergency kits during 1943 were also largely of RAF origin.

Adaptations were made to the American A3 rafts so that equipment could be stowed, and a selection of both British and American rescue equipment was taken on a tour around all air force bases in the USA so that future combat crews would be familiar with them. By the summer of 1943 the combination of training and greater coordination had brought about a distinct improvement in rescue figures. In June 1943, 28 per cent of aircrews that had ditched had been saved – seventy-one out of 255. During a raid on St Nazaire on 28 June no less than six 8th Air Force bombers were lost, but three whole crews were rescued. In the following month the figures were even better; 196 Flying Fortress aircrew ditched and 139 were rescued. Perhaps the best achievement occurred on 25 July when eighty men had to ditch and seventy-eight were rescued.

Of particular significance on 25 July was that an airborne lifeboat saved one of the Flying Fortress crews, the first time an American crew had been saved in this way. On this occasion three Fw 190s bounced the aircraft just off the Danish coast. The pilot was forced to ditch nearly 80 miles (130 km) north-west of Borkum. The crew managed to evacuate the aircraft and tied their two dinghies together. They used their dinghy radio, transmitting an SOS every half-hour. They drifted for nearly twenty hours and at dawn they began to paddle in a roughly westerly direction. Around noon two Lancasters passed overhead and one of them spotted the dinghies and dropped a Lindholme nearby. The Lancaster returned later and dropped two more Lindholmes. All the crew put on their waterproof suits. That evening three Hudsons appeared overhead and one dropped an airborne lifeboat. The Flying Fortress crew easily managed to get aboard and abandoned their dinghies, which were subsequently sunk by gunfire from the Hudsons. After around three-quarters of an hour the Flying Fortress crew managed to get both of the airborne lifeboat's engines running and to erect the mast. One of the Hudsons signalled to them to indicate the right course and it proceeded without incident through the night. In the early hours of the next morning a Danish fishing boat was sighted and the four crew welcomed the Americans and agreed to take them to

England. They hauled the lifeboat aboard and just as they were about to get under way two RAF high-speed launches arrived. After enjoying a bottle of rum, the fishing boat and the two high-speed launches reached Great Yarmouth at 2245.

On 28 July an American Flying Fortress crew was again able to take advantage of an airborne lifeboat. The aircraft was hit on its way back from a bombing raid of Kiel. Numerous attacks from Fw 190s had put three of the engines out of action and had set fire to the starboard wing. The aircraft ditched, hitting the water very heavily tail first. Five men were able to abandon it but the other five lost their lives. The aircraft was sinking rapidly and its dinghy had not been blown out, so one of the crew went back on board and managed to pull it out just in the nick of time. Luckily it inflated and the five survivors climbed aboard, they had no rescue equipment, however, apart from distress flares, and they had not managed to send an SOS. Nevertheless another Flying Fortress from their squadron saw the dinghy and circled for a time before heading back to base. Later in the afternoon the crew saw three search aircraft, but the aircraft did not see them. Just as they were about to give up hope they fired another flare and this time they were seen. Two Hudsons arrived, one carrying an airborne lifeboat. The crew clambered aboard and followed the course given to them by one of the Hudsons. They made good progress on one engine and the following morning additional fuel was dropped to them. They had an aircraft escorting them throughout the whole of the day and that evening they were picked up nearly 100 miles (160 km) from Great Yarmouth by a high-speed launch and taken to Great Yarmouth. The crew had managed to travel 100 miles (160 km) by themselves in around twenty-eight hours.

In August 1943 the 8th Air Force agreed to make a single aircraft available to each group for air sea rescue. Lindholme equipment and later the Bircham barrel were cleared for use on Flying Fortresses, Liberators and Mitchells. As a result of this and further training and cooperation, during August 60 per cent of all ditched 8th Air Force crew was saved. In September this rose to 61 per cent. On two fateful days, 6 and 7 September, a total of 121 aircrew ditched, of whom all but three were saved.

Between July and December 1943, 1,346 men had been involved in ditching and of this number 524, or 40 per cent, had been rescued. This was a huge improvement compared to the first half of 1942, when the rescue rate had been just 6 per cent. In December the service had saved ten men from two B-24 Liberators that had ditched. This was the first time men crewing these aircraft had been involved in an air sea rescue operation.

It was clear that the Americans were now taking air sea rescue very seriously. In September 1943 the Headquarters of American Air Forces in Washington created a special branch known as the Emergency Rescue Branch. They were also making preparations to set up, along with the RAF, an air sea rescue service that would cover the Pacific Theatre. In early 1944 the Air Sea Rescue Agency was created in Washington, charged with coordinating the research and development of air sea rescue procedures, methods and techniques and, above all, maintaining liaison with the RAF Air Sea Rescue Service. In February 1944 an air sea rescue officer became part of the RAF delegation in Washington. The first person to fill this post was Wing Commander R. Bicknel.

From records of No. 277 Squadron A Flight, Martlesham Heath, in March 1944, we are able to piece together the story of the loss of HSL 2706, which was operating out of Gorleston. The relevant entries relate to 23 March 1944. The weather on that day was fair and at 0520 Operations informed A Flight that there was a problem and that they would be called back with further details later. At 0550 the position of a bomber that had ditched the previous night was given. A launch was already searching, but it was too dark to see anything. The launch had stayed out on patrol. A section of Spitfires from the flight were to begin their search at 0630.

At that time Flight Lieutenant Roden and Flight Officer Parisse took off, but Roden was forced to return to base because of an engine problem. He landed at 0635 and took off again in another aircraft at 0650. The two aircraft began to search; they reported that visibility was about 25 miles (40 km) and that the sea was calm. Having found nothing at all they returned to base at 0820. A relief flight, consisting of Flight Officer Dechamp and Pilot Officer Ormiston was airborne at 0805 and they searched until 0915. Two Walruses and three Spitfires were placed on standby and at around 1200 hours Roden and Parisse were again airborne, patrolling 20 miles (30 km) east of Felixstowe. Again Roden ran into aircraft difficulties and was forced to land at 1215. His place was taken by Dechamp, who proceeded to Felixstowe.

On the way back the flight passed over Orford Ness, where they saw a Flying Fortress that had ditched 15 miles (25 km) east. A Walrus was brought to the scene, which picked up the ten American crew. Then, 45 miles (70 km) east of Orford Ness, they saw a column of smoke rising into the sky. The Walrus set off to investigate and discovered that the smoke was coming from HSL 2706. Nearby there was a raft with three men on it. The Walrus saw an American P47 flying low, heading for the coast; it did not respond to signals. The Walrus returned to base, landing at 1200 hours.

At around 1300 hours Flying Control Martlesham Heath had received word that HSL 2706 had been attacked by a P47, which had mistaken it for a German E-boat, at around 1205. By 1250 hours the Walrus that had picked up the American pilots was airborne again, under the command of Flight Lieutenant Mackertich. They headed for the column of black smoke, escorted by a section of Spitfires. Three of the launch's crew were on a Carley float. Because of the heavy swell the Walrus could not land and directed a second launch to the position. Two Typhoons also arrived on the scene at this time. Also in the air were a P47, a Mustang and a Lightning, around 15 miles (25 km) to the east. A Hudson was circling a large patch of oil and a Lindholme dinghy, believed to contain seven corpses.

While all this was taking place one of the Typhoons reported that he was going to ditch, so the Walrus headed off for Orford Ness. The crew of the Walrus managed to pick up the airman but despite their efforts he died.

This was the second time that a launch operating out of Gorleston had been lost.

Another significant step in the improvement of the ASR took place at a meeting at the Air Ministry on 8 May 1944. The United States Strategic and Tactical Air Forces Headquarters agreed to establish a VHF fixer service at Saffron Walden and to allocate twenty-five P47 Thunderbolts, based at Boxted, specifically for ASR work. They would be equipped to carry M-type dinghies and smoke floats. The RAF agreed to make available six

Warwick aircraft, equipped with airborne lifeboats for every major 8th Air Force operation. Walrus aircraft, based at Martlesham, would also be able to respond instantly and all ASR craft along the east coast, within No. 6 Group's area of operations, would be fitted with equipment so that they could pick up signals on the ASR frequency.

A new rescue squadron, later known as the 5th Emergency Rescue Squadron, was established on 9 May 1944. It was involved in its first operation on 19 May when a B-17 ditched some 240 miles (390 km) north-east of Great Yarmouth. Warwicks were sent out to try to locate it. Because of the distance, the P 47s could not be deployed and as a result four Mustangs were despatched. At around 1812 hours the crew were spotted and an airborne lifeboat was dropped. The rescue aircraft patrolled the area throughout the night and at 0600 hours on 21 May saw a Danish fishing vessel haul the lifeboat aboard and begin to head back to Denmark. The circling Warwick fired shots close to the fishing boat and four P 47s managed to persuade it to halt. A high-speed launch out of Great Yarmouth located it and the ten Flying Fortress crew were picked up and taken back to Britain.

There was another example of the new cooperation on 29 June. At around 1135 hours the pilot of a Flying Fortress contacted Saffron Walden and informed them that he was about to ditch. Additional signals were obtained from the bomber's fighter escort, who informed Saffron Walden that eight of the crew from the Fortress were in two dinghies, about 20 miles (30 km) west of Alkmar. A high-speed launch was immediately despatched and one of the American fighters covered the dinghy until it came. HSL 2551 arrived three hours later.

It had unhesitatingly taken a course into a German minefield; it was so close to the Dutch coast that the crew could see German soldiers patrolling the harbour walls of Ijmuinden. None the less they managed to haul the eight men aboard, as well as the body of Second Lieutenant Mayall. The escorting American fighters were forced to head back to base, as they were running low on fuel. Their replacements had not yet arrived when a Ju 88 which had been watching the operation swooped down on HSL 2551, shattering the craft and setting it ablaze. One of the Americans was killed and two others were wounded, whilst at least one of the high-speed launch crew was killed and seven others were wounded.

Fortunately, they had managed to send a distress signal, which was picked up by two other high-speed launches, 158 and 184 out of Gorleston, near Great Yarmouth. They rescued all the survivors at around 1640. Flight Lieutenant Lindsay, Corporal Stewart, Leading Aircraftmen Sykes and Wood and two American airmen had either been drowned or killed in the action. What is perplexing about this incident is that the subsequent board of inquiry does not reconcile the statements of the witnesses. One account states that ten survivors were picked up and that two American airmen were either killed or drowned, and there is no mention of the fact that HSL 158 had fifteen survivors as well as the body of one man who had drowned.

We do know that an RAF Walrus from Martlesham carried two USAF doctors to HSL 158 and tended to the wounded. Both launches were back at Gorleston shortly before midnight.

Another example of cooperation occurred on the same day, when No. 11 Group passed on a report that a pilot had been seen in a dinghy about 10 miles (16 km) west of the Hook of Holland. Two P 47s escorted a Warwick carrying an airborne lifeboat to the area. They came under heavy fire from flak near the coast and the Warwick was hit, but they spotted the dinghy and two more P 47s and two ASR Hudsons were sent to the scene. A high-speed launch was also scrambled, with additional P 47s as air cover. After seven hours, involving the combined efforts of fifteen aircraft and the launch, the Australian Beaufighter pilot was picked up. The body of his navigator was picked up by another high-speed launch later.

The damaged Warwick tried to make its way back to base, but its wireless had been damaged. Some US fighters operating in the area reported seeing a dinghy with several men aboard and, via 6th Control Wing, Saffron Walden, a high-speed launch was directed to the spot. The men were picked up and brought home.

In May 1944 the RAF had taken delivery of four 70 ft (21 m) motor gun boats. They were immediately allocated to air sea rescue duties as MTBs 82, 83, 88 and 89. One of the craft was sent to Pembroke Dock, two to 48 Air Sea Rescue Unit (ASRU) Tenby and one to ASRU Tayport.

The vessels were based on the original British Power Boat Company design by Hubert Scott-Paine, but had been built by Elco at Groton, Connecticut. Scott-Paine had sold Elco a 70 ft (21 m) motor gun boat and the design in 1939. The original vessel was allocated to the United States Navy with the designation PT 9. Subsequently Elco built a further ten vessels (PT 10–19), which were completed towards the end of December 1940.

During their sea trials, off Miami Beach and in the Caribbean in January 1941, the United States Navy had been singularly unimpressed. The primary concerns were that the vessels were not suitable to carry the four 21 in (53 cm) torpedoes required and that they were rather too light. None the less, the USN were impressed by the low engine noise produced by the three 1,200 hp Packard engines.

When fully loaded, they were capable of around 45 knots, easily the fastest vessels the Americans had in their arsenal. At maximum speed, they had a range of 350 miles (560 km), but at cruising speed this was increased to 420 miles (675 km).

The Royal Navy took possession of these vessels in April 1941, under the Anglo-American lend-lease programme, and renamed them MTB 259–68. They were sent to the Mediterranean to join the 10th MTB Flotilla. The original Scott-Paine PT 9 became MTB 258. Also under lend-lease the non-Elco vessels PT 3–7 became Royal Navy property, but these were sent for duties with the Royal Canadian Navy and the Royal Canadian Air Force.

Elco had also built twelve 70 ft (21 m) PTC craft (1–12) by March 1941 which were also transferred to the Royal Navy under the lend-lease agreement.They became MGBs 82–93. Modifications were made to the vessels, including moving turrets (which housed five Vickers machine-guns) to either side of the bridge.

MTBs 82, 83, 88 and 89 began their air sea rescue duties on 1 May 1944. They were returned to the Royal Navy between August 1945 and August 1946.

Towards the end of 1944 the ASR received the first nineteen long-range rescue craft (LRRC); a further twenty-one were delivered later. The new Fairmile D Class had been a long time coming, the Royal Navy had been promising the RAF delivery since 1942. Norman Hart had originally designed the Fairmile as a motor torpedo boat. Former Royal Navy Volunteer Reserve (RNVR) officer Noel Campbell Macklin, who had set up the Fairmile Marine Company, learned that the navy was in need of fast, small boats. He proposed to the Admiralty that by using the skills of woodworkers and furniture makers it would be possible to mass-produce prefabricated motor launches from waterproof plywood. The Admiralty placed an initial order for twelve of his first version, the A series. These were 110 ft (33.5 m) motor torpedo boats powered by three Hall-Scott Defenders and capable of between 22 and 24 knots. Initial trials, however, showed that the vessel was too slow and too flimsy to be used as an all-purpose craft.

Subsequently Macklin enlisted the aid of designer Sydney Graham, who drew up a new design using two Hall-Scott V12 engines. The vessel was now 112 ft. (34.1 m) long, with a speed of around 16 knots. Some 568 of this B series were built, of which fifty were transferred to the ASR (numbers RML 492–500 and 511–553). It was relatively well armed, with a single two pounder, one 20 mm gun and four .303 machine-guns.

The C series, which was classed as a motor gun boat, could achieve 23–26 knots using three supercharged Hall-Scott Defenders. It was 110 ft (33.5 m) long and was not sufficiently better to warrant mass-production.

Finally, in 1942, the D series came on stream, using four Packard 4-M 2500 engines. Designed by William Holt in 1939, its significance was that it used a planing type hull, with a convex line running towards the keel. The concept behind the planing was that when the vessel reached a certain speed the hydro-dynamic lift reduced the friction between the planing surface and the water. This meant that the D series could now achieve speeds of 34 knots.

The Admiralty ordered a total of 229 of these craft (they cancelled just one). The ASR received nineteen initially, followed by twenty-one more by the end of 1944, although by the time certain modifications were made they were not available for active service until 1945.

The RAF soon discovered that the boats' weapons and shrapnel mats impaired the performance of the craft. They therefore removed the shrapnel mats, on the basis that they would never stop a direct hit anyway.

The Fairmile D was extremely useful, particularly in the Far East where it had become apparent that the Japanese would shoot at anything. At 115 ft (35 m) and with an array of weapons, it was perfectly capable of looking after itself.

So far Anglo-American cooperation and the acquisition of faster and more efficient vessels had strengthened the ASR, but a vast operation was about to get under way that would stretch all parties to breaking point, the campaign for the liberation of Europe was imminent. An enormous redeployment of ASR resources would be necessary in order to cover the operation, which would see men and aircraft deployed in numbers hitherto unknown in a single mission.

Coastal Command and Fighter Command needed to be reinforced, both in terms of search aircraft and MCUs all along the south coast. Nos. 276 and 278 Squadrons with their Warwicks moved to Bradwell Bay. The Spitfire and Walrus flights settled in at Martlesham. There were now ASR search flights with eighty aircraft at Bolthead, Bradwell, Hawkinge, Martlesham, Portreath, Shoreham and Warmwell. These aircraft would cover the immediate assault area of Operation Overlord – D-Day. Outside the assault area, four Coastal Command deep search squadrons and the American Thunderbolt rescue squadron would act as cover.

MCUs were redeployed along the south coast. Some units were disbanded, others were enlarged with transferred craft and crews, and some new units were created specifically for the Overlord operation. There were new units based at Poole, Portland and Plymouth, while another nine units covered the area from Felixstowe to Falmouth and Newlyn. In all there were seventy-six highspeed launches plus seaplane tenders based at Lyme Regis and Sheerness.

By May, ninety high-speed launches were available, based at Cowes, Dover, Felixstowe, Littlehampton, Newhaven, Newlyn, Plymouth, Poole, Ramsgate, Salcombe, Torquay and Weymouth. A mobile reserve of fourteen 68 ft (20.7 m) high-speed launches was also based at Calshot.

The Royal Navy was also available in strength; two flotillas of rescue motor launches were based at Dartmouth and a flotilla each at Falmouth, Newhaven and Plymouth. This, however, meant that rescue motor launches had to be withdrawn from Milford Haven, Appledore, Larne and the Clyde region. To back

HSL 2629 of 232 ASRU at Colombo, 1945 to 1946. *Courtesy of Don Thurston*

HSL 2712 of 243 ASRU in Galle Harbour, Ceylon, 1945 to 1946. *Courtesy of Don Thurston*

Miami Launches 2530 and 2534 at Calcutta, 1943 to 1944. *Courtesy of Don Thurston*

A dinghy on the stern of an HSL at Chittagong. The HSL is an unidentified craft of 228 ASRU that picked up a Warwick's air crew in 1944. *Courtesy of Don Thurston*

Crew members of HSL 2704, 243 ASRU in Ceylon, 1945 to 1946. *Courtesy of Don Thurston*

MCS men enjoy several Tiger beers in Singapore, 1953 to 1954. *Courtesy of Owen Newlands*

Ernie Beeching in the radio cabin onboard HSL 2680 of 231 ASRU in Penang, Malaya in 1945. *Courtesy of Don Thurston*

Members of 226 ASRU at the Bengal Railway Offices, Garden Beach, Calcutta in 1943. *Courtesy of Don Thurston*

Members of 229
ASRU in the
canteen aboard
accommodation
barge, *Henzada*,
Chittagong 1945
Courtesy of Don Thurs

A Liberator crew
on the bridge of
HSL 2709 of 228
ASRU, after being
picked up near
Chittagong in 1944.
Courtesy of Don Thurston

Flight Lieutenant
Derek West on th
stern of HSL 270
of 228 ASRU in
Hong Kong, 194
Courtesy of Don Thurst

Lady Mountbatten and 4 members of 239 ASRU waiting to cross a creek on the Burma coast in January 1945. *Courtesy of Don Thurston*

The *Hatiali* accommodation barge, with 231 ASRU at Penang, Malaya in 1945. HSL 2628 is alongside. *Courtesy of Don Thurston*

The forward base of 239 ASRU, manning HSLs 2692 and 2716 at Teknaff, Arakan in 1944. *Courtesy of Don Thurston*

HSL 2686, formerly of 230 ASRU at Seletar, Singapore in 1946. *Courtesy of Don Thurston*

HSL 2685 of 230 ASRU in Pazzundung Creek, Rangoon 1945-46.
Courtesy of Don Thurston

MT 2560 at Seletar during Operation Monsoon. *Courtesy of Ted Shute*

up all of this there were fifteen lifeboats from the RNLI, although these would carry out rescues outside of the main attack area.

By 31 May 1944 the total strength of ASR craft amounted to ninety high-speed launches, six seaplane tenders, forty rescue motor launches and, as a back up, fourteen Naval motor anti-submarine boats. The Americans also contributed by sending sixty coastal cutters from the US Coastguard rescue flotilla. They would deal with crews from vessels in the invasion area.

As a further precaution, large numbers of H-type dinghies were stowed on board ASR craft and the US cutters. They would be kept on deck and distributed to men in the water if the craft was unable to pick them up. They were primarily aimed at ship's crews or men who had had to abandon landing craft. Above all, all surface craft were ordered to paint a large, five-pointed star on their foredeck so that they could avoid the unwanted attentions of Allied aircraft.

The coordination of all of these activities required thousands of concentrated man-hours. Every air operation was carefully mapped and ASR surface craft would be deployed along the paths of aircraft passing over the sea. High-speed launches were also attached to the diversionary force which would sweep towards the enemy coast, far to the east of the actual assault area in Normandy. High-speed launches were also attached to marker ships, which were used to indicate turning points for the airborne forces and, at first light on D-Day they would sweep the area for downed crews. More would be deployed south of the Channel Islands.

Allied fighter pilots were urged to bale out rather than ditch, because if they attempted to ditch they could easily be mistaken for hostile enemy aircraft and would be shot down. Pilots of larger Allied aircraft, however, were told to ditch. They were instructed to land to the north of an Allied surface craft and to make sure that they signalled that they were friendly. All Allied aircraft had distinctive black and white stripes on their wings and fuselage and at night they were told to switch on their navigation lights if a surface vessel fired an aircraft recognition signal.

All ASR personnel were told that maximum effort was expected on D-Day and for at least three days afterwards. Some of the rescue motor launches were detailed for use as casualty clearing vessels. Airmen that were picked up would be taken straight back to the launches' bases, unless of course they needed immediate medical attention.

Two high-speed launches from Calshot's No. 32 ASR/MCU would be allocated to each of the three fighter direction tenders, and would take up station at first light on D-Day. They would be relieved each day by another six launches.

In the early hours of the morning of 6 June 1944, with ASR Spitfires and Walruses already on patrol, the surface craft began to take up their positions. In truth, with the number of surface vessels and aircraft around, the chances of aircrew being missed would be negligible. During the day some sixty aircrew were rescued by ASR; and very few were lost. Five US aircrew from a Liberator were saved, a Thunderbolt pilot was picked up, as well as forty-four soldiers and sailors who had jumped over-board from either ships or landing craft. So complete was the coverage that when one RAF Spitfire pilot sent out an SOS informing his base that he was about to bale out, a high-speed launch was immediately on hand and he had barely got wet before the crew pulled him out.

On another occasion an American Dakota carrying para-troopers was hit by flak just as it reached the French coast. The flak had damaged the port engine and the starboard engine was burning itself out. The pilot realised he would have to ditch and strangely chose to do so near the enemy-held Channel Islands. He had been involved in airborne operations over Sicily and remembered that on some occasions Allied aircraft were shot at by their own vessels. The co-pilot, however, recalled the briefing to ditch to the north of a surface vessel. Using landing lights they ditched at 0010 hours. The eighteen paratroopers abandoned the aircraft, but the co-pilot remained in his cockpit and signalled a destroyer that they had spotted with a torch. The destroyer got to them so quickly that the co-pilot was able to walk off the wing of the Dakota, straight onto it without even getting his feet wet. In all, fourteen Dakotas ditched during D-Day and all the crew ended the day safely back in Allied hands.

CHAPTER FIVE

Closing Phases of the Second World War

In the first ten days of Operation Overlord the ASR services picked up at least 163 aircrews, fifty-eight other Allied servicemen and two Germans. This was in addition to the many that were picked up by Royal Navy vessels and landing craft. Over the same period the four rescue squadrons had saved over 300 lives and had flown nearly 1,500 operational sorties.

On 26 June 1944 a number of high-speed launches were operating in the Seine Bay. Two were allocated to the Mulberry Harbour at Arromanches and two each to the Gooseberries at Ouistreham and Courselles. Throughout this time they enjoyed considerable fighter protection. An RAF maintenance party was also established aboard HMS *Adventure* off Arromanches to give immediate assistance and repair. It was further decided that the launches would operate along the whole coastline of Normandy and Brittany. On 20 June it had been decided to create No. 32 Mobile ASR Unit and that two units, Nos. 32 and 33, would be allocated to the command of Headquarters Allied Expeditionary Air Forces. Each unit would have nine high-speed launches and one general service pinnace. It was further decided that these units should be responsible for the coastal areas to the north and west of France, running from Dieppe to Spanish territorial waters. Initially it was proposed that one of the units would be based at Cherbourg, with detachments operating from Lorient and Le Havre. It would be supported by Warwicks with airborne lifeboats, Spitfires and Walruses.

On 7 July, three launches were attached to Cherbourg prior to No. 32 ASR/MCU moving into the port. The unit moved into

Cherbourg on 27 July and on 1 August A Flight of No. 276 Squadron, consisting of four Walruses and four Spitfires, began operating from the Cherbourg peninsula.

There had been a number of incidents, including the attack on HSL 2551 on 29 June, which has already been mentioned. On 12 June a high-speed launch from Calshot received a signal from a tug, indicating that some men had ditched and were in the sea. Assisted by two US Coastguard cutters, they hunted for the men, who were believed to be on board a raft. They were subsequently picked up and it was discovered that they were the crew of a pontoon bridge unit that had been swept out to sea in high seas.

Two days later two high-speed launches from Weymouth saw clouds of smoke rising from a group of destroyers. They headed off to investigate and discovered that HMS *Blackwood*, a Royal Navy frigate, had been badly damaged when it had hit a mine. There were a number of injuries and, with great difficulty, in heavy seas the two launches managed to take off 115 survivors, of whom fifty were stretcher cases. Two other launches came to assist and the walking wounded were transferred to these vessels. At times the 68 ft (20.7 m) craft had as many as eighty-six people on board.

On 19 July a high-speed launch operating out of Salcombe was heading for its rendezvous position when it received information that the survivors, who were believed to be in dinghies, might be hostile. An aircraft was circling over the position. As it turned out, the launch's crew had to take the survivors on board at the point of Sten guns and revolvers, as the three officers and twenty-five other ranks were in fact the survivors of a German U-boat crew. The crew took the men to Plymouth, where they became prisoners of war.

The Marine Craft Policy Committee was never entirely convinced that the Royal Navy would ever relinquish any of its Fairmile craft to the RAF. Consequently, in 1944, they began to approach several smaller manufacturers for new designs. At a meeting on 22 September they coined the description 'long-range rescue craft' to distinguish the type of vessel they were after.

Amongst the many submissions they received, three appeared to be good enough to be deployed. Camper Nicholson was authorised to produce two prototypes, powered by Griffon engines and fixed propellers. Similar permission was given to the British Power Boat Company which proposed a vessel with four Napier Sabre engines and variable-pitch propellers and Thorneycroft, whose design included six Rolls- Royce Griffon engines, also with variable pitch propellers.

As a back-up to these three main designs, Vosper was at hand with a vessel powered by four Griffons and with variable pitch propellers. In addition, the British Aeroplane Company was pushing ahead with its Fred Cooper design, spending its own funds on a variant of the Fairmile F using Bristol Hercules engines. Fred Cooper had been with the British Power Boat Company, and in many respects his design was very similar to the Fairmile F 2001. It was powered by four Bristol Hercules air-cooled engines and had a speed of 36 knots. The long-range rescue craft differed in several ways, notably in that it was constructed of wood (with extra strengthening), as opposed to metal. This craft would be named Celerity. It underwent sea trials but it was discovered that because of the amount of power the intake cooling fans needed, the vessel was in fact under-powered. In late March 1945 it was revealed that only reconditioned Mark XI Hercules engines were available; the alternatives were Pegasus XVIIIs and Wright R2600s. It was finally decided that a modified Mark XVII Hercules would be used. The vessel was bound for the Far East on ASR service.

Since breakthroughs have been made in Normandy and military operations were now taking place further east, the ASRUs based on the Cherbourg peninsula started to move east. On 17 September 1944, Operation Market Garden was launched against German positions in Holland. It was to stretch the ASR to its absolute limits. The operation involved landing many thousands of British and American paratroopers and glider-borne troops from Nijmengen to Arnhem.

Vast streams of aircraft towing gliders left Britain and ASR surface vessels and aircraft covered their passage over the sea. Over the period of the operation, thirty-five gliders and a Dakota came down into the sea and the service picked up around 181 men. An RNLI vessel and a minesweeper picked up twenty-one others. The heaviest day was 19 September when ninety-two men were picked. It was later said that so complete was the cover provided by the ASR that many of the aircraft simply had to follow the track of its launches, without even looking at their navigational equipment.

By October, allied land forces were deep into Belgium and Holland and, once again, ASR cover had to be moved east. Fighter and Coastal Commands and the Second Tactical Air Force were now responsible for the coasts of Holland, Belgium and France. No. 32 ASR/MCU provided four high-speed launches and No. 33 nine, to be based at Ostend.

Because of the danger of the bulk of their U-boat bases being overrun, the Germans decided to move them from the Bay of Biscay to Norwegian ports. It was clear that anti-submarine warfare was now imminent, primarily in the North Sea, and, several Coastal Command squadrons therefore moved to the north of Scotland. ASR units followed. Whilst this reorganisation was taking place another historical event took place in August 1944. No. 269 Squadron, operating at Lagens in the Azores, was finally re-equipped with six Warwicks and this meant that there were now no longer any Hudsons working in the ASR.

By November 1944 there was very little German activity in the English Channel or in the Straits of Dover, and it was suggested to both Fighter and Coastal Commands that Spitfires were no longer needed in air sea rescue. It was proposed that the Spitfire units be disbanded and any remaining Warwicks or Walruses transferred to Coastal Command. A meeting on 13 December confirmed this decision. It was also decided that Warwicks and amphibians were now perfectly adequate for the task. Coastal Command would now be responsible for the coordination of rescues. In January 1945, it was also decided that the Fighter Command Warwick flights based on the south coast were no longer necessary, as there were already Coastal Command Warwick units covering the area from St Eval and Beccles.

In the last six months of 1944, ASR had picked up some 936 aircrews, compared with 1,225 in the previous six months. Unfortunately accurate figures beyond this are not available, as no separate records of lost aircraft were kept during the D-Day period.

On 15 February 1945 responsibility for all ASR operations was formally transferred to Coastal Command. Five search squadrons would provide air cover, and a flight was based in the Azores. It was intended that all the rescue squadrons would be equipped with Sea Otters, Walrus Mark IIs would be used until enough had been transferred from the Royal Navy. On the same day Nos. 275 and 277 Squadrons were disbanded and No. 278 Squadron was transferred to Coastal Command. No. 276 Squadron was to have a complement of five Spitfires and six Walruses or Sea Otters, which deemed to be sufficient to cover ASR operations on mainland Europe. Fighter Command maintained responsibility for scrambling aircraft for searches close to shore and both Bomber Command and Flying Training Command were also to be used. The cooperation with the Royal Navy, the Merchant Navy, the RNLI and fishing vessels would continue.

In March 1945 Allied forces crossed the Rhine and considerable numbers of paratroopers and glider-borne troops were dropped to the east of the river. Only two gliders were lost, but rescue aircraft and ASR launches were on hand to pick them up. Indeed in March some 291 aircrew were forced to ditch in seventy-nine incidents. Eighty-four were rescued, a success rate of just over 28 per cent. Although figures for rescues around the British Isles are difficult to assess, it has been calculated that 5,658 took place between the founding of the ASR and the end of March 1945, including both aircrew, non-aircrew and both Allied and German personnel.

Arguably the last major air sea rescue in Europe before the end of hostilities there began on 30 March 1945. It was a considerable epic, undoubtedly one of the longest and most daring operations undertaken. It involved six US airmen, the crew of a rescue Catalina belonging to the 5th Emergency Rescue Squadron. They had been scrambled to find a Mustang pilot who was aboard his dinghy, about 3 miles (5 km) off Schiermonnikoog. They were not to know that they were about to trigger a series of events that would see them adrift for 109 hours.

The Catalina was escorted by two Thunderbolts and managed to land just feet from the Mustang pilot's dinghy. Suddenly a wave smashed one of it's engines. None the less the crew threw out ropes and lifebelts towards the pilot. He drifted away, however, and was lost. The crippled Catalina also began to drift and a distress signal was routed to No. 16 Group Headquarters, who immediately despatched a Warwick to find both the Mustang pilot and the Catalina, but it could see nothing.

The following morning a Warwick, escorted by four Mustangs, was scouring the area. They found the Catalina after around two hours of searching and the Warwick managed to drop an airborne lifeboat. The crew was still on board their aircraft and the pilot decided to taxi towards the lifeboat. However, in doing so he hit heavy waves that smashed the Catalina's tail and it promptly began to sink. A further Warwick with a fighter escort dropped a second lifeboat, but as the crew clambered aboard it began to sink and they swam back towards their nearly submerged Catalina.

A jet-engined German Me 262 now added to the chaos by shooting up the sinking Catalina, which forced the crew to jump aboard their three dinghies. The German aircraft disappeared and a Flying Fortress belonging to the US Rescue Squadron managed to drop an American airborne lifeboat. This time, the Catalina's crew managed to get on board and start the engines. They were now about 15 miles (25 km) north-west of Nordeney Island. They motored along for 36 hours in a broadly north-westerly direction, then ran out of fuel.

Poor weather at first prevented search aircraft from finding the lifeboat, but on 2 April a Beaufighter managed to penetrate the area. It crashed into the sea, however, and the crew were lost. On 3 April two Warwicks, escorted by Mustangs, began to patrol the area and they picked up an SOS signal transmitted by the lifeboat's dinghy radio. They eventually managed to find the lifeboat and the Warwicks dropped petrol droppers, another lifeboat and Lindholme equipment.

The Catalina's crew managed to row to the dropped equipment, which they transferred into their American lifeboat. It was a poor decision as, despite their best efforts, they could not get the lifeboat's engines working again. Additional Lindholme equipment and petrol were dropped during the day, but they could still not get the engine started.

On the evening of 3 April, with poor visibility and a cloud base of just 700 ft (215 m), a fifth airborne lifeboat was dropped. The Catalina's crew were too exhausted to even attempt to reach it, but before the search aircraft left the area they dropped sea markers around it. Meanwhile, high-speed launches were despatched to the area, but they could not find the lifeboat, despite the sea markers.

At 0840 hours on 4 April, with more Warwicks and Mustang escorts searching the area, a message came in from a high-speed launch, with the good news that they had picked up the Catalina's crew around 20 miles (30 km) off Heligoland. The crew were safely brought ashore at Great Yarmouth in the early hours of the morning of 5 April. The launch had covered 200 miles (300 km); this was arguably not only the last but also the longest ASR operation in Europe.

CHAPTER SIX

ASR Far East

In October 1941 Air Headquarters Far East received their first ASR officer. His remit was to try to organise a rescue service that would cover Malaya and Singapore. He had at his disposal a single pinnace and a marine tender, but he did also have the support of the Royal Navy. The service went into operation in December 1941, and in its first month it managed to rescue eleven pilots. In January 1942, with the assistance of Moth aircraft from the Malay Volunteer Air Force, a further twelve pilots were rescued. These Moths were capable of dropping smoke floats and lifejackets to ditched aircrew. On 23 January a Moth assisted in the rescue of the first Hurricane pilot to ditch in the Far East. It kept sight of the pilot in his K-dinghy, despite bad visibility, until a high-speed launch picked him up.

The fall of Singapore severely curtailed efforts to organise a rescue service in the Far East. Elsewhere the situation was really no better. India did not receive its first rescue craft until the spring of 1943. Few resources were available and this theatre of war continued to be relatively low on London's list of priorities. Those rescues that took place before 1943 were the work of the Fleet Air Arm and the Royal Navy.

In 1942 Air Headquarters India began asking for marine craft and aircraft for rescues. As a result, in February the Air Ministry asked the Admiralty to release sixteen Walruses so that new ASR search squadrons could be formed in both the Far East and the Middle East. The Royal Navy was also short of Walruses, but by April they had conceded that if they were available locally at Royal Navy bases and not needed for other operational duties they would be made available for ASR. Air Headquarters India then asked for Lysanders, but again they were told that the priority was to construct other aircraft and, ultimately, marine craft. They were promised that marine craft would be available as early as possible in 1943. In the meantime they would have to rely on the Royal Navy and any operational craft that may be available for rescue missions.

There had been protracted discussions at the Air Ministry and with the Directorate of Air Sea Rescue regarding the number of marine craft that should be earmarked for overseas commands. Indeed in January 1942 the thirty-three marine craft initially suggested had been increased to sixty-six. The success of the Japanese in the early years of the war had highlighted the fact that in the medium to long term level of air operations would far exceed initial estimates. Far East Command would need a minimum of eighty marine craft to cover the Far East and Australasia. When the Japanese occupied Singapore and the Dutch East Indies, this demand was scaled down, but all concerned knew that marine craft must be available for future offensive operations.

By the summer of 1942 the United States had agreed to take responsibility for search and rescue missions in their areas of operation in the Far East. This now meant that the RAF would need thirty high-speed launches for India, ten for the East African coast and a further thirty for future offensive operations. It was agreed that the first twenty, which should be available during 1943, would be sent to India.

In July 1943 No. 203 ASRU was established in India and allocated two high-speed launches. A second unit was created in October. However, because of increased operations in North Africa and the Mediterranean, craft earmarked for India were being diverted to that theatre. As a result, by the beginning of July 1943 India had just five launches. By the end of the month they had nine, but there was a hiatus until January 1944 during which no other launches were sent to India.

In February 1943 the Air Staff had set the operational target figures they intended to achieve by March 1944. A squadron of twenty long-range search and rescue aircraft was intended to provide air cover for India although it was anticipated that it would not receive any Warwicks until June 1944. In March 1943 an ASR officer was appointed to India. He had few assets to work with, but fortunately air operations were not heavy at that time. Major activity, however, was taking place around Chittagong, where the Miami launches were based. In these early months they rescued a number of aircrew, including three men from a ditched Wellington.

The general reconnaissance squadrons, also based in India, had a major success in August 1943. A Blenheim flying out of Trichinopoly ditched near the China Bay area of the coastline. A Catalina, escorted by two Hurricanes, were sent to find the crew. One of the Hurricanes saw the M-dinghy and a high-speed launch sped to the area and picked up the three survivors just two hours after the first distress call.

The next major development was the creation of No. 292 Air Sea Rescue Squadron. It was to have a strength of sixteen Warwicks plus four in reserve. It was hoped that the squadron would be operational, at least in part, by February 1944. The first ten Warwicks would be delivered at some point during January 1944, and they would be reinforced by five Walruses that would be available from the Royal Navy, although these would not be available until September.

In November 1943 India took delivery of its first Lindholme gear and Bircham barrels. The first successful use of the Lindholme equipment took place that month when it was dropped to aid the crew of a USAF bomber. The ASR broadly modelled on that of Britain, officially came into existence that month, and it was hoped that by March 1944 it would be fully operational. Also in November it was decided to merge the ASR effort of Middle East Command beyond the Mediterranean with that of the Indian Ocean. It now effectively became part of South East Asia Air Command. As a result No. 222 Group, based in Ceylon, took over operational control of East Africa.

In December 1943 South East Asia Air Command was informed that the ten Warwicks that would form the initial backbone of No. 292 Squadron would probably not be available by January 1944 after all. This threw their plans into disarray; technical difficulties were holding up production and distribution and at this stage no one could give South East Asia Air Command any indication of when they might arrive.

Despite all problems, however, the first Warwicks did begin to arrive in April 1944. Moreover, Sea Otters had been despatched by merchant vessels and the Royal Navy had begun to hand over some Walruses. The long-awaited establishment of 292 Squadron, based at Jessore, could now begin. When sufficient aircraft had arrived, Warwicks would also operate from Bombay and Ceylon, Sea Otters from Chittagong and Walruses from Ceylon. This would mean that the aircraft could give cover along the west coast of Burma.

In the meantime search and rescue missions were being undertaken by Wellingtons of No. 231 Group. US Catalinas ably assisted them from Eastern Air Command. The crew of a Beaufighter were rescued in the Chittagong area by two of these Wellingtons on 17 April 1944. The Wellingtons found the dinghy and dropped Lindholme equipment, and the crew climbed aboard. Using fluorescent markers to indicate their position they began drifting towards the south-east. Search aircraft kept them in sight and on the morning of 18 April a Wellington found them again and a US Catalina managed to land nearby and pick them up.

By June 1944 the situation regarding high-speed launches had considerably improved. More vessels were able to get through to India and deliver the much-needed launches. By June there were some forty-five covering India and Ceylon, from Karachi to Chittagong. There were also enough to man Jiwani and Jask in the Persian Gulf by August.

Unlike the operations in north-west Europe and the Mediterranean, ASR services and communication between commands were difficult because of the vast areas involved. In order to improve this ASR liaison officers were allocated to Eastern Air Command, the 3rd Tactical Air Force and other operational groups in the area.

On 5 June 1944 the ASR at Chittagong received a distress call from the crew of a B29 Super Fortress that had ditched in the Sangu River estuary. Spitfires were scrambled from Chittagong to find the aircraft and a high-speed launch made for the river mouth. In just twenty minutes the Spitfires saw the aircraft on a muddy riverbank. One of them circled the area whilst the other flew back to lead and escort the launch. The launch managed to pick up six men from two dinghies, including one who was severely injured. They then noticed that another member of the crew was sitting on the fuselage of the aircraft. The launch crew launched a dinghy to rescue him and he told them that four other crewmates were trapped in a pressurised aft compartment near the aircraft's tail.

Another launch was called, and with the water now over the main and tail planes, they tried to break into the fuselage. They failed and had to wait for low tide. A minesweeper arrived to assist, but all efforts were frustrated. Moreover, there was still no positive evidence that the men were still alive. Indeed, the hull of the aircraft was waterlogged and it became clear that the four men were dead. The aircraft was blown up.

By the summer of 1944 it had become abundantly clear that the Indian climate did not suit Warwicks. The fabric on the aircraft deteriorated rapidly and the engines needed much more maintenance. The Lancaster Mark III was earmarked as a suitable replacement, but India would have to wait as these aircraft were sorely needed in Europe.

In November 1944 the ASR in India came under criticism from the commander of XX Bomber Command. He was particularly concerned about the lack of rescue cover for the Bay of Bengal. He pointed out that the RAF marine craft did not have the range to pick up some of the ditched aircraft and that when Royal Indian Navy launches were available they took too long to get there. He illustrated his point with two examples, one of which involved the crew of a B29 that had ditched in the Bay of Bengal. It was located in three hours, but a Royal Indian Navy motor launch had not picked them up for two days. On the other occasion two B29s had been lost whilst searching for a third missing aircraft. On this occasion a single Catalina undertook the search and the commander was forced to divert other US aircraft from operational duties.

With the Warwicks proving to be more of a liability than an asset, the temporary solution was to use Catalinas and general reconnaissance Liberators. As a result No. 212 Catalina Squadron was transferred to ASR. Based at Karachi, it would now cover the Bay of Bengal and India's west coast. A detachment of No. 292 Air Sea Rescue Squadron was subsequently moved to Ratmalana in Ceylon.

By January 1945 two flights of the US 1st Emergency Rescue Squadron were redeployed from Italy to create No. 7 Emergency Rescue Squadron. Together with No. 212 Squadron, the Indian Ocean could at long last be covered.

The ASR was perfectly aware of the shortcomings of its high-speed launches' range. They also knew that the existing launches were not entirely suitable for the Indian Ocean and the Far East. Steps were therefore taken to create what would become known as long-range rescue craft. These craft would have to have a cruising speed of around 35 knots, sufficient fuel capacity for extended missions of up to fourteen days and adequate accommodation onboard for the crew for this period. Above all, the craft needed to have a range of between 1,500 and 2,000 miles (2,400–3,200 km).

The Admiralty was first approached to see if they could provide a craft that would fit the bill. In August 1944 they agreed that facilities would be made available to produce such a vessel. Obviously development and production would take time and in the interim the Royal Navy agreed to supply the RAF with some D-type Fairmile launches. These vessels had a maximum cruising speed of 24 knots and at normal speed a range of 1,500 miles. They estimated that around forty of these craft could begin to be despatched from Britain in March 1945. It was anticipated that there would be problems with this vessel since the hull was made of wood and, would therefore be prone to attack by the Toredo worm. Two solutions were possible: either the craft could be hauled ashore every few weeks for a detailed inspection or the RAF could sacrifice speed for protection and cover the hull in copper. The first solution would prove difficult, as India was not blessed with sufficient docking facilities. The second also presented problems, as it would mean that the launch would have a maximum speed of only 18 knots. There was really no other alternative, however. Either there would continue to be delays to the Fairmiles or the Royal Navy would have to hunt for an alternative craft. As a result of these problems, coupled with production difficulties, if the Fairmiles were delivered at all it would not be until July 1945.

In that month two units of Fairmiles had completed their acceptance trials and immediately began their long passage to India. In the meantime the Royal Navy had agreed to provide naval craft from those already stationed in the Indian Ocean. However, the Fairmiles were stopped in the Mediterranean and on 4 August Air Command South East Asia was told that they would not receive them after all. They would not be used at all east of the Suez Canal, as the Royal Navy was proposing to use twelve corvettes for long-range air sea rescue in South-east Asia.

As it happened these wrangles between the Air Ministry, the Admiralty, the Royal Navy and the RAF became academic because on 15 August 1945 the Japanese surrendered.

Exact rescue figures for the ASR in the Far East are difficult to come by, as no record of rescues was kept prior to June 1943. What is clear, however, is that from then to the end of the war around 150 aircraft and 700 aircrews were involved in ditches. The ASR managed to make successful rescues in eighty-eight of these cases and rescued 327 aircrew. Operational aircraft rather than ASR aircraft in fact carried out many of the searches for these crews. Meanwhile, of course, the general reconnaissance Catalinas of Air Command South East Asia, operating over a twenty-seven-month period up to the end of July 1945, saved 1,304 ship crew.

The ASR in the Far East remained very much a Cinderella organisation until the war in Europe was over. It was only after the German surrender that aircraft, long-range marine craft and other rescue equipment could be sent to that theatre. By the beginning of June 1945, however, No. 292 Squadron had been disbanded and re-formed as seven separate flights, with Warwicks and Liberators based at Agaterla and Kankesanturai and Sea Otters based at Akyab Ratmalana and Mingalanden.

In July the flights received Warwick Mark Is, which were treated with an aluminium dope to help prevent deterioration in the tropical climate. It was expected that Lancasters would replace them towards the end of 1945. It was also proposed that No. 212's Squadron's Catalinas would be re-equipped with Sunderland Mark Vs in August. There were also plans to deploy Lincoln bombers and a special ultra-long-range rescue unit would be provided with Lancasters and Catalinas. These proposals were scrapped, however, when the Japanese surrendered.

The isolated Cocos Islands were an important base to protect the sea lanes between Australia and South Africa. Although the Japanese did not make an attempt to occupy them, they were bombed on three occasions. The base was manned during 1944 and 1945 by a squadron of Spitfires (No. 136 Squadron), two Liberator squadrons (Nos 99 and 356) and an MCU.

HSLs 2562 and 2698, which had been working between Calshot and the Normandy beaches between June 1944 and Christmas of that year, were then posted to Dumbarton prior to being shipped to the Far East. They were fully fitted and re-furbished. On arrival in Bombay, however, the crew discovered that they had been stripped of everything that was not nailed down at some point in transit and they had to start again. They were joined by HSL 2702 from Ceylon and, together with a GP pinnace, a seaplane tender and marine tenders, they were loaded aboard the SS *Salwen* for an undisclosed destination. Only when they were on board were the crews told that they were bound for the Cocos Islands to set up an ASR unit.

They were joined aboard the *Salwen* by fresh Spitfires and pilots and a contingent of the RAF regiment to guard the new installation. It took around six months to clear sufficient vegeta-tion for the army to build a landing strip and camp, but the MCS was already busy dealing with the comings and goings of Catalinas from Australia.

The Cocos base became operational in mid-1945; by then the majority of the aircraft had been posted to India, as the number of Japanese aircraft in the area had trailed off significantly. Officially, the base became 129 Staging Post, and its primary activity of the post was to use Sunderlands to drop supplies to prisoner of war camps. It had a largely uneventful existence, although the high-speed launches covered a huge distance at sea.

With the cessation of hostilities in the Far East, the ASR units and the MCS still could not rest. The Japanese had established innumerable prisoner of war camps all around South-east Asia, and with the collapse of the Japanese infrastructure, command and control, the few supplies and medical equipment they received dwindled to nothing. The hunt was now on to find these isolated camps, whose guards were probably totally unaware that Japan had finally surrendered.

Mosquitoes of 684 Squadron, flying out of the Cocos Islands, were pressed into service on this vital mission. One was forced to make an emergency landing at Kallany airfield, which was still in the hands of the Japanese. It was close to the prisoner of war camp at Changi Jail. The Japanese offered no resistance and hastened to find an RAF technical officer and a fitter from the jail to attend to the Mosquito. This was the first landing of British servicemen in Singapore since the ignominious surrender back in February 1942.

Kogalla, in Ceylon, was the base for Nos 205, 230 and 240 Squadrons. They too dealt with the dropping of supplies and the repatriation of prisoners of war and civilians. During October 1945 alone, some 457 prisoners of war were flown out of Singapore via Kogalla to Madras.

In May 1946, with just ten Sunderlands left at Kogalla (Nos 230 and 240 Squadrons had been disbanded), No. 205 Squadron's five aircraft moved to Singapore, whilst No. 209 Squadron sent five to Singapore and a further five to Hong Kong. Six of the remaining serviceable Sunderlands were converted to passenger aircraft and these, under the guise of the newly formed No. 88 Transport Squadron, also headed for Hong Kong.

By April 1948, No. 88 Squadron had reconverted their Sunderlands, replacing the nose and tail turrets, and began operating out of Kai Tak, Hong Kong. Between September 1946 and April 1948 they had carried nearly 2,400 passengers and 400,000 lb (180,000 kg) of freight and mail to the occupation troops in Japan. These operations would have proved impossible had it not been for the MCS.

Towards the end of 1943, with the war in the Middle East at an end and operations going well in Italy, there was an opportunity to transfer high-speed launches from the Middle East to the Arabian Sea and the Indian Ocean. In January 1944 HSL 2649, which had been based at Basra since November 1943, accompanied HSLs 2650 and 2738 to Al Faw, Bahrain, Sharjah, Muscat, Ras al Had and on to Mesirah. This placed the launches on the Far East air supply route, which cut along the Aden coastline. It was the base of ASRU 206. The rest of the route to India was covered at Karachi by ASRU 234 and in northern India and Calcutta, by ASRU 229 and ASRU 225.

ASR veterans frequently refer to the problems of maintaining their launches in tropical climates, with the wood-boring marine life. As we have seen, aircraft were also affected by the humidity. Mosquitoes had problems with the glue that kept them together. Many of the veterans feel that their activities in the Far East are all but forgotten, yet they were a vital safety net for many hundreds of aircrew that ditched. They were involved in a number of key operations. In February 1944 No. 230 Squadron, then based at Koggala on Ceylon, sent two Sunderlands to Assam to provide a shuttle service from Brahmaputra to Lake Indawgwi, deep inside Japanese-occupied Burma. Nicknamed Gert and Daisy, they were involved in a thirty-two-day airlift, which brought in much-needed supplies, equipment and ammunition and brought out 237 men. They were a vital link for Orde Wingate's Chindits, locked in a vicious struggle with the Japanese occupying forces.

The Sunderlands of No. 230 Squadron were used in a very similar operation a year later in March 1945. They flew from Calcutta to Shwegyin, on the Chindwin River, covering a distance of 1,200 miles (1,900 km), often crossing mountains 10,000 ft (3,000 m) high. The operation began on 9 March and during 220 hours of flight they carried in 400,000 lb (180,000 kg) of equipment. They were supported by a similar effort running between Bombay and Calcutta.

Sunderlands were also used to make attacks in the Rangoon area against Japanese shipping. It should be remembered that none of this work would have been possible had it not been for the tireless work of the MCU and, of course, the high-speed launches provided the much-needed ASR cover.

In one incident, in March 1945, a Flying Fortress ditched, and four crew were trapped in a pressurised compartment in a vast delta of islands, marshlands and swamps. The area was covered by Pinnace 1341, commanded by Flight Officer L. E. G. Ambler, who had joined it in November 1944. He had previously been a sergeant coxswain on HSL 112 in the North Sea and had worked with seaplane tenders at Porthcawl in 1941. His undated sortie report states:

It was now the fourth day of the search, already we had been fortunate enough on the second day to land six of the eight survivors at our base, a seventh had made his own way there by various means and now the eighth and last survivor was being searched for.

The area we were combing consisted of mangrove swamp jungle interlaced with hundreds of *khals* [streams], it was in fact like looking for a needle in a haystack. Just before noon one of the search aircraft gave a position of a parachute and with all speed we made for it, the over-hanging jungle growth of a narrow part carried away the aerials, ensign and all the halliards. Finally we were in a position, with the anchor dropped and a search party made ready to enter the jungle.

It was absolutely impossible to get through on foot owing to the flooded conditions and so our small dinghy was used, with this, we had little difficulty in penetrating. To put it bluntly it was really grim inside, dirty brackish water, dankness and smell with just sufficient light filtering through. After going some six to eight hundred yards we suddenly heard a shout, we listened and heard another. Our hopes raised we cheered in reply knowing that we had found our last survivor.

Furiously we propelled the dinghy in the general direction of the shouts and shortly grounded, not far away we saw the man we had been searching for. He was covered in mud from head to foot and came stumbling through the mud towards us. We were impressed by his obvious cheerfulness, his fortitude must have been second to none when it is considered that during the four days and nights he had been alone in that utter desolation without food or drink except the rainwater which dripped off the leaves and with only the animals and land crabs for companions. We all felt good about this for it was the job we had set out to accomplish and it had come off.

On 27 May 1945 the same crew spotted a C 47 flying low over the river. Its engine was misfiring and it then disappeared. At around 0910 hours they headed to where they thought the crash had occurred and ten minutes later they informed No. 231 Group that they were responding. The three crew were picked up just to the north-east of Khulna.

Compared to the previous operation, which lasted ten days, this was a mercifully quick and successful mission.

Less successful was an operation on 23 March. Pinnace 1341 was told to investigate an aircraft crash in the Sundarbans area, to the north of the Bay of Bengal. They left base at 0605 and were in position at 1455 hours. With the crash site marked by a circling Harvard and a Mosquito, a shore party was sent to investigate. They discovered the wreckage of a Mosquito belonging to No. 684 Squadron. Human remains were found, which turned out to be Flight Lieutenant K. J. Newman. They searched for the navigator for nearly three days, but unfortunately could find nothing.

Another example of their kind of work occurred between 3 and 6 September 1945, this time with the aid of Pinnace 1327. They were hunting for a Liberator crew and found three of the men on the 4th, just over a mile (1.5 km) south of the crash site. Three more were found 3 miles (5 km) further south. On the 6th they discovered the seventh man. The last man made his way back to an Allied base under his own steam.

The development of ASR aids had continued throughout 1944 and 1945. As the war in Europe came to an end, the problems of aircrews who had ditched in tropical climates began to take precedence. One particularly difficult problem had been providing enough stowage space for water. Improvements began to be made in the desalination kits. These kits were being produced in 1944, but experiments were under way to produce a better design. The problem was that the RAF and the Fleet Air Arm alone wanted 2,500 sets per week. Early tests showed that the existing container became warped in tropical climates, and a Perspex container was a far better solution.

Fighter pilots had some water in a water cushion in their K-dinghy pack; this contained 3 pints (1.7 litres). The USAF in the Pacific was already developing solar stills, which produced drinking water by condensation. The simplest version was known as the pillow model. The pilot filled the pillow with sea water and left it in the sun. The moisture on a sponge evaporated, and condensation took place inside the cover. It could produce 35 fl oz (1 litre) per day. Initial orders were placed for 50,000 of these stills.

Work was also done to make locating dinghies in the vast oceans of South-east Asia easier. Most of the larger aircraft carried the US-made dinghy radio, and fighter pilots had the Walter as part of their K-dinghy packs. Both had their disadvantages. The dinghy radio was manually operated and therefore not ideal, particularly if the crew was injured, unconscious or exhausted. The Walter was battery-powered, but in the tropical climate the battery's life expectancy was very short. The USA had developed a device known as Emily. This was a reflector that opened like an umbrella. It had three reflecting planes that directed radar back to its source. Some RAF units took possession of these devices before the end of the war in the Far East.

There were also improvements to rescue equipment, particularly the personal pack. It had been shown that, with the emergency packs stowed in the fuselage, many of the aircrews failed either to get them or to reach their dinghy. A personal pack, to be strapped to each member of the aircrew, was developed. Production was authorised in December 1944, but the pack did not become available until August 1945. It contained a desalination kit, a heliograph, signal cartridges, a water storage bag and emergency rations, and was designed to be slipped over the head and then tied to the waist.

Inflatable exposure suits were also under development in 1944 and by July a design had been sufficiently developed to go on trial. It was made of a double thickness of rubberised fabric and had a valve that allowed the wearer to inflate it. The idea was that the layer of air between the two sheets of rubberised fabric would help to retain body heat. It was designed for use both in Europe and in the Far East, but a shortage of rubber meant that it did not go into mass production.

Another problem for pilots who ditched in the Pacific was the sharks. The USAF developed a mixture of chemicals that produced a black cloud and acted as a shark repellent. It was proposed that this should be fitted to a pack attached to the Mae West. The USAF provided the RAF in South-east Asia with these packs on an unofficial basis.

Further work was done to improve the Thornaby bag and the Bircham barrel. Trials were carried out in 1944 for a supply-dropping apparatus known as Type F. This comprised a cylindrical container that could be dropped by parachute by virtually any type of aircraft. It housed a Walter, a torch, distress signals and water. Early versions also had a flame float to help the ditched crew find it. It was also fitted with nearly 200 yards of buoyant cord to enable the crews to haul it towards their dinghy. Around 500 of these were available by August 1945.

A petrol-dropping container was also developed during 1944.

It consisted of a large tube that held slightly less than 2 gallons (9 litres) of petrol. As the tube was only part-filled, the air kept it buoyant and it was designed to be dropped close to a lifeboat that was either short of fuel or had run out. These petrol-droppers became operational in the spring of 1945.

CHAPTER SEVEN

Mediterranean, Middle Eastern and West African Operations

I n addition to operations around the British Isles, a huge
amount of ASR work was undertaken in the Mediterranean
and in the Near and Middle East, not to mention the coast of
West Africa. There was little formal organisation prior to Italy's
entry into the war in June 1940; indeed there was little flying in
the Mediterranean at that time. There were important operations
to come however, including the siege of Malta, the invasion of
North Africa, and the invasion of Sicily and then mainland Italy.
Later there were also engagements in the Aegean and a large
amphibious landing in the south of France.

In February 1941, with the formation of the Directorate of Air
Sea Rescue at the Air Ministry, a number of officers had been
appointed to investigate and develop search and rescue procedures abroad. They were broadly to follow the pattern that was
being established around the British Isles. Consequently, on
13 May 1941, a flight lieutenant was attached to Headquarters
Mediterranean in Malta, Headquarters West Africa in Freetown
and Headquarters Far East in Singapore.

As the pace of the war stepped up in the Mediterranean
during the summer of 1941 it became clear that the deployment
of search and rescue units would need to be speeded up. It was
decided on 3 September 1941 that a squadron leader would be
sent to Headquarters Middle East in order to organise ASR cover

in the eastern Mediterranean, but this post was not actually filled until February 1942.

When war broke out in 1939 there were only four high-speed launches deployed beyond the British Isles, based at Singapore, Aden, Basra and Malta. Subsequently, Coastal Command deployed some at Gibraltar, but owing to the need for cover around Britain, precious few were available for overseas commands. In April 1940 the launch based at Basra was moved to Port Said, and then to Hurghada on the Gulf of Suez. During this period the Royal Navy and merchant ships were still carrying out the bulk of rescue work. In August 1940 the launch in the eastern Mediterranean was transferred to Mersa Matruh, where it was supported by a converted cabin cruiser.

It was the siege of Malta that proved beyond any doubt that ASR services were vital in the Mediterranean. Above all, as there were very few aircraft in the Mediterranean in these early years, the lives of the pilots were precious as, particularly in the case of Malta, they meant the difference between the island remaining free or being conquered by German and Italian forces.

Compared with the British at the beginning of the war, the Italian air force had a far better developed ASR service. They deployed Cant Z seaplanes at most of their seaplane bases in operational areas.

In May 1941 the Directorate of Air Sea Rescue made their initial estimate of the number of high-speed launches needed for overseas commands: thirty-four, with ten in reserve. It was soon apparent, however, that it would be some months before any of these craft would be available. As an interim measure it was decided in the June that six should be transferred to Malta and the Middle East: three to Malta and one each to Port Said, Aboukir and Mersa Matruh.

During the summer of 1941 Malta was under constant attack, but the only ASR cover was HSL 107. Between 1940 and 1944 she alone was to rescue sixty-seven Allied aircrew and sixteen Italians and Germans. She was based at Kalafrana and was primarily concerned in picking up pilots from the two squadrons of fighter aircraft based on Malta. Initially at least it was very much a make-do arrangement; small craft were pressed into action and seaplane tenders were used, even in the most inclement of weather.

In June 1941 it was decided to allocate a third fighter squadron to Malta. The ground personnel were taken there by Royal Navy vessels, along with one of the ASR launches and crews that had been allocated to Malta. Unfortunately, although the crew was on board, the launch was left behind. The reinforcement of Malta's ASR cover therefore became all the more imperative. In July it was decided to ship the three launches to Gibraltar, where they would be fitted with extra fuel tanks and proceed to Malta under their own steam. The Royal Navy scotched the operation on the grounds that they would have to provide a tanker to refuel them; at that time they considered this to be far too hazardous. However, two of the launches did get through in October 1941.

Although the records prior to November 1941 are somewhat inaccurate, it is suggested that the ASR units on Malta picked up around thirty British pilots of whom, HSL 107 accounted for around seventeen. Other vessels were available to the unit: three seaplane tenders and twelve other craft of varying types.

By the late summer of 1941 the Mediterranean was now a very active operational area, and the Directorate of Air Sea Rescue decided that rather than rely on other vessels, only high-speed launches would be deployed as ASR cover abroad. They decided that thirty-three would be needed, based at Aden, Alexandria, Bathurst, Cyprus, Freetown, Gibraltar, Haifa, Khota Bahru, Kuantan, Malta, Mersa Matruh, Port Said and Singapore.

The late summer also saw the creation of an ASR flight in the Middle East. It was under the operational control of No. 201 Group and consisted of three Wellingtons. It was initially formed in August at Kabrit, but in September it was moved to Burg-el-Arab, to work in conjunction with the Middle East's only high-speed launch. The idea was that they would be used to drop rubber dinghies to ditched crews until they could be reached by surface craft. The unit became operational in the September and it registered its first successful rescue that month, in response to a report that a ship's lifeboat, carrying ten men, had been seen 100 miles (160 km) north of Ras-el-Kanazis. One of the Wellingtons located the lifeboat and dropped supplies and instructions on what course to take. The Wellington patrolled the area until dark. When the occupants were rescued they turned out to be fugitives from the Greek island of Crete, which had been occupied by the Germans.

In November 1941 a Walrus was loaned to the unit by the Royal Navy and based at Mersa Matruh. A Grumman and a Fairchild, which had been given to the RAF as a private American donation for use as air ambulances, also reinforced the flight. Most significantly, two more high-speed launches finally arrived. ASR operations in the Mediterranean were finally properly established.

In January 1942 an ASR detachment was brought up to El Adem (Tobruk) as a result of ground advances on the North African coast. However, it was withdrawn in February 1942 when the situation deteriorated there, moving first to Gambut and then to Fuka. In the next six months some seventy-five individuals were rescued from the sixty-seven crash calls answered. By June 1942 the situation on the ground had become extremely perilous and the unit was moved back to Abu-Sueir.

No. 230 Squadron was formed in the Middle East in August 1941, using Sunderlands. It was already experimenting with a supply-dropping device very similar to the Thornaby bag.

Unfortunately detailed records were not kept until the following year. The turn of the year 1941–1942 had seen the two new launches based as Mersa Matruh and the original launch based at Port Said. The old cabin cruiser that had worked with the original launch was returned to Alexandria. An improvised rescue Pinnace was at work on Cyprus. By December 1941 there were three launches at Malta, three in the Middle East and one in Aden.

Although the Middle East rescue service had anticipated that they would have a minimum of twelve high-speed launches, it was not until May 1942 that any other launches were sent out to overseas bases. The overriding concern was the British Isles and over the same period, December 1941 to May 1942, only ten high-speed launches were added to the home strength. None the less, in February 1942 an ASR officer was sent to the Middle East to try to develop the service as far as he possibly could given the resources available. His brief would be to organise cover for Cyprus, the Red Sea, the Persian Gulf and the Levant.

In August 1942 the Commander-in-Chief Mediterranean took over operational control of the rescue craft and with it the power to divert Royal Navy vessels to assist in rescue work. In the period February to September 1942, eighty-six lives were saved by the rescue service in the Middle East.

Meanwhile, on Malta, the arrival of the two new high-speed launches allowed a combined ASR/MCU to be created in November 1941. Two of the launches and the headquarters were based at Kalafrana. The third launch, supported by a seaplane tender, was based at St Paul's Bay. In December alone they answered thirty-eight crash calls and saved twelve RAF aircrew and an Italian pilot. Whilst carrying out all of this work the MCU was busy loading, unloading, handling and refuelling seaplanes, which provided a vital lifeline for Malta during the siege. In addition to this, it rendezvoused with submarines, which also brought in much-needed supplies.

There was a great deal to be done: merchant vessels were frequently hit and the crews had to be saved and as much salvaged as possible from the wrecks. A prime example was the merchant cruiser *Breconshire* which was towed into Kalafrana in May 1942. The supplies she was carrying were vital to the island and she had frequently been attacked; at one point she was set ablaze by enemy aircraft attacks. The unit salvaged everything they could possibly get off her before she sank three days later.

The unit was also engaged in fire fighting and managed to save thousands of gallons of petrol and equipment by their prompt actions. By the end of 1941 they had picked up thirty-five Allied crew and twelve enemy personnel. The following year saw eighty-five allied and forty enemy crew saved.

In July 1942 it was decided that overseas high-speed launches would be organised in pairs, and that when additional craft became available they would be allocated on a needs basis. By July thirteen were *en route* to newly formed units abroad, but there were still only nine actually in operation. An additional launch had reached Malta, but it had only replaced one that had been lost in June during an air raid.

The first two Miami launches reached the Middle East on 26 July and by the autumn of 1942 the Directorate of Air Sea Rescue began to make serious plans for overseas needs. It was decided in October that 135 craft would be allocated to overseas commands: they included a mixture of high-speed launches, pinnaces, Miamis and naval rescue motor launches. Overall this would mean that there would be forty-seven ASRCs, including the thirteen that had been authorised back in June and were already formed. It was anticipated that the other thirty-four would be operational by May 1943. They would cover the Middle East, West Africa and India, with a unit in the Bahamas.

Montgomery's 8th Army had finally broken the back of Rommel's *Afrika Korps* and was streaming west along the North African coast, and a vast amphibious landing, known as Operation Torch, was made in 1943 to establish Allied forces firmly in the region. ASR units were not deployed in the initial phases of this operation, but as soon as the Anglo-American units had established themselves in North Africa, the need for them became apparent. High-speed launches began arriving in November 1942 and in December two additional units were created, each equipped with three pinnaces.

In February 1943 the first overseas ASR squadron was formed. Six Walruses were transferred from No. 700 Fleet Air Arm Squadron, Algiers to create No. 283 ASR squadron. Initially it was part of Eastern Air Command, but later came under the Mediterranean Air Command. It was formed at La Sebala, Tunis, and was to be the first combined ASR organisation, comprising two ASRUs and a rescue squadron of Walruses.

Meanwhile, in the Middle East, the number of Wellingtons had been increased to six by August 1942 and during September and October six more much-needed high-speed launches arrived.

There were a number of incidents which illustrate the type of work the Middle Eastern units were involved in during this period. One took place on 2 November 1942. At around 1330 hours a Beaufighter went missing near the Bay of Sollum. The Middle East ASR flight was ordered to send an aircraft to search, but since the position was nearly 250 miles (400 km) away, there was no chance that it would get there before dark. An aircraft was therefore sent to Aden with instructions to begin the search in the morning. Shortly after arriving in the area, it spotted two men in a dinghy. No. 201 Group despatched a Sunderland and a Beaufighter to ensure that the dinghy remained in sight, but the original aircraft, which was low on fuel, had to leave the position before they arrived. The Sunderland and Beaufighter could not find the dinghy, but on 4

November another Sunderland did find it. Owing to rough seas, however it could not land to pick up the men.

The following day two of the ASR flight's Wellingtons, supported by a Baltimore from No. 203 Squadron, headed out to find the dinghy. The plan was that the Baltimore would indicate its position for the Wellingtons to drop supplies and emergency kit. The Baltimore failed to find it, however, and the Wellingtons therefore did not take off.

On 7 November the Baltimore finally managed to find the dinghy and dropped flares to mark its position. Then one of the Wellingtons found it shortly before dark. The search continued into the next day, but it was not until 9 November that it was again found by a Wellington. There were Royal Navy motor torpedo boats operating in the area, but they could not be guided to the position. On 10 November a high-speed launch at Mersa Matruh was given the dinghy's position from the previous day and managed to locate the survivors and bring them home.

By July 1942 HSLs 159, 161, 2515 and 2516 had arrived at the Marine Repair Base, Port Said. Ultimately HSLs 121, 141, 251 and 2561 would be based at Alexandria and by November 166 was at Mersa Metruh. HSLs 159 and 161 covered Cyprus and Haifa, whilst HSL 165 was operating in the Red Sea.

HSL 165 had a busy time, picking up a Blenheim crew on an inaccessible beach by rowing to their aid in a clinker-built dinghy, and also extracting a Baltimore crew from No. 203 Squadron. In this latter episode a pair of Wellingtons that had been ordered to search for the aircraft had spotted it. They had dropped emergency kits and circled the site. A Magister was sent with a medical officer, and an Oxford arrived to pick up the men. The Oxford could not lift off from the sandy beach and HSL 165 was despatched to help bring off the Baltimore survivors. There was still the problem of the marooned Oxford, however, and for the next eight days, ground crew managed to work at the site, supplied by ASR Wellingtons and eventually get the Oxford out.

On 3 January 1943 HSL 2517 left Tobruk with instructions to search for the crew of a Mitchell. They left at 0500 hours but were stopped twice by Royal Navy patrols before 0630. At 0700 hours they reached the position they had been given and commenced a series of patterned searches. They continued the search for four hours, only to be told that they had been given the wrong coordinates. With the weather turning foul, they made off for the correct position and a Walrus flew overhead and directed them to the ditched crew. By 1500 hours the seven American crewmen were safely on board. They were exhausted, having been in the sea for twenty-four hours.

With the weather closing in, the launch made 1,400 rpm on the way back to Tobruk. After just over an hour they had to reduce to 1,200 rpm as they were in the midst of a gale. At 1720 hours they had again to reduce to 1,000 rpm, and shortly after to 800. They were forced to stop shortly before 2000 hours and when they started up again they had difficulty in making any headway. By 2100 hours they were within sight of the search-lights on the boom at Tobruk. The wireless transmitter was inoperative and there was a force 6 to 7 gale blowing. The master ordered engine oil to be poured into the water to prevent the sea breaking on board. By midnight the crew estimated that the launch was drifting to the north-east at around 4 knots.

At around 0830 hours on 4 January two destroyers were seen to the south, but all attempts to contact them failed. The weather had not improved and the launch was still drifting. The crew continued to use the oil to avoid being swamped. On the morning of 5 January there were still squalls with rain. At 1515 hours a Wellington was spotted heading south-west, but all attempts to attract its attention failed. By 0500 hours on 6 January the weather had abated enough for the launch to get underway.

They headed south at 800 rpm and half an hour later increased speed to 1,200 rpm. At around 0720 hours daylight revealed land and at 0740 they set course for Bardia. By 0900 they were off Bardia and shortly before 1000 alongside in the harbour.

A medical officer and an ambulance attended to the Mitchell's crew and the master headed off to inform the officer in command at Tobruk of his whereabouts. At 1250 hours the engines were restarted and ten minutes later HSL 2517 left Bardia for Tobruk. She was off Tobruk by 1555 hours and crossed the boom at 1614 hours. She was safely alongside by 1630 hours.

On reaching Bardia, one of the Mitchell's crew said, when he was told that HSL 2517 was a lend-lease Miami: 'Well you needn't pay for this one; we'll write and tell our President to chalk it right off.'

The Middle East ASR flight had remained at Abu-Sueir until November 1942. As the 8th Army continued its advance, however it was moved to Burg-el-Arab. Detachments were posted to Benghazi, Gambut and Sidi Barani. This was an enormous stretch of coastline to patrol and in January 1943 a Blenheim flight was added and a Walrus joined the flight in the February. There were still very few high-speed launches, and seaplane tenders and general purpose Pinnaces were still being used to cover wide areas.

By the beginning of 1943 the war in the desert was virtually over. Any future operations, possibly aimed at Italy, the south of France or the Greek islands, would inevitably mean that there would be increased numbers of operational flights over the Mediterranean. Headquarters Middle East began a radical reappraisal of their needs in the eastern Mediterranean. They needed a mix of amphibians and twin-engined, land-based aircraft. They wanted sixteen Catalinas and thirty-two land-based aircraft to cover an enormous area, which included Aden, Central and East Africa, Iraq, Malta, Persia and Tripoli. Further light aircraft would be needed to maintain communications and carry out searches overland. The Air Ministry broadly concurred and actually suggested that the rescue squadrons would need sixty aircraft. Forty of these would need to be long-range and twenty high-speed. Unfortunately the supply of both Catalinas and Hudsons were inadequate at this time, and in March 1943 the Middle East was offered ten Walruses and twenty Warwicks. They would have to cover the whole of the Mediterranean, and none would be available until August.

The Middle East was also desperately short of high-speed launches; in the five months leading up to March 1943 just eight marine craft had been allocated to this region. The Middle East Command had asked for fifty-five marine craft, but by March there were only seventeen available, including those based at Malta.

Despite the lack of resources the early months of 1943 saw considerable successes. On 9 January a high-speed launch arrived in Malta from Benghazi and although the crew knew little about the local waters, it was despatched in the early hours of the morning of 10 January to find a Wellington crew that had ditched nearly 90 miles (145 km) away. The launch had gone around 65 miles (105 km) when a red flare was fired about 2 miles (3 km) to their port. The launch's crew fired a green flare, indicating that the dinghy occupants, if indeed that was what it was, should fire more red flares. Four more red flares were fired and with the aid of a searchlight the Wellington's crew was found within another ten minutes.

Nearly a month later, on 5 February, a high-speed launch left Benghazi to take up station in Tripoli. By this stage of the war Tripoli had become a very important port. In March the same launch was in the process of rescuing a fighter pilot when it was attacked by enemy aircraft. One man was killed and another injured. But during February the high-speed launches in the Middle East managed to pick up fourteen aircrew, including six enemy personnel.

By April 1943 a new Mediterranean Air Command had been created and preparations to invade Sicily and Italy were well under way. It was decided that at least one ASRU and an ASR squadron would be needed. Consequently, No. 253 ASRU was formed, with six high-speed launches, and No. 284 ASR squadron with six Walruses. It was immediately clear, however, that this was probably insufficient and in May No. 254 ASRU, with eight high-speed launches and two pinnaces, was formed. Immediate preparations were made to transfer the necessary launches from Britain and the Walruses from the Royal Navy at Gibraltar. It was hoped that during June and July the number of rescue craft would be increased to thirty-eight. By 20 May it had reached thirty-one. There was still a problem obtaining rescue aircraft and marine craft and with Operation Husky, the invasion of Italy, imminent, the planners had to cope with the resources they had available.

As an interim measure, a number of what were known as 'bastard' bomber Warwicks were supplied. However, they could not carry airborne lifeboats and it was unlikely that suitable Warwicks would be available until at least September or October.

During the summer of 1943, Operation Beggar took place.

This involved Halifaxes towing Horsa gliders from Britain to North Africa, to be used for airborne operations in the forthcoming Sicily and Italy campaigns. At this time there were no ditching drills for gliders, so it was lucky that only one broke away from its tug on 3 June, ditching into the Bay of Biscay. The Perspex panels in the cockpit began leaking almost immediately and after five minutes the glider was up to its wings in water. The crew broke out the M-dinghy, along with their emergency packs, including food and hot tea, and clambered aboard the dinghy. Luckily the Halifax that had been towing the glider circled the position and rescue units were able to home in on the position. Soon afterwards a Sunderland found them and guided a Royal Navy frigate to the position. When the crew saw the frigate they fired their Very pistol and continued to do so every twenty minutes. When they were picked up after ten hours, the glider was still afloat, so it was sunk with a depth charge. This episode proved, if nothing else, that glider crews needed to have clear ditching drills.

Whilst the pigeon service had been phased out fairly early in the British Isles, it was still being used in the Mediterranean until at least the summer of 1943. The pigeons were still proving their worth, as was illustrated when a Baltimore ditched around 100 miles (160 km) from its base. The crew were able to send out an SOS and a fix was obtained, but owing to poor visibility the dinghy was not spotted. The crew had taken the precaution of bringing their pigeon containers into the dinghy. One of the birds had drowned and the other was very wet, but they allowed its feathers to dry and then attached a message that said 'Crew safe in dinghy 10 degrees west of Tocra.' The pigeon got home safely and a high-speed launch picked the men up the following morning.

The impending amphibious landings in Sicily and Italy threw all the plans that had been formulated in October 1942 into disarray. It had been decided that overseas commands needed 135 rescue craft, distributed amongst forty-seven ASRUs, but in July 1943 all of this had to change. Some sixteen ASRUs were operational in the Mediterranean: seven in North Africa, eight in the Middle East and one in Aden. Collectively they had a strength of forty-three high-speed launches and twelve pinnaces. The new plan was to provide Mediterranean Air

Command, which included the Middle East, with eighty-seven marine craft. This would mean that thirty-two more high-speed launches would be needed in order to equip all the ASRUs that were under formation, and it was proposed that twenty-four of these craft would be delivered by the end of August. This would take the existing units up to full strength. It would also be a start in providing an additional unit for the Middle East, as well as three for Iraq and Persia and four for East Africa.

In order to cover all eventualities for Operation Husky, ASR facilities at Malta, in the Middle East and in north-west Africa, would each be given its own area of responsibility. Three zones were set up, and each of the three commands would handle distress calls in their own areas. Catalinas and Wellingtons, based at Bizerta, would deal with deep searches and carry out rescues where the Walruses were not suitable. During the first two weeks of July, No. 230 Squadron's Sunderlands were also attached to rescue duties. Also available were a handful of Walruses at Hal Far in Malta, forming the newly established No. 284 Squadron.

The ASR work began well before the first allied soldier set foot on Sicily. The amphibious landing was to be preceded by an air offensive. On 2 July a Beaufighter involved in this offensive was forced to ditch about 80 miles (130 km) out to sea from Tunis. Two Walruses were sent to find the crew; one landed and rescued the men, but was unable to take off. It attempted to taxi all the way to Bizerta, but after seven hours ran out of fuel. A high-speed launch was sent to pick up the Beaufighter's crew and assist the Walrus.

In preparation for Operation Husky the ASRU on Malta was reinforced. It now had eight high-speed launches, six seaplane tenders and four Pinnaces. However, over thirty-five squadrons were based in Malta, and even with this reinforcement the unit was stretched. In the first seven days of the invasion, thirty pilots were lost.

The invasion of Sicily began on 10 July and by 17 August the Allies had taken the island. Throughout the period ASR aircraft and marine craft hunted tirelessly for ditched crews and between 3 and 10 July alone, forty-five lives were saved. Throughout the battle for Sicily Allied aircraft pounded the Italian mainland. There were heavy casualties and on 17 July a

Sunderland, with some P 38s acting as escorts, was told to search
for no less than seven dinghies that were said to be south-west
of Naples. Enemy aircraft drove the Sunderland off, however,
and the following morning another Sunderland was sent. This
one managed to pick up six aircrews. A third returned to search
for more dinghies. The Sunderlands were always escorted by
P38s and on this last mission the escorts intercepted fifteen Ju
52s and shot them down.

A Catalina undertook a second difficult mission on 2 August.
It landed in the water around 4 miles (6 km) to the south of
Cagliari to pick up the crew of a Beaufighter. When it tried to
take off the starboard propeller hit the waves and was damaged.
When it tried to taxi away enemy shore batteries fired on it.
Luckily it had a fighter escort and when enemy fighters came
out to destroy it three of them were shot down. Unfortunately in
the ensuing battle one of the enemy fighters managed to hit the
Catalina and it burst into flames. The crew baled out and joined
the Beaufighter survivors, as their own dinghy had been shot to
pieces. The survivors started drifting towards the Sardinian
coast, but despite heavy fire from the land batteries a high-speed
launch swept in and picked them all up.

Three days later a Walrus from No. 283 Squadron, now operating a flight at Palermo, Sicily, took off to look for a dinghy that
was believed to contain three enemy aircrew. It found them and
dragged them aboard. It could not take off, however, because of
the heavy seas and the crew decided to taxi towards Sicily, but
it was clear that they would not make it before they ran out of
fuel. They altered course for Salina island, although they were
unsure whether it was still in enemy hands. As luck would have
it, a British garrison had just arrived. Their squadron was
completely unaware that they were safe and posted them as
missing, as there was no signals equipment on the island at that
stage. When a high-speed launch arrived with supplies for the
garrison on 10 August the Walrus's crew could eventually be
reunited with their squadron.

By the end of August 1943, No. 283 Squadron was at Palermo
with detachments at Monte Corvino and Sidi Achmed. In May
No. 284 Squadron had been created in Britain and had arrived in
Gibraltar in the June. This squadron became operational at

Cassibile on Sicily on 27 July and on their very first day they picked up an American fighter pilot some 10 miles (16 km) south-west of the Italian mainland. During the first three weeks of August the squadron picked up eight Allied and one German aircrew. With Sicily safely in Allied hands it moved to Lentini on 22 August and established a flight at Milazzo on 9 September. Between 8 July and 17 August Air Sea Rescue aircraft flew some 427 sorties, and in the first fourteen days of Operation Husky at least forty-five aircrew were rescued.

On 17 August a large number of USAF Flying Fortresses flew from Great Britain on bombing raids on the Messerschmitt works at Regensburg. After the raids they flew on to bases in North Africa. ASR deployed sixty-five aircraft and a number of high-speed launches over the next three days to find the crews of seven Flying Fortresses that had ditched to the north of Bone. A US Catalina belonging to No. 1 Emergency Rescue Squadron, which had just arrived in North Africa, managed to pick up ten crew, but was damaged when it tried to lift off. It began taxiing towards Bone and rendezvoused three hours later with a high-speed launch, which took the Flying Fortress's crew aboard. The Catalina continued on its journey towards Bone and picked up two more dinghies full of aircrew. Beaufighters and Bisleys found another four dinghies, with the result that a total of forty-two aircrew were picked up.

Attention now turned to the invasion of mainland Italy. It was proposed that two ASR flights would be based in North Africa, one in Sicily and another in the Middle East. This meant that two new squadrons had to be created. The Air Ministry decided that it would be more efficient to have two large squadrons rather than four smaller ones, and as a result of further discussions on 30 August Nos. 293 and 294 were formed, to conduct longer-range search and rescue. They were to have ten Warwicks and three Walruses each, but despite this agreement it was clear that no Warwicks were going to be available in the Mediterranean until at least the end of September. The bulk of the work was therefore carried out by Walruses, Bisleys (of No. 614 Squadron), Wellingtons and some Hudsons that had flown in from West Africa. To cover the invasion No. 614 Squadron operated out of Borizzo, along with a number of high-speed launches. There were Walruses based at Salerno and Milazzo, more launches at Ustica and Salina and a supporting depot ship that would be on hand to refuel launches and flying boats. No. 1 Emergency Rescue Squadron of the USAF also moved up and operated from the North African coast.

The Allied crossings began on 3 September and continued until 8 September, when they attacked Salerno. In the first eight days ASR picked up at least twenty-seven aircrews, and an unknown number of others were saved by the Royal Navy and convoy vessels. With the Germans desperately trying to prise the Allies from their toehold on the mainland, there were a great many air operations throughout September.

On 15 September a Beaufighter flying out of El Aouina was forced to ditch between Elba and Capraia. The pilot and navigator clambered aboard an H-dinghy and had two K-type dinghies with them, along with the pilot's parachute and emergency supplies. They even managed to salvage 30 pints (17 litres) of water from the aircraft's water tank, which was floating nearby. They were picked up by an Italian launch and taken to Capraia. The Italians were at a loss to know what do with them and eventually the authorities decided that they should take them back to Allied territory using an Italian E-boat. It reached Ponza shortly before it fell into Allied hands. From there the men were taken to Malta and eventually, after nine days, returned to their unit.

Six days after the first Beaufighter's adventure began, a second, having attacked fifteen Ju 52s and fought an aerial duel with two Me109s, was forced to ditch north of Sardinia. When it hit the water both the pilot and the navigator were knocked unconscious. By the time the pilot regained consciousness the cockpit was almost submerged. He managed to rouse the navigator and get him out, despite the fact that the man had a broken leg. Their dinghy had been ejected and was inflated, and after a struggle the two men scrambled aboard. They could see that they were in sight of land and tried to paddle towards Sardinia, but the current was too strong. In desperation the pilot jumped overboard and began hauling the dinghy with one arm whilst swimming with the other. He was not making a great deal of progress, so he wrapped the rope ladder around his head and continued swimming with both arms. He towed the dinghy to the shore, where Sardinian nuns at a nearby convent carefully tended them.

September 1943 also saw the beginning of a desperate struggle for the Dodecanese islands in the Aegean. They had been occupied by Italian troops since the general British withdrawal during 1940 and 1941. Throughout 1941 to 1942 the islands had seen the comings and goings of numerous agents and commandos, who were conveyed there by Royal Navy Fairmiles, Harbour Defence motor launches and Greek caiques.

By September 1943, with the Germans fully engaged in Italy and Italian resistance crumbling, it was decided to launch a series of operations against the Dodecanese and other Greek islands held by the Italians. These operations were to be called Accolade, Bigot and Actress. If the British could gain control of the islands near the Turkish coast, to the north of Crete, then supply bases could be established to link up with partisans operating in Greece and Yugoslavia, and ultimately the Russians could be supplied through the Black Sea. The idea of capturing the islands was scotched, however, when the Germans moved 7,000 men to Rhodes. The British still believed that they could take Rhodes by storm, occupy Kos, Leros and Samos and link up with Cyprus, but the Allied Supreme Command gave this operation an extremely low priority. The major priorities were Operation Husky in 1943 and Operation Overlord in 1944.

The situation changed radically on 3 September 1943 when Mussolini was arrested and, in effect, the Italians were no longer allies of the Germans. The Germans on Rhodes acted with great speed and ruthlessness, despite the fact that they were outnumbered five to one, and seized the island for themselves. None the less Operation Accolade, the allied assault on Rhodes, was earmarked to take place towards the end of October.

Elsewhere in the Greek islands the Germans were gradually occupying many of the Italian-held bases. The British managed to occupy Kos and Leros and staged air raids on Rhodes from squadrons based in Cyprus and North Africa.

In order to counter the British moves, Kampfgruppe Muller was hastily pulled together, including the 22nd *Panzer* Grenadier Division, which had been fighting on Crete against the Italians. The target was Kos, which had a garrison of the 1st Battalion of the Durham Light Infantry, 5,000 Italian troops, No. 7 Squadron of the South African Air Force and anti-aircraft units belonging to the RAF Regiment. These men, supported by Royal Navy units, had actually been earmarked for the invasion of Rhodes.

HSL 2517 carried British officers to the island of Castelrosso, the first island in the chain and only 150 miles (240 km) from Cyprus. The officers accepted the Italian garrison's surrender without a shot being fired. Subsequently 400–500 British troops were ferried to the island by a pair of Free French vessels. HSL 2517 now moved to Leros, filled to bursting point with armed men eager to accept the Italian garrison's surrender. This having been achieved, the troops took possession of the island. Over the next few days Salino, Samos and Symii were similarly occupied, but the Germans were building up a counter-attacking force that would include sixty-five Ju 87 Stukas, ninety Ju 88s and HE 111s and fifty Me 109s. In due course they would hinder the operation for British surface vessels and land-based troops.

HSLs 2516 and 2517 were busy over the next few days picking up downed aircrew and victims of German aircraft attacks. It was not long before the Germans launched their own counter-offensive, first striking against Kos at the beginning of October. The British infantry was quickly overrun, but the RAF Regiment continued the unequal struggle until at least 0600 hours on 4 October. On the 3rd HSL 2517 and a seaplane tender managed to evacuate ninety army personnel and Italians, who they transferred to a Royal Navy vessel off the coast of Turkey. They then headed for Castelrosso with four ground crew, six pilots and a number of other personnel.

With the Germans seemingly determined to reoccupy all the islands, it was decided that Leros would be evacuated on 20 November. The Germans pre-empted this move and launched Operation Typhoon on 12 November. Despite heavy losses over five days the island was taken and over 3,000 British troops and 5,350 Italians were taken prisoner. German losses were estimated to be in excess of 1,100. HSLs 2516, 2517 and 2539 were actively involved in evacuating troops from the island and later from Samos.

The British had not finished with the Greek islands, however, and since the Germans had committed considerable numbers of men to the area, it was decided that a series of raids would keep them pinned down. HSLs 2516 and 2539, based at MCU Alexandria, were converted during October and November 1943, to look like Greek caiques. They were repainted, a false mast was erected, the gun tubs were removed and underwater exhausts were fitted. Extra lockers were constructed to carry weapons and the two vessels were used to ferry raiding parties into the Aegean. A number of raids were launched and so successful were they that Vice-Admiral Willis congratulated the master of 2539 and his crew.

Once operations in the Aegean came to a close the launches were transferred by stages to Benghazi, as additional rescue cover was now required for the continuing operations in Italy. Malta was given the responsibility of dealing with all ASR operations around Sicily and the toe of Italy. There was still feverish activity, but the workload had been reduced after Naples had fallen to the Allies on 1 October. By November, with Corsica, Sardinia and southern Italy in Allied hands there was now a need for long-range search aircraft. Mediterranean Air Command made yet more appeals for the long-awaited Warwicks. By this stage only thirteen had been delivered; they were promised that another twenty might be available in January 1944.

By January there were some forty-five high-speed launches operating in the Mediterranean, compared with a paper establishment of thirty-three. The Middle East had twenty-one. In early 1944 the new 68 ft launches arrived and with their increased ranges they were to be of great use. One of them proved its worth on 26 February 1944, when it was sent out to find a dinghy at the absolute limit of its range.

The crew searched unsuccessfully for thirty-seven hours, returned to base, refuelled and left again immediately. Back on search on the morning of 29 February they saw an aircraft overhead, which signalled that they should follow. Around the same time a destroyer appeared on the horizon and was seen to be steaming in the same direction. This was clearly going to be a race to see who got to the dinghy first. The launch won easily and picked up two crewmen who had been adrift for seven days at a point about 20 miles (30 km) south-east of Crete. Having won the race with the destroyer the launch crew were happy to pass the survivors on to the larger vessel, which rewarded them with hot food and drink. In addition to the launch's operation, Wellingtons, Baltimores and Beaufighters had flown for nearly 230 hours searching for the dinghy.

By the spring of 1944 the three ASR squadrons had finally been equipped with Warwicks, but they had a huge area to cover. No. 283 Squadron, based at Hal Far on Malta, launched its first operational search on 26 April. No. 284 Squadron was established at Alghero and No. 293 Squadron at Pomigliano. Between them they covered Sardinia, Corsica and the Italian coast. An ASRU was also operational in the Adriatic by March 1944. These units were supported by a pair of flights of US Catalinas based at Foggia and Grottaglie. In May alone this small branch of the ASR effort in the Adriatic responded to ninety-seven ditches and was successful on thirty-three occasions.

With Italy one of the Allies, Cant aircraft of the Italian air force were available. They were based at Brindisi, Lake Varano and Cagliari, and during April they responded to forty-three rescue calls and made at least four successful rescues.

In May 1944 No. 283 Squadron received its first airborne lifeboats, and the first operational drop was on 22 July. A Spitfire had engaged a Ju 88 and had developed engine trouble. The pilot baled out south-east of Malta. His flight leader gave the approximate point and he circled the dinghy until an ASR Warwick arrived. It dropped some Lindholme rescue equipment and the Spitfire pilot managed to get aboard. With darkness closing in another Warwick arrived with an airborne lifeboat. It was dropped, but the release equipment failed and the parachute broke away in mid-air. The lifeboat was smashed when it hit the water. The pilot was, however, picked up by a high-speed launch soon afterwards.

During June and July 1944 ASR were involved in 143 incidents, eighty of which were successful rescues. In all, 235 Allied personnel were picked up, as well as four Germans. Two incidents show the service's continuing commitment to finding survivors. In June a Spitfire pilot baled out 5 miles (8 km) east of Grossette. He managed to get on board his K-dinghy, which drifted towards the shore. He was quickly located by an ASR Walrus, which despite rough seas managed to land and pick him up. No sooner had this been accomplished than the Walrus sprung a leak and the crew, along with the Spitfire pilot, had to evacuate and get into their M-dinghy. All the survivors were picked up by a high-speed launch.

In the same month a USAF Liberator, which had been hit by flak, ditched north of Ancona. The seven survivors managed to get into their dinghy and were picked up by a German hospital ship. Amazingly the captain offered them the choice of becoming prisoners of war or returning to their dinghies. They chose the latter and the captain broadcast their position, which allowed a Catalina to come and pick them up.

The next major operation that involved ASR was Operation Dragoon, the invasion of southern France. The service would be responsible for all search and rescue missions outside a 15 mile (24 km) radius of the assault area; Mediterranean Allied Tactical Air Forces would deal with the central area. In order to cover this operation Walruses and high-speed launches were positioned at Alghero, Cagliari and Calvi. Launches alone were based at Ajaccio and Borgo. Warwicks would also be based at Alghero and Cagliari, supported by Italian air force Cants. The landings took place on 16 August and despite forecasts of heavy opposition there was in fact very little in the way of aerial combat. Once the Mediterranean Allied Tactical Air Forces had set up their bases in the south of France, ASR became responsible for all rescues up to 40 miles (65 km) from the coast. For this task three high-speed launches and three Walruses were stationed at Calvi.

With German opposition fading away in the Mediterranean, many of the ASR units were deployed on convoy and escort work, and this remained the pattern towards the end of 1944.

By the end of the year No. 323 Wing of Mediterranean Allied Coastal Air Forces, based at Foggia, effectively controlled the majority of rescue aircraft and marine craft in the Adriatic. They continued to be supported by Catalinas of the US 1st Emergency Rescue Squadron, part of No. 293 Squadron and their Warwicks and high-speed launches based at Manfredonia. As reserves they could call upon 293's Walruses, Flying Fortresses and Liberators of the US 15th Air Force, innumerable fighter escorts and Cants of the Italian seaplane wing. In the last six months of 1944 No. 323 Wing picked up 512 personnel from the sea, mainly Allied aircrew, but also some Germans, Poles deserting from the German army and Yugoslav partisans.

A US pilot flying a Catalina carried out a daring rescue on 18 July 1944. He volunteered to pick up a Hurricane pilot in the Mljetski Channel, under the very noses of German shore batteries. As he came in he began to draw fire, but he landed the aircraft, picked up the survivor and evaded the fire whilst taking off, managing to get the man home. He was subsequently awarded the Distinguished Flying Cross by the British.

No. 293 Squadron, now operating from Italy, had picked up thirty-two aircrew during October. On the 21st alone they had made three successful rescue missions.

Although operations in the Mediterranean were being scaled down by 1945, two quite amazing air sea rescues took place in March and April. On 10 March a Mosquito was forced to ditch off German-occupied northern Italy. Every time an ASR aircraft attempted to drop flares to rescue the crew it came under intense fire. Once the fog had cleared the next morning a Walrus and a Warwick, escorted by Spitfires, once more tried to locate the two men. One man was spotted standing on the beach beside the wrecked Mosquito, which had floated ashore inside a minefield. The Walrus managed to land outside the minefield and two of the crew paddled their dinghy through it, but were forced to turn back by strong currents. The Warwick then dropped an airborne lifeboat near to the Walrus and the two crew used it to get them through the minefield. They picked up the pilot and discovered that the navigator was dead. They then paddled back through the minefield, boarded the Walrus and, with a constant escort of Spitfires, returned to base.

On 2 April 1944 Lieutenant Veitch of No. 260 Squadron, South African Air Force, was in action over Yugoslavia in his Thunderbolt. As a result of a near miss by enemy flak his Thunderbolt developed engine problems and he was forced to bale out in the Gulf of Venice, just 5 miles (8 km) from the Istria Peninsula. He had, however managed to send an SOS before doing so. A Catalina of No. 1 Emergency Rescue Squadron arrived and could see that his dinghy was drifting close to a minefield; there was no hope of it landing. A Warwick of No. 293 Squadron managed to drop an airborne lifeboat and Veitch boarded it and steered it through the minefield so that the Catalina could pick him up.

Not content with this close escape, three days later his

replacement aircraft was hit whilst he was attacking a German train in Yugoslavia. Again he baled out, this time over the Gulf of Trieste. Once again he had chosen a minefield. None the less he climbed into his K-dinghy and saw a German torpedo boat heading towards him. A Mustang fended it off and a Warwick managed to drop an airborne lifeboat. He climbed aboard, but no sooner had he done so than the shore batteries began to fire at him and another German vessel came out to capture him. Luckily the Warwick had a fighter escort and it swooped down on the ship. It would not turn back, however, so a Mosquito came down and sank it. The Mosquito remained protecting Veitch for the rest of the day, as he steered the lifeboat out of the minefield and towards a Catalina that had landed in the rough sea; it was another successful rescue.

Veitch seemed to make a habit of close shaves. On 30 April he again baled out into a minefield, this time south of Lake Marano. On this occasion a US Flying Fortress dropped a lifeboat to him and he steered through the obstacles and was taken in tow by a high-speed launch. In these three amazing escapes Veitch did not suffer so much as a scratch. For his persistence, if nothing else, he was awarded the Distinguished Flying Cross.

Particular mention should be made of ASR operations in West Africa. In the early years of the war, this was a vital southern reinforcement route to the Middle East. It was later used as a stopping point for aircraft from America and, above all, it was used by several reconnaissance units in their hunt for German U-boats in the South Atlantic.

In August 1941 the Director of Air Sea Rescue allocated four high-speed launches to operate out of Freetown and Bathurst. Owing to the service shortage of marine craft, however, the first two did not arrive until October 1942, and the units had to make do with these two until more marine craft arrived in July 1943. An ASR officer was appointed to Air Headquarters West Africa in October 1942; up until this point a single Sunderland, based at Jui, had carried out all rescue work. It was equipped with a local version of a Thornaby bag, which was in fact made from kitbags and parachute bags.

Sunderland crews were responsible for air sea rescue on a rota and perhaps one of their first successful rescues took place in

October 1942, when they saved the passengers and crew of SS *Oransay*. The vessel had been torpedoed 300 miles (500 km) off the African coast. The Sunderland spotted six lifeboats the following morning and managed to drop rescue equipment and radio for a Royal Navy vessel to pick up the survivors. On the following day they found nine more lifeboats and three more the next day. Despite the distance and relative lack of search and rescue units, all the passengers and crew were saved.

In December 1942 No. 200 Squadron, flying Hudsons, became the first overseas unit to receive Lindholme rescue equipment. Whilst this considerably improved the chances of aircrews that ditched in this area, work was still severely hampered by the lack of marine craft. In the interim Royal Navy launches filled this role.

In July 1943 it was decided that five ASRUs should be established in West Africa, each with two marine craft. By July two high-speed launches were on station and four pinnaces supported them. This meant that a unit could now be established at Takoradi, in addition to the two existing bases. When more high-speed launches became available two more units were to be based at Pointe Noir and Port Etienne. This was still inadequate coverage for this vast stretch of coastline and for a time they would be supported by the USAF in Dakar, who had two of their own rescue launches, as well as Free French naval vessels.

A bizarre incident occurred in August 1943. A U-boat shot down a Liberator, but it was crippled during the engagement. The Liberator's crew died when the aircraft crashed, but their dinghies were blown out of their stowage and seven of the German U-boat crew managed to clamber aboard one of them. The German survivors, who were thought to be the Liberator's crew, were picked up. The captain of the Liberator that had crippled the U-boat, Flying Officer L. A. Trigg was subsequently awarded the Victoria Cross.

By January 1944 two high-speed launches were based at Port Etienne, two Pinnaces were at Bathurst, two more launches at Freetown and one launch and a pinnace at Takoradi. These last two marine craft also covered Banana, where they were supported by a Belgian launch.

In August 1944 the ASRU at Banana was transferred to Lagos,

and by the end of that year, ASR operations around West Africa had reached an all-time low. Between March 1943 and February 1945 they had responded to thirty-two incidents and rescued 201 aircrew out of a total of 270. In addition to this they had also saved the lives of 649 merchant seamen.

ASR During National Service

Even before the end of the war in Europe, not to mention the war in the Far East, the contraction of the RAF had begun. Many thousands of RAF ground crew and trades people had been transferred into the army or the Royal Navy before the end of hostilities. With hostilities over, a mad, chaotic rush was under way to demobilise as many people as possible, often with absolutely no regard to how it would affect units that would still need to operate in the post-war world.

As a result, many of the younger aircrew that still had time left to serve in uniform were forcibly remustered as motorboat crews. They had to fit in as best they could with the nucleus of career marine craft personnel, and there were inevitably mis-understandings and hostility towards these 'fly boys' who had been dumped on the Marine Craft Section.

In the Indian Ocean and the Far East many thousands of British military personnel were still deployed well into 1946. Not only was the situation in these areas rather more complex, with occupation duties to perform, the impending closure of many bases and the very real prospect of independence being granted to a number of countries that had been part of the British Empire, but it was also compounded by shipping problems. The logistics of getting home many thousands of people, from the other side of the world were proving to be a headache that nobody seemed to be able to solve.

An interim solution was found in the conversion of what had been strike aircraft in 1945, such as Halifaxes, Liberators, Flying Fortresses, Sunderlands, Lancasters and Stirlings. These aircraft were fitted with the most basic seating and huge convoys of them plied between far-flung territories to transit camps and then back to the British Isles. Many of the men were desperate to return home, but for the MCS and the ASRUs these huge aerial armadas needed protection, maintenance and support. Many marine craft had to be deployed along the routes taken by aircraft returning not only from the Far East but also from mainland Europe. It would have been politically and morally unacceptable for men who had served in the forces to be lost on the eve of their resumption of civilian life.

As far as the Air Sea Rescue and Marine Craft Section was concerned, there were 300 high-speed launches and perhaps thousands of other craft dotted around the world, all of which needed to be assessed, documented and probably disposed of either locally or back in Britain. These vessels, and the men who had manned them, had saved 13,269 lives during the course of the war in all theatres. The men who had operated at first from the British Isles and then from bases in various parts of northwest Europe had picked up 5,658 aircrew, in addition to many hundreds of other personnel.

The future of the marine craft seemed rosy, for as long as there were flying boats they and their crew would always be needed. There was also an assumption that as long as aircraft flew over the seas there would be a need for air sea rescue facilities. Moreover the craft and personnel would continue to be needed for survival training, torpedo recovery, range safety and target towing. In fact, however, everything was veiled in a fog of uncertainty. What would the peacetime RAF look like? What would it do? Where would it be based? What would be the impact on the marine craft and their crews when the heavy bombers, flying boats and piston-engined fighters were phased out?

The Second World War had proved beyond any doubt that, despite the fact that many of the vessels used were at best worn out and at worst obsolete before they had even entered service, the men who used them were masters of self-sufficiency and improvisation. They had continued a tradition of coping, sometimes excelling, in adversity. Vessels that had not been designed for a particular job had more than exceeded expectations in the capable hands of experienced crews. A pinnace, No. 96, had travelled from Colombo to northern Sumatra at an average speed of 10 knots, a non-stop journey of over 900 miles (1,450 km). Not only was this a record for its time, but given the fact that the pinnace had never been designed to do this, it was a testimony of the RAF sailors' seamanship and abilities.

Gradually, as the coxswains, motorboat crews, mechanics, fitters and wireless operators returned to Britain, they were demobbed. Those that remained within the MCS discovered that all the ASR pinnaces were marked for disposal and only the 60 ft (18.3 m) general service pinnace would be retained. A handful of 40 ft (12.1 m) and 41.5 ft (12.6 m) seaplane tenders would also be retained, but all the 37.5 ft (11.4 m) versions were surplus to requirements. Some would be converted into fire floats. The numbers of all the other vessels, including planing dinghies, bomb scows, smaller marine tenders, refuellers and ferryboats were to be reduced dramatically

The experienced crews who wished to stay within the RAF were severely disadvantaged by the scaling down of the service. Many of them were offered posts within the RAF in different branches – The masters of the high-speed launches were often offered posts in the catering branch, administration or equipment – but very few decided to take these postings.

It rather belatedly dawned on the Air Ministry that at least in the short to medium term they would need marine craft and air sea rescue arms not only to cover the bases that would be retained but also be available for any new conflicts that might occur. They began to address the problem by recruiting direct entry marine officers. They had a ready reservoir of experienced non-commissioned officers in the service, but they were not invited to apply for appointment as officers. More generally, the recruiting figures for the RAF had dropped markedly, perhaps not as drastically as the Royal Navy or the Army, but still enough to cause major concern.

A significant event for many of the men who were to serve on marine craft in the late 1940s and 1950s, occurred in 1947. In recognition of the fact that the peacetime army, Royal Navy and RAF were under strength and would probably remain that way if drastic action were not taken, National Service was introduced. To begin with it had little impact on the Marine Craft Section as, traditionally, the majority of the crews had been regulars.

Other moves were afoot which would, at least for the next forty years, ensure the continued use of marine craft by the RAF. The MCS was granted full branch status on 11 December 1947. Henceforth it would be known as the RAF Marine Branch and it would be responsible for many of the activities and planning that had hitherto been the responsibility of other commands. It would be responsible for its own training, for running recovery and depot ships, and for framing the role of high-speed launches. It would be responsible for range safety and support the flying boats and the Moorings Branch. The latter was responsible for laying and servicing RAF moorings around the world and operated twelve moorings drifters. They were commanded by civilian officers, now effectively controlled by the Marine Branch.

On 25 June 1948 there was another considerable boost to the Marine Branch when it was agreed that all RAF marine craft of 68 ft (20.7 m) or more would henceforth be called His Majesty's Air Force Vessel (HMAFV). They would be commanded by RAF officers and manned by RAF personnel. This was the first time that any other British military organisation was allowed to fly the Union Jack between dawn and dusk, an honour that had previously only been accorded to the Royal Navy.

Corporal Coxswain 'Johnnie' Sutherland, who had joined the Marine Craft Section in June 1943, at Cardington, was subsequently posted to St Eval, Cornwall. He had been trained as a radio telephonist, but was told by the station commander that they already had too many of these, so he was posted to Padstow to train as motorboat crew. He attended the MBC course at Corsewall and was subsequently assigned to the Marine Craft Section, Wig Bay, where he joined a maintenance unit for flying boats. He was also duty ASR crew twenty-four hours on and twenty-four hours off. In September 1944 he was transferred to Aden, but was at Mesirah two days after VJ Day. By 1946 he was back with ASRU Aden and was then posted to Fenara. He returned to Britain and served at Calshot from February 1947, attending the coxswain's course at Pembroke Dock in 1948. He was then transferred to HMAFV Bridport. In June 1951 he joined RAF Lyme Regis as the Coxswain of a seaplane tender and was finally demobbed in January 1952.

He recalls several incidents in this career, notably one

regarding HMAFV *Bridport*. In 1948 she was on a recruiting tour, starting at Margate and finishing at Rothesay in Scotland. At Rhyll she was moored some distance from the pier. The skipper and the chief engineer had been invited to a meal and drinks ashore with the local civic dignitaries. Corporal Sutherland was the duty coxswain and had been told by the skipper to pick them up at 2230 hours. The ferryboat arrived at the pier at the appointed time; there was a stiff breeze, but no sign of the skipper or the engineer. The pier watchman offered the crew a cup of tea, but there was still no sign of the passengers. It was agreed that they would go back to the *Bridport* and the pier watchman would signal their passengers' arrival with an Aldis lamp.

The crew waited and waited and finally, around 0130 hours, the Aldis lamp flashed from the pier, with the message 'Your passengers are here.' The wind was now stronger and on the return trip, about halfway to *Bridport,* the skipper lost his hat overboard. He had taken to wearing a small pork pie hat for his jaunts ashore and it blew off. The engineer said, 'We've got to save his hat corporal.' They had an Aldis lamp and after ten minutes they spotted the hat and managed to get alongside it. The engineer leaned over the side, grabbed it and shoved it straight back onto the skipper's head, regardless of the fact that it was still full of seawater. The Skipper did not mince his words and told the engineer in no uncertain terms what he thought of him.

There were still problems in clarifying not only the role of the new Marine Branch, but also what types of marine craft would be needed. Only when decisions on the type of craft had been made would the branch be in position to determine how many men it would need to recruit, what skills they would need, and how it would train them. This problem fell to the Marine Craft Policy Committee. They faced a difficult task and they knew, as did many of the crews, that their decisions would increasingly be determined by economic constraints rather than operational needs.

The main high-speed launch to be retained in the 1950s was the Hants & Dorset, which had been effectively converted into a rescue target-towing launch. It had lost it guns and armour plating and was now painted with a black hull and a light grey superstructure. Even the serial numbers had changed; they were now painted in white and the yellow ring around the roundels had been removed. Vessels operating overseas were painted white and had their serial numbers in black.

Many of the ASR seaplane tenders, mainly operating with 37 ASRU Lyme Regis, 29 ASRU Littlehampton and 46 ASRU Porthcawl during the war, were 'reduced in rank' to the role of range safety launches. They were involved in patrolling practice ranges and a handful were still employed with flying boat squadrons. Technically at least, the marine craft that continued to support the flying boats retained the title Marine Craft Section. The marine craft repair units became maintenance units and were placed under Maintenance Command. The last of the maintenance units, 238 MU Calshot, was disbanded and moved to Mount Batten in 1961. Meanwhile some marine craft were placed with the marine craft training schools.

Many of the units that had been ASRUs, were scaled down and became MCUs. The new units were distinctly different from the old ASRUs. Whilst an ASRU might have had up to twelve high-speed launches, most of the MCUs now had three or four rescue target-towing launches or range safety launches, supported by marine tenders or general service dinghies. Other MCUs differed entirely and still had pinnaces which had to cope with innumerable different roles.

The continued development of the helicopter was a dark cloud on the horizon for the Marine Branch. The RAF had already combined many aspects of its ASR and other rescue services as search and rescue. Pessimists felt that the life expectancy of the new Marine Branch was limited, but it continued to soldier on, despite their fears, until the 1980s.

On 29 February 1940 Harland and Wolff had completed and launched two Royal Navy Bangor Class fleet minesweepers. They were J50, the *Bridport* and J65, the *Bridlington*. Some fourteen of these vessels were built and their wartime complement was a crew of around sixty. They were officially handed over to the RAF in 1946, but they were not manned until the following year. Squadron Leader George Coats commanded the *Bridlington* and Squadron Leader E. H. Roberts the *Bridport*. The vessels were handed over at Chatham, with the *Bridport* joining 19 Group, being based at Portsmouth and the *Bridlington* joining 18 Group, to be attached to HMS *Sea Eagle* at

Londonderry. The new designation that had been granted meant that they became HMAFV *Bridport* and HMAFV *Bridlington*. The *Bridlington* worked with combined services on NATO fleet exercises. Over the years many masters of high-speed launches from the war years commanded both vessels.

In July 1948 HMAFV *Bridport* was transferred from work with the Ministry of Supply to undertake operations connected with the Berlin Airlift from June 1948 to May 1949. The crisis had been precipitated by friction between NATO and the Soviet Union. The latter was attempting to blockade the British, French and American sectors of Berlin, with the result that the population of these sectors suffered dire shortages of food, fuel and other essentials. The Allies created air routes, or corridors, and provided virtually unlimited,twenty-four hour supply into and out of the beleaguered city. Each of the corridors was a single lane of traffic and could only go at the speed of the slowest moving aircraft. Russian aircraft patrolled these corridors and it would have caused huge political repercussions if any Allied aircraft had strayed. The *Bridport*, commanded by the former Malta skipper, Squadron Leader E. W. T. Hardie, made a number of voyages to Blankenese, near Hamburg, to support the marine craft crews and the Sunderland flying boats. During this period virtually any aircraft that could still fly headed for Tempelhof airport, laden with food, fuel and provisions, and evacuated German civilians, notably orphans.

The *Bridlington* was involved in postings rather further afield. In October 1955 she set sail for Gan in the Maldives. Gan had long been associated with the RAF as a transport, supply and service base between the Far East and Australia. With India gaining its independence, followed by Burma and Ceylon, many of the air routes had changed. RAF aircraft would no longer overfly India, Pakistan or Ceylon and cover was needed for the areas around Aden, Bahrain and Singapore. *Bridlington* left Plymouth and stopped at Gibraltar, Malta and Aden before arriving in Colombo. A survey party then set off for Gan.

It had been an eventful journey. When *Bridlington* was sailing between Gibraltar and Malta a small boat had been spotted. On investigation it was found to contain two men who were badly dehydrated and heavily sunburned. They turned out to be Germans who had deserted from the French Foreign Legion and had been adrift for three days. They were handed over to the German consul in Malta.

Representatives visited the Sultan of the Maldives, who ruled over 2,000 uninhabited and 200 inhabited islands. The natural choice for a base was at Addu Atoll, which had an RAF presence dating back to 1942, when an airstrip had been constructed there. The *Bridlington* deposited the survey crew and continued to supply them until Sunderlands arrived to take over that duty. Gan lay on the southern most point of the atoll. There was a ring of about twenty-five islands in the area, four of which were inhabited. What was particularly useful about Addu Atoll was that it had an ideal natural harbour, which had been capable of housing RMS *Queen Mary* in 1942. The *Bridlington* finally left Gan for Plymouth in February 1956, arriving on 26 April.

Gan was due for development from January 1957. It took two years to build a 400 ft (120 m) jetty and required the services of nearly 2,000 locals and others to complete the work. All the time it was supplied by Sunderlands from RAF Seletar, which arrived twice a week until an additional service was provided from Colombo. Gan remained a British base until 29 March 1976. At its peak 550 Marine Branch personnel served there. There were no married quarters available, and prefabricated bungalows were provided for all ranks. The airmen constructed an eighteen hole golf course, the cinema showed four different films each week and the NAAFI club was well appointed, with a good restaurant. It was a popular posting for the Marine Branch, as things were cheap and everything was duty-free. Many of the men used postings there to save for their weddings or house purchases.

The Defence White Paper of 1975 sounded the death knell for the station and Gan began to be run down in the same year. As far as the Marine Branch was concerned, the busiest months were the first three of 1976, when they had to carry out an inventory of everything on the base and then load it onto freighters for disposal. One of its last tasks was to erect a monument, which was set up near the former station headquarters. The inscription simply read 'Royal Air Force Gan, 1956–1976'.

Meanwhile HMAFV *Bridlington* had returned to Plymouth and had been effectively mothballed. The *Bridport* was still working with the Ministry of Supply, but in May 1958, after ten years of service with the Marine Branch, they were both sent to the scrapyard.

The increasing number of helicopters coming into service had initially appeared to be more useful in land than in sea rescues. Moreover, they lacked the ability to fly at night or in poor visibility and they had a limited range. They also lacked carrying capacity. However, those that were coming into service in the 1960s were beginning to be able to cope with the job.

The Marine Branch was still using their Hants & Dorsets, many of which had entered service during the Second World War. Indeed one craft, 2552, had joined the RAF in 1943 and had served at around fifteen bases at home and abroad before being disposed of in April 1958 from 1113 MCU Holyhead. No. 2746 had been delivered to Fanara in March 1946, the last of her kind to be produced. She had served at 1153 MCU Cyprus, and had operated with RTTL 2713 against the EOKA terrorists. After seventeen years another Hants & Dorset, 2743, which had become the longest serving vessel, finally left service, also at Holyhead, in October 1962.

It was not until 1950 that a replacement was approved for the Hants & Dorset. By this stage the British Power Boat Company had closed (in 1946) and Vosper provided the only viable solution. They had designed a 68 ft (20.7 m) long, 19 ft (5.8 m) beam, RTTL Mark Ia. It was far bulkier than the original Hants & Dorset, but still had the diagonal double planking. It offered more space inside and the deckhouse had an aluminium tripod mast. To many trained eyes it very much looked the part, but everyone was to be extremely disappointed.

It began to enter service over the period 1953–1955, but was dreadfully underpowered. It had a top speed of just 24 knots and if it had a fouled bottom or the hull had absorbed water, it struggled. This was no great surprise, as it was powered by Napier Sea Lion engines. This had never been the intention, but delays with the Rolls-Royce Sea Griffons had forced the RAF to accept this compromise. In other respects the vessel was not too bad: the quarters and the sickbay were good, and even the engineer had room in which to work. In 1959 the craft were retro-fitted with Rolls-Royce Sea Griffons and could now boast a speed of 38 knots. The first craft to be converted was RTTL 2747, and 2748, 2749 and 2750 soon followed.

Meanwhile, whilst new gearboxes were being developed, Vosper produced five more craft with the old Napier Sea Lion engines. These vessels, Nos. 2751–55, had a different-shaped deckhouse, which was made from aluminium. They had re-positioned the master's cabin and had relegated the wireless operator's cabin to a tiny position on the starboard side. One of the major drawbacks with this new design was that there was no way of getting from the wheelhouse to the engine room or the wireless operator's cabin without either walking through the sickbay and the crew quarters, then up a ladder or going round the boat and approaching from the side deck. It was abundantly clear that this would be hazardous at high speed or in poor weather conditions. Ultimately these vessels were also con-verted to house the Rolls-Royce Sea Griffons.

There were three types of Hants & Dorsets by 1956: the wooden-topped version with three Napier Sea Lion engines, the Vosper version with an aluminium top and Napier engines, and the Vosper type with an aluminium top and Griffon engines. By the early 1960s all the Mark Ia launches had been converted to the Mark Ib, but 2751–5 still retained their Napier engines.

A new Vosper Mark II was on the drawing board in 1955. The prototype, RTTL 2756, had a confusing designation; the proto-type drawings gave the number as 2762E, with the letter E standing for experimental. It was subsequently changed to RTTL 2772E. It was built entirely of aluminium; the only wood used was for the teak deck. It was capable of 52 knots, but the aluminium tended to corrode and had to be replaced with diagonal double planking, which reduced its speed.

In the early 1960s the MCMU at Calshot, subsequently based at Mount Batten, was given the job of converting all vessels to Mark IIs. This meant that they had to secure components from Rolls Royce, Vosper and a multitude of other suppliers. It is to their great credit that they managed to complete the job much faster than any civilian shipbuilder. By the time the conversions had been completed RTTLs 2751–61 and 2767–72 had all become Mark II launches. Both they and the Mark Ib were now equipped with two 1700 hp Rolls-Royce Sea Griffon engines. Their cruising speed was between 32 and 36 knots, but their maximum speed was 40 knots. They were difficult to handle, however, as their slowest speed was 10 knots. These vessels formed the back-bone of the Marine Branch's fleet from the mid-1950s to the early 1970s.

During the 1950s the 60 ft (18.2 m) pinnaces had been phased out, with two notable exceptions. Pinnace 1196 was not removed from operational duties until 1966, when it was serving with 1107 MCU Newhaven, and 1198 survived another year before it was retired at Seletar. These vessels had served the Marine Branch for twenty years.

Groves and Gutteridge built their successor. They were 63 ft (19.2 m) long and bore more than a passing resemblance to their predecessors. They were powered by two Rolls-Royce C6SFLM diesel engines and were capable of speeds of up to 17 knots. The first one, 1371, entered service in 1955 and the last one, 1392, joined the Marine Branch in 1965.

Cuts continued to affect the Marine Branch, both directly and indirectly. The last Sunderlands left Pembroke Dock for Seletar in 1956. This meant that all the bomb scows, ferryboats and re-fuellers were now surplus to requirement after forty years. Recruitment was frozen, as the Marine Branch was considered overmanned. Moreover, the technical advances made by heli-copters were beginning to have a marked effect; the branch was shrinking.

We are indebted to Rick Mortby who served with the Marine Branch during the 1950s, for an account of a typical search and rescue operation off the British Isles. In 1957, whilst stationed at Gorleston, 2579 received a call to respond to an incident off the coast of Winterton, near Great Yarmouth. A Black Hunter III squadron had lost its 'tail end Charlie', which had ditched in the North Sea. 2579's crew were on standby and had seen the flight pass over their heads. They received a bearing from the river cruiser *Norwich Belle* and immediately put out to sea to investigate. Despite a systematic search by local lifeboats, 2579 and a Shackleton there was absolutely no sign of the aircraft. It was later believed that the aircraft had hit the water at considerable speed, aquaplaned and then sunk without any visible wreckage.

CHAPTER EIGHT

The 1960s and the End of an Era

As the numbers of MCU bases in the Britain were gradually reduced, personnel found themselves increasingly required to serve overseas. An MCU man could comfortably expect to be posted abroad for a two-year stretch, in theory accompanied by his wife and children. In practice, however, it was difficult to obtain married quarters and many married men served much of the two years abroad alone. If the man was single he could expect at least a year overseas.

One of the busiest MCU bases overseas was at RAF Seletar, Singapore. The marine craft maintenance unit there handled all the repairs in the Far East, and it fell to 1124 MCU to provide search and rescue services, as well as target towing. It also dealt with weapons recovery and sonar practice. The search and rescue function was carried out in cooperation with Shackletons and helicopters flying out of Changi airbase.

An example of the cooperation between different units occurred on Boxing Day 1962. RTTL 2755 was on anti-pirate patrol duties in the South China Seas, *en route* to Borneo. During the voyage she hit a floating object and no matter what the crew did, they could not prevent her shipping water at an alarming rate. They radioed back to Seletar with an SOS, but it was taken to be a routine position report. Fortuitously, a Hastings aircraft of Transport Command spotted her and stayed aloft of her position until the arrival of a Shackleton.

Back at Seletar, a crew manned a pinnace and headed for her. It was beaten there by a Westland Belvedere helicopter, which was being air tested and lacked a winch. With great precision the pilot managed to get all the crew off with a knotted rope. Eventually RTTL 2755 was towed back to Seletar, where it was patched up, fitted with a cannon and despatched to resume its abortive anti-pirate patrol mission.

The writing was on the wall for 1124 MCU by 1966; they were busy training local crews that would eventually replace them. The unit, like many others around the world, took this self-driven redundancy move in its stride. It was ultimately disbanded in October 1970. The two rescue target towing launches (2750 and 2755), along with the single range-safety launch (1652) were handed over to Singapore Armed Forces Maritime Command. One of the pinnaces (1385) was brought back to the UK, whilst the older 1198 was sold off.

Elsewhere, the Kai Tak base was closed in January 1967 after a long and effective period of service. The base at Glugor had been set up in 1945 and was for a short time 231 ASRU. It became an MCU the following year. The RAF used the depot barge *Hataili* as a mobile ASRU during the offensive in Burma in 1945. It was given back to its owners when hostilities ended. As a more permanent solution, the MCS was re-established at Penang. In 1955 the section was redesignated as 1125 MCU and worked in tandem with Royal Australian Air Force Butterworth, providing not only search and rescue cover, but also range safety and survival training facilities.

An incident which showed the RAF's ability to handle search and rescue missions occurred in July 1966. It ended in tragedy, but none the less provides a good example of inter-service co-operation. On the evening of 23 July, 1125 MCU received word from RAAF Butterworth that three men had not returned from a skiing trip to the north of Penang. By this stage it was getting dark and one of the men should already have been dropped off at Penang, whilst the others should have been back at the Yacht Club at Butterworth.

RSL 1645 and 1656 were made ready and were out in less than twenty minutes. News arrived that a Malay fishing boat had picked up one of the survivors, who stated that their boat had sunk near to the wreck of a First World War Russian ship that had been sunk by the German cruiser *Emden*. This, at least, gave the crews something to work on, particularly as he also said that the other two men had probably been swept out to sea.

Working on a sweeping pattern with their searchlights scanning the water, the two launches began searching for the two missing men. A Shackleton, operating out of RAF Changi, dropped flares to illuminate the surface of the ocean and the launches examined anything that could be wreckage or survivors.

They were reinforced in the morning by RSL 1652 whilst helicopters and other aircraft from RAAF Butterworth assisted in the search. The Royal Malaysian Customs Service sent out their own high-speed launches to assist, but it was not until the evening that two ski rope handles were found, along with some other wreckage. Unable to find the men, the search was recommenced the following morning. A body was found and then a second two days later.

The MCU's first major search and rescue success of the 1960s took place in March 1960 out of RAF Gan in the Maldive Islands. As we have seen, despite being a haven for mosquitoes and a generally inhospitable place, Gan was a popular posting; indeed many Marine Craft Section personnel repeatedly volunteered for duty there. Initially they operated tugs and landing craft to offload supplies from vessels visiting the atoll, but eventually a landing craft general purpose Pinnace, 1374, and a marine tender replaced them.

Life on the atoll was basic, but at least there was chilled Tiger Beer at the NAAFI, there was sunbathing, scuba diving and a cinema. In 1959 Flight Lieutenant Bernard Saunders was appointed commanding officer of the Marine Craft Section there. He was an experienced high-speed launch master and the commander of 1113 MCU at Holyhead.

He was appointed to deal with a tricky diplomatic situation that had erupted. With some volunteers and RTTLs 2747 and 2748, he was despatched to help deal with the somewhat ramshackle 'invasion' of the atoll by the newly independent Maldives government. He arrived in the nick of time and the invasion, never a very serious affair, was called off. The arrival of the two launches, coupled with the occasional posting of a Royal Navy vessel dampened the Maldives government's interest in 'liberating' the atoll. Moreover, 205 Squadron's Shackletons provided for defence as well as search and rescue missions.

Saunders was therefore on hand for a mission in March 1960. An RAF Hastings carrying twenty Royal Navy personnel went down in treacherous waters just 1½ miles (2 km) south-east of Gan's airstrip. Saunders, aboard RTTL 2748, picked up eighteen of the men and the crew of P 1374 saved the remaining two.

RAF Gan was developed somewhat during the 1960s (better quarters and a hospital were built), but it was finally closed in 1976.

One of the most significant developments in the 1960s was the use of helicopters, which ultimately was to spell the end of the MCS. The first helicopter rescue could be said to have taken place at RAF Khormaksar, Aden, in 1963. One evening a Royal Navy Vixen was forced to ditch just outside the harbour. The duty crew of RTTL 2767 was despatched to pick up the two crew, but before they had even left the port an RAF Wessex had rescued them.

The Marine Craft Section at Khormaksar during the 1960s was not only concerned with regular rescue duties for the transport and strike aircraft using the airfield, but also with supporting the Hunter squadrons being used in the brush-fire war that had ignited in Radfan.

The section had a rescue target towing launch, a Pinnace and a range safety launch, as well as landing craft, including a Zebra craft that was later posted to Masirah. The Z-12, as it was known, was some 145 ft (44 m) long and 30 ft (9 m) wide. The aft contained the bridge, cabins, mess deck, gally, storage rooms and engine room. The remainder of the craft was like an enormous landing craft. It was prone to breaking down, did not like the salty water, lacked engine parts, did not have any air-conditioning and the superstructure was often hot enough to cook a breakfast on. None the less it was a workhorse and used to ferry equipment, stores and vehicles from merchant ships to the shore.

Shortly after the rescue of the Vixen crew, an Argosy cargo aircraft went down in the inner harbour in Khormaksar. Once again the helicopter squadron was at hand to rescue the crew. Meanwhile, the launch and the pinnace were making for the downed aircraft. Seeing the crew in the safe hands of the heli-copter, the MCS men sprinted aboard the rapidly sinking Argosy and extricated several thousand pounds' worth of equipment and avionics. Later, the Argosy was refloated and towed onto the slipway at Khormaksar.

MCS Khormaksar's pinnace, 1380, was involved in a major rescue operation in June 1966. The MCS was then under the command of Flight Lieutenant Whitchurch and had responded to a sinking Arab dhow some 20 miles (30 km) from Steamer Point. With a Shackleton and a search and rescue helicopter lending assistance, the pinnace managed to get alongside and decided to tow the dhow into the port. It took them five hours, but they saved the fifty-one passengers onboard.

The political situation in what was then the Aden Protectorate deteriorated markedly during the 1960s and British troops were often targeted by rebels. RTTL 2767 came under fire on one occasion from Yemen shore batteries on the Red Sea and on another occasion a terrorist bomb put a hole in its hull.

In 1967 MCS Khormaksar was disbanded and the marine craft were transferred either to Masirah or Bahrain. During the re-deployment RTTL 2767 motored for twenty-five hours and covered 563 miles (906 km).

Masirah, a somewhat desolate island off the Arabian penin-sular, had long been an inhospitable home for pre-Islamic and possibly Neolithic inhabitants. It had been used as a base for air sea rescue during the Second World War and in August 1945, after VJ Day, it had become No. 33 Staging Post, not only for British troops from India and the Far East who were being flown home to be demobbed, but also for the innumerable former prisoners of war who had been held in Japanese camps. In order to ensure that the prisoners, who in some cases had suffered over five years of imprisonment, returned home safely, ASR facilities were put on standby around the Persian Gulf. Normally the flights would route via Sharjah and Bahrain, with Masirah covering the southern Arabian route. By April 1946 there was less strain on the air routes and RAF Masirah was reduced to a skeleton force consisting of a junior officer, ten airmen and nineteen civilians. They were supplied on a weekly basis by a flight of Wellingtons.

When the MCS men arrived there in the 1960s little had changed. Buildings constructed of tins filled with concrete which had housed personnel during the war were again pressed into service.

There were also still MCS personnel in Tobruk, where they dealt with cargo, ferried personnel and transported fresh water for the garrison. They were also engaged in laying underwater pipelines and cables.

In 1967 Pinnace 1373 arrived from Malta to take up search and rescue duties in Tobruk. It recorded what was probably the section's oddest rescue of all time. Flight Sergeant Anderson and Senior Aircraftman Chase, manning a 24 ft (7.3 m) marine tender, executed a perfect search and rescue mission on a calf that was swimming out to sea.

The MCS at Muharraq maintained a presence into the 1960s, primarily serving Dahran airbase on Bahrain. In addition to military flights in the area, they also found themselves dealing with civilian ditchings. At 2332 hours on 17 April 1964 Middle East Airlines Flight 444 out of Beirut lost radio contact with the Dahran control tower. The aircraft was a Caravelle with eighty seats and a crash call was sent to the MCS. They received it at 2350 and scrambled RTTL 2751. The airliner had been approaching Dahran over an extremely hazardous section of reefs and its only hope had been to ditch in what was a very poorly marked channel. To add to the difficulties, there was a gale blowing and the crew of RTTL 2751 knew that any attempt to find the airliner in the dark would not only prove fruitless, but would probably result in their own deaths. When they commenced their search at first light they could barely see 200 yards in front of them. They tried to make it into the channel on several occasions, but failed and had to return to base.

At around 1100 hours a Dakota and a US Marine Corps helicopter spotted the Caravelle. They immediately informed the launch, which on this occasion managed to make it into the channel. Visibility was still extremely poor and the only hope any survivors might have had lay in an immediate response. The launch's Gemini, swept the area despite a surging swell. The launch itself looked to the south, in the hope that any survivors had drifted in that direction, but nothing was found. Not a single survivor had managed to get out of the wreck, which was lying upside down in 2.5 fathoms of water. The crews of RTTL 2751 and RSL 1649 undertook the unenviable task of ferrying the bodies back to the port.

Aerial view of the Aden base 1948. *Courtesy of Owen Newlands*

The men of MCS Aden 1948 to 1950. *Courtesy of Owen Newlands*

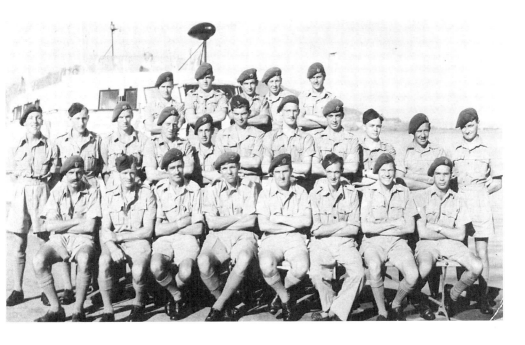

HSL 107 at speed off Malta in 1943. *Courtesy of Ted Shute*

HSL 2713 at Aden. Despite its unlucky number, the vessel always went to sea on a Friday. *Courtesy of Owen Newlands*

HSL 129 at
Kalafrana when it
was bombed in a
hangar in February
1942.
Courtesy of Ted Shute

Captured Italian motor anti-submarine boat in use by the RAF at Port Said, 1944-5.
Courtesy of John Sutherland

Flight Lieutenant Eric Price, Skipper of HSL 107 on the conning seat in wheelhouse in front of pickup scoreboard 1943. *Courtesy of Ted Shute*

HSL 107 on Boxing Day 1942, returning from a successful pickup of a Wellington crew. Note the empty German dinghy on the foredeck. *Courtesy of Ted Shute*

HSL 100 at Silema in October 1942. Pictured at the back are LAC Taffy Groves, LAC Sid Mountford and Corporal Ted Shute. In the front LAC Laderney Bisson, Flight Officer Richards, Sergeant Coxswain Tommy Thomas and LAC Hilton. *Courtesy of Ted Shute*

HSL 107 underway on a crash call at St Paul's Bay 1942. During the siege of Malta, HSL 107 picked up 63 allied aircrew, 10 Germans and 11 Italians. *Courtesy of Ted Shute*

HSL 166 at Malta, having run the gauntlet along the North African coast from Alexandria in January 1943. *Courtesy of Ted Shute*

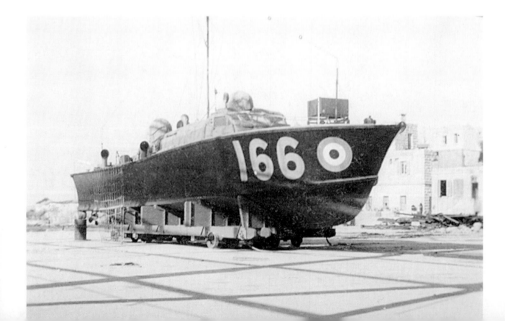

Owen Newlands steering
Pinnace 92 at Aden in 1948.
Pinnace 92 was used for
ammunition dumping and
ferrying troops to and from
troop ships. *Courtesy of Owen
Newlands*

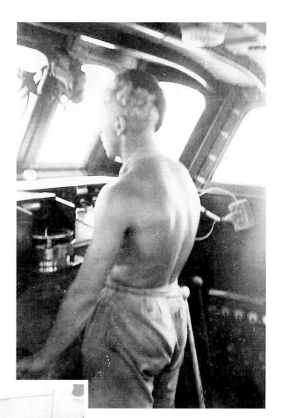

Duty Crew Room
at MCS Aden
1948 to 1950.
*Courtesy of Owen
Newlands*

George Head, the
Flight Sergeant
Coxswain onboard
ISL 128. He is
standing by the
hatch to the
ickbay, where the
ickup scoreboard
as painted on the
pened hatch.
Courtesy of Ted Shute

Rescue by HSL 107 off Malta 1943. Ditched crewman is Pilot Officer Taggart. He was forced to abandon his Spitfire after it was hit in the oil cooler by a Bf-109 on 3 March 1943. *Courtesy of Ted Shute*

Pinnace 1235, having been picked up from Algiers in May 1943 prior to its service during Operation Husky. *Courtesy of Ted Shute*

Pinnace 22 on the day that the snatch block broke when they were pulling an HSL over the craters in the slipway to the water. *Courtesy of Ted Shute*

A captured Cant at Kalafrana. Corporal Bill Bilton seen posing beside the propeller. *Courtesy of Ted Shute*

HSL 128, which during the seige of Malta, picked up 118 personnel, including 22 Germans, 6 Italians and a spy. *Courtesy of Ted Shute*

A GP Pinnace 1205 at Gibraltar in May 1946. The vessel is being readied for relaunching after a refit. *Courtesy of Ted Shute*

71 ASRU at Gibraltar on 31 March 1946. Depicted is the crew of HSL 2583. Ted Shute is first left in the front row. *Courtesy of Ted Shute*

HSL 128 at speed outside Malta as photographed by an escorting Spitfire. Note the checkerboard on the foredeck, indicating that the HSL has VHF onboard. *Courtesy of Ted Shute*

Seaplane Tender 447 at Aden, 1948 to 1950. *Courtesy of Owen Newlands*

HMAFV *Bridport. Courtesy of John Sutherland*

HSLs 2603 and 2604 at Port Said 1943. *Courtesy of John Sutherland*

HMAFV *Bridport* at Gibraltar 1948-9. *Courtesy of John Sutherland*

Seaplane tender 1539 at Aden 1944. *Courtesy of John Sutherland*

Miami 2542 in the Middle East in 1945. *Courtesy of John Sutherland*

A Mk III Miami off Aden in 1944. *Courtesy of John Sutherland*

Pinnace 1229 in the Middle East in 1944. *Courtesy of John Sutherland*

Miami Mk II 2520 in the Middle East in 1944. *Courtesy of John Sutherland*

HSL 2604 being escorted by HSLs 141 and 166 from 208 ASRU at Alexandria. King Farouk of Egypt can be seen on the flying bridge. He was being shown an airborne lifeboat exercise in August 1945. *Courtesy of Ted Shute*

Luckily not all the rescue attempts in this period ended in tragedy. Indeed in 1965, whilst under the command of Flight Lieutenant Terry Fryirs, RSL 1649 succeeded in saving five members of the Parachute Regiment. The paratroopers had purchased an Arab dhow in Bahrain and had christened it *Red Wolf*. Their intention was to sail it home. For several months it had been in plain sight of the MCS's jetty whilst the men fitted it out and carried out running repairs. They were well aware of the hazards of the enormously long journey that faced them and prudently decided to give the dhow a few tests in local waters before they started.

On their second practice trip they were caught in a storm around 40 miles (65 km) from Muharraq. Despite the fact that the wind was blowing a gale and there was an ever-present danger of shoals and sandbanks, RSL 1649 managed to find them without radar. The vessel had a problem with its bilge pump, which had become blocked, and as a result it was sinking. The five men were not only suffering from extreme seasickness but were also exhausted. After several attempts RSL 1649 managed to come alongside and get the men off the sinking vessel.

This was the second amazing rescue that RSL 1649, under the command of Fryirs, achieved in 1965. In the January they had managed to rescue a seaman, who had had his legs crushed in an accident on a merchant ship. Once again the weather conditions were extremely hazardous and it had taken the crew thirteen hours to get to the ship and back. Fryirs was later rewarded with the MBE and awarded RAF Man of the Year. In September 1971, however, MCS Muharraq was closed and all the marine craft were sold off to local buyers.

Throughout the 1960s and 1970s, 1153 MCU, based at Limassol, Cyprus, covered the bulk of the Middle East. It was ideally located as it lay beneath the main air routes from the eastern Mediterranean to the west, as well as being a frequent passing point for merchant and naval vessels.

1153 MCU undertook a number of dramatic and potentially hazardous search and rescue missions throughout the period.

The first notable one took place in July 1963. Squadron Leader T. H. Finn, commanding RTTL 2769, found and towed back the

Israeli hydrofoil vessel *Aleigal*, complete with its eighty passengers and crew. In the same year RTTL 2769 saved a soldier who was adrift off the Syrian coast, whilst Pinnace 1383 towed back the soldier's vessel.

In September 1966 Flight Lieutenant C. Clark, commanding HMAFV 2771, was sent to find and rescue the crew of a Greek ship, the MV *Alexis*. He was ably assisted by Pinnace 1383, commanded by Squadron Leader P. Greenall. Their persistent search yielded only a number of dead sheep and wreckage but seven crew finally drifted ashore on a life raft. Regrettably two deck boys, the captain's wife and a seaman were lost.

On 17 February 1967 Pinnace 1384, commanded by Clark, was despatched to the assistance of the *Three Stars*, a Greek ship that had sailed from Piraeus. There were reports that she was on fire 4 miles (6 km) south-west of Cape Zevghari, the most southerly point on Cyprus. Pinnace 1384 sailed at 0730, followed half an hour later by RTTL 2771, commanded by Flight Lieutenant G. Hubbard. As back-up Pinnace 1383 was also despatched, as it had fire-fighting equipment onboard. The vessels arrived in time to see a helicopter taking off the crew of the *Three Stars*. RTTL 2771 came alongside and a salvage party was quickly assembled, supported by a fire crew. Pinnace 1384 managed to attach a towline and despite a 25 knot wind and heavy seas it began to tow the enormous vessel. A second towline was attached to Pinnace 1383, and they headed towards Episkopi Bay. By the late afternoon, with the fire under control, the ship was anchored and safe. Pinnace 1383 had on board Duncan Gibbons, who had led the fire crew and had brought the flames under control. He was awarded the Queen's Commendation for Brave Conduct.

Since the Suez crisis of 1956, Anglo-Egyptian relations had been tense to say the least. However, an episode that began on 18 August 1968 proved that despite the political mistrust the MCS harboured no grudges. At 1440 on August 18 HMAFV 2769, commanded by Flight Lieutenant G. Hubbard, responded to a report of an aircraft accident that had been sent to the unit by an RAF Argosy. The aircraft in question was a Russian-built Antonov AN 24 airliner owned by the Egyptians. The report stated that it had broken up when it hit the water. It was a considerable distance from Cyprus and it took Hubbard and his crew around five hours to reach the scene. A scene of absolute devastation greeted them; there were bodies floating in the water and no sign of any survivors. Worse still, there were innumerable sharks in the area feasting on the corpses. While Hubbard's crew were engaged in the recovery of the bodies, they were joined that night by Pinnace 1378, commanded by Squadron Leader Greenall. They ceased operations when it became too dark, but continued their unpleasant task at dawn the following morning. By noon it was clear that there were going to be no survivors, around twenty-five corpses had been recovered. The bodies were laid out inside and on the decks of HMAFV 2769, which then began its voyage to Egypt. Meanwhile Pinnace 1378 headed back to base.

HMAFV 2769 arrived in Alexandria after a six-hour journey. Hubbard was to have been escorted by a flotilla of Egyptian motor torpedo boats, but they had been unable to find him. He ordered the RAF ensign to be lowered as the launch entered the harbour. The RAF personnel were welcomed with open arms and they spent the night as guests of the Egyptian government. The British Consul noted:

> To them [the Egyptians], this was a friendly gesture by the British coming to the help of Egypt in distressing circumstances and the expressions of gratitude to the RAF personnel and to me were so profuse as to be almost embarrassing, it has added greatly to our prestige.

On 11 September 1968 HMAFV 2769 was despatched to assist another Greek vessel, the MV *Podromos*, which was in difficulties some 60 miles (95 km) east of Cyprus. As it happened the crew were not in peril nor was the ship damaged in any way. Duncan Gibbons commanded the launch, and was guided to the position by an RAF Argosy. The vessel was stationary and listing severely to port. Four of the crew were already in a lifeboat and five others were standing on the deck. The RAF men got the crew aboard their launch and three of them clambered aboard the Greek ship to find out what was wrong with it. It turned out to be very simple: the cargo had not been secured in the hold and a heavy swell had shifted it to the port side. Other than this the vessel was completely seaworthy. It was apparent, however, that the launch was not going to be able to tow it anywhere. Pinnace 1378 was called up to assist and after twelve and a half hours managed to bring the ship into Akrotiri.

The situation on Cyprus became very difficult in 1974 when a military coup swept aside Archbishop Makarios. There was chaos in Limassol, with Greek and Turkish Cypriots engaged in running battles through the streets. A few days later Turkish troops landed on the north of the island, which only served to escalate the bloodshed.

No. 1153 MCU's buildings came under fire, and a mortar round had hit the officers' mess. Squadron Leader R. J. M. Manson was given permission to evacuate and the two launches and one pinnace left the base amidst small arms fire. They were forced to abandon Pinnace 1384, which was unserviceable. They made for Akrotiri, where they found a chaotic situation, with many hundreds, if not thousands, of service families on the dockside. Many of them had nearly died as they struggled towards the safety of the RAF airfield.

Regardless of the deteriorating situation and knowing that air activity would be increasing in the area, 1153 MCU set up a twenty-four hour watch system. It was a prudent move as just a few days later the Turkish air force sank one of its own destroyers, the *Kocatep* around 30 miles (50 km) from Paphos. RTTLs 2759 and 2769 were directly involved in hunting for survivors that had been swept away from the main area of search and rescue. They managed to find ten Turkish sailors, whilst RAF helicopters, Royal Navy frigates, a supply ship and a Turkish destroyer picked up the other seventy-two survivors.

A fortnight later the service families were allowed to return to their homes and 1153 MCU returned to Limassol. This move, however, coincided with a major Turkish land offensive, and the situation was now even more dangerous. The unit moved back to Akrotiri whilst the RAF organised the evacuation of many thousands of RAF families, civilians and holidaymakers from the airfield.

When the situation stabilised the Turks dug in along the Atila Line and 1153 MCU returned to normal duties. They first went to retrieve Pinnace 1384, which they towed back to Akrotiri. In the meantime Pinnace 1385 was involved in bomb disposal at sea, attempting to deal with the huge numbers of bombs, mines and other explosive devices dropped by the Turks during the invasion.

Malta, which had been the scene of desperate action during the Second World War, was now the home of 1151 MCU. It was based at Marsaxlokk and was primarily involved in target towing, training, ferrying the sick and injured and assisting with the rescue of over-confident water skiers, divers and swimmers. The highlights of their stay in Malta were perhaps in 1967 and 1968, when RTTLs 2758 and 2768 were used in the films *A Twist of Sand* and *Hellboats*.

The unit was due to close in 1972 but actually did so in 1978, after sixty years of RAF marine craft presence on the island. The launches subsequently became the property of the Maltese government.

Gibraltar had operated for many years as an RAF base, and in December 1941 had become the home of No. 71 ASRU. During 1942 and 1943 HSLs 142, 181 and 2582 had saved seventy-four British aircrew, seventeen Allied personnel and had towed home five Sunderland flying boats. Bizarrely, in the post-war period, RAF North Front, as it was known, was up against smugglers who had purchased RAF high-speed launches and Royal Navy motor torpedo boats and had stripped them down and modified them for maximum speed. There was even one occasion when pirates attempted to steal a harbour launch. Flight Lieutenant Smith and Deckhands M. Eardley-Stiff and Peter Turton, in Pinnace 1388, gave chase. The pirates tried to ram the pinnace but their engine seized and the RAF men jumped aboard the launch and overpowered them.

Following the closure of 1102 MCU Falmouth, RAF North Front assumed that designation. They were still using RTTLs 2753 and 2754, which had been delivered in the 1950s, and were primarily concerned with range safety, surveillance and target towing.

In January 1976 RTTL 2754 left base to take up position for a ten-hour surveillance to the east of Gibraltar. The vessel was commanded by Flight Lieutenant George Bell, the weather was reasonable and the launch made good progress. At around 1730 hours Chief Technician John Crouch, the senior fitter, burst into the wheelhouse and told those assembled that there was a hole in the port side of the launch. No sooner had he spoken than the bows dipped and the launch slowed to a crawl. The foredeck and the wheelhouse were soon awash and it was clear that they were about to sink. With the vessel rapidly flooding, the crew were in imminent danger. They had lost radio contact and the lifejackets were inaccessible, apart from five in the wheelhouse and two in the engine room, there were nine crew. The Very pistol's locker was also under water. With great difficulty, the men managed to retrieve lifejackets, a Very pistol and a key that was essential for pyrotechnics.

The inflatable, which was stowed on the foredeck, broke free and floated away. The crew now had seven serviceable lifejackets and one life raft. By this stage, however the launch was not sinking any faster. Shortly before dark the crew saw a ship heading in their direction. It was MV *Kapatanikos*. They fired six rockets and several Very cartridges to attract its attention, and it managed to bring a boat alongside. The two officers and fitter Mike Wray stayed on board the launch.

A message from the *Kapitanikos* was passed on to 1102 MCU, apprising them of the situation. Their only reserve pinnace was being serviced and frantic attempts were made to make it seaworthy as soon as possible. In the meantime the Royal Navy was trying to collect together the crews of the frigate HMS *Keppel* and the tug *Sealyham* in order to respond.

By midnight, both ships had left Gibraltar and an RAF salvage party was onboard. The three men still on board RTTL 2754 had managed to extract the remaining life raft, but it had inflated upside down and they had lost their survival kit. The weather was deteriorating and the sea was getting rougher. The hull was being pounded, and the three men had an extremely uncomfortable night.

Shortly after dawn a French cargo ship appeared and a US Orion, flying overhead, passed on their position to HMS *Keppel*. At around 0930 hours the three men were on board a whaler and the RAF salvage crew, led by Flight Lieutenant Cairns, had gone aboard the launch to see if it could be saved. They could not make a temporary repair and there was too much water for the portable pumps. Indeed only the tank space bulkhead had stopped the craft from sinking. They inflated a twenty-man life raft inside the sickbay to help with buoyancy.

HMS *Keppel* towed the stricken craft for a time but it was clear that it was still sinking, the tank space bulkhead had finally given way. The stern dipped and the bows rose and the vessel sank.

By 1972 there were just five MCU bases still operational in the British Isles; 1100 MCU Alness, 1102 MCU Falmouth, 1104 MCU Bridlington, 1113 MCU Holyhead and Mount Batten's Marine Training and Engineering Squadrons, which had detachments at Gorleston and Tenby. The vast majority of the units were still using pinnaces, range safety launches and rescue target towing launches. Despite their age, and plans as far back as 1966 for steel and reinforced plastic replacements (building was delayed), these vessels continued to be effective and seaworthy.

On 29 September 1969, however, a disaster overcame Pinnace 1386, operating out of 1104 MCU Bridlington. It had been engaged in helicopter activities off Dundee and was returning to base via Amble, which was often used as a stopover point. It was also due to assist in an exercise with helicopters from No. 202 Squadron based at RAF Acklington.

The entrance to Amble harbour had two concrete jetties and about 1 mile (1.5 km) offshore was Coquet Island, which housed a lighthouse. Between the lighthouse and the harbour entrance was a shoal, known as Pan Bush. As the pinnace approached the harbour the crew could see that there were heavy seas hitting the north pier. They decided to head to starboard and cross the tip of Pan Bush, where there would still be at least 3 fathoms under the keel. They were about to make their turn when a huge wave hit and lifted the craft making it list to starboard. They could see that the wave had swept the water away from Pan Bush and there was nothing beneath the craft. Another wave hit them and rolled the pinnace over.

The local coastguard launched the first distress signal. He then called for a helicopter to be scrambled from RAF Acklington; the time was about 1830 hours. The inshore rescue boat was scrambled minutes later and at 1839 the RNLI's *Millie Walton* set off. There were also some fishing boats heading towards the stricken pinnace. The master, Flight Lieutenant Ken Bell and Coxswain Sergeant Danny Coutts had been swept away and motorboat crewman William Traynor had been caught on board when the wave hit but managed to escape. However, none of them had a lifejacket. The wireless operator, Donald Ivil, the fitter Sergeant Robert Moore, a second wireless operator, Geoffrey Benson, Deckhand Charles Chase and Motorboat Crewman David Ashton were all trapped inside. Moore, Chase and Ashton were in the forecastle and opened the forward hatch. Chase managed to swim out first; Ashton would not attempt it and Moore reluctantly left him behind.

A helicopter arrived on the scene and managed to save Coutts. Traynor and Chase were hanging onto a lifebelt and the inshore rescue boat saved them. The RNLI lifeboat came alongside the inverted pinnace and pulled Moore aboard. They managed to attach a line and proposed to tow the vessel into the harbour. Four divers returned in the inshore rescue boat and tried in vain to get into the pinnace. The towing operation proved to be a disaster when the pinnace got stuck. It was now nearly 2000 hours. Still more rescuers arrived and after an hour the wreck started to move.

At around 2130 a Royal Navy diving team managed to clamber onto the hull; they could hear tapping. At around 2315 they managed to smash a hole in the hull and pull out Ashton; he had been in the pitch darkness for five hours. Ivil, Benson and Bell had all been lost.

The Marine Branch had not been immune from the post-war cuts and in the 1960s and beyond further cuts were implemented. Economies were sought everywhere and towards the end of the 1960s there were moves to create a combined service. The Air Ministry was absorbed into the Ministry of Defence and simply became the Air Department. In November 1969 Coastal Command was absorbed into Strike Command. At this stage the Deputy Director of Marine Craft was Group Captain Les Flower. He knew that despite cutbacks and closures, his Marine Branch would still have to carry out their duties. It was still operating with pinnaces, rescue safety launches and rescue target towing launches, many of which had been in service for years. The pinnaces and rescue safety launches were still adequate, but the rescue target towing launches' range was far too limited.

Flower had commanded a Fairmile D Type during the Second World War. He believed that the Marine Branch sorely needed an updated version, with greater speed and diesel engines. Above all, it needed a craft that had been designed for the purpose from the very beginning.

In 1965 The Admiralty approved the design phase of a craft that was to become known as the long-range recovery and support craft (LRRSC), but the Marine Branch would have to wait a considerable time before any of these would be available to them. Flower searched for an interim measure and found it in the shape of three Royal Navy inshore minesweepers powered by a pair of Paxman diesel engines. The minesweepers were 170 ft (51.8 m) long with a 21 ft (6.4 m) beam, but only had a maximum speed of just over 13 knots. They became known as interim recovery vessels (IRVs). Consequently, in April 1966, HMS *Bottisham* became HMAFV 5000, HMS *Chelsham* became HMAFV 5001 and HMS *Hailsham* became HMAFV 5002. Later these number designations were transferred to the first three long-range recovery and support craft and the interim recovery vessels would become 5010, 5011 and 5012 respectively.

Surprisingly, the first long-range vessel, HMAFV *Seal*, was virtually completed and officially named on 2 August 1967. It had been constructed at Brooke Marine in Lowestoft, a boatyard that had a history with marine craft dating back to the 1920s. Unlike the previous, this new craft was made of steel. She was a little over 120 ft (36.5 m) long and had a 23 ft 6 in (7.16 m) beam. It drew just under 6 ft (1.8 m) and was powered by a pair of Paxman Ventura 16YJCM 2,000 hp engines. She had a top speed of 24 knots and a cruising speed of 17 knots. She could carry 31 tons of fuel oil, which gave her a maximum range of 2,000 miles (3,200 km) assuming an average speed of 12 knots, or 950 miles (1,530 km) at an average of 20 knots. Compared to the Mark II rescue target towing launch, which had a displacement of 45 tons, HMAFV *Seal* had a displacement of 159 tons.

As for the interim rescue vessels, when the first long-range recovery and support vessels came into service, two of them, the former *Botisham* and *Chelsham*, were returned to the Royal Navy. The remaining vessel, HMAFV 5012, remained at 1107 MCU

Newhaven, operating as a laboratory the for Royal Aircraft Establishment, Farnborough, until 1972. In 1972 she sailed from Newhaven to Malta and then headed for Campbeltown, the Clyde and the Scilly Isles. She was formally handed over to the Royal Corps of Transport on 17 October 1972 and two weeks later 1107 MCU Newhaven closed.

The new craft had a crew of eighteen. There was comfortable accommodation on board, and for the first time since the scrapping of HMAFV *Bridport* and HMAFV *Bridlington* an RAF marine vessel had a cook. The first master of *Seal* was Flight Lieutenant Parkin. The vessel arrived at Mount Batten on 7 August 1967for trials. She later carried out additional trials from Port Rush, operating with Shackletons. Tests still needed to be carried out as to her long-range abilities and in 1968 it was decided that she would take part in torpedo-recovery exercises at the Atlantic Undersea Test and Evaluation Centre in the Bahamas. She had four 500 gallon (2,275 litre) reserve fuel tanks fitted at Mount Batten, which now meant that she could cruise for 2,500 miles (4,000 km). In addition to her sophisticated navigational aids and communication systems she had additional radio systems and electronic location equipment fitted.

She was due to arrive at the Bahamas by 18 March 1968. On 1 February she left Mount Batten and headed for Lisbon. She was in Madeira on 7 February, leaving again on the 14th. She then made for the Cape Verde Islands, arriving there on the 19th, and then Barbados, where she arrived on 25 February. The voyage was largely uneventful, and she made RAF history in becoming the first launch to complete an Atlantic crossing without a problem. She now headed for the Bahamas, over 1,500 miles (2,400 km) away, arriving on 6 March. She was involved in the exercise for the next six weeks and left the Bahamas on 15 April, reaching the Azores on 2 May.

The crew had been told that the weather was fine and they decided to move on to Portugal after just an eight-hour refuelling stop. The weather reports were hopelessly wrong, however, and after about thirty hours the vessel was caught in a gale. To the crew's delight she handled the situation perfectly and they continued the remaining 350 mile (560 km) journey to Leixoes in Portugal. They were trapped there for five days by storms, but on 10 May began their trip to Plymouth. When she arrived, *Seal* had covered 12,500 miles (20,100 km) and been away for 101 days. Again she had made history: this was the longest ever voyage undertaken by an RAF marine craft.

Two years later, after huge delays and changes to specifications, LLRSC 5001 *Seagull* was commissioned. Six months later LLRSC 5002 *Sea Otter* came into service. An unexpected problem arose from the size of these craft: Mount Batten could no longer handle their servicing and supply. Consequently they were serviced at naval dockyards.

In January 1970 the Deputy Directorate of Marine Craft became the Directorate of Marine Craft and in the same year, after thirty-six years' association with marine craft, Les Flower retired. Group Captain D. T. Beamish replaced him. Flower had already put in motion plans to replace what remained of the wooden craft. He had proposed the creation of a 73 ft (22.2 m) Mark III rescue target towing launch, a 60 ft (18.3 m) general service launch and a 24 ft (17.3 m) boat. The general service launch would replace the pinnaces and range safety launches, whilst the 24 ft boat would replace the marine tenders. Ultimately, however, the general service launch project was cancelled.

James and Stone, based in Brightlingsea, Essex, constructed a new launch, which was launched in January 1973. It was 72 ft 9 in (22.17 m) long, had a beam of 18 ft 6 in (5.64 m) and a draught of just 5 ft 4 in (1. 63 m). It was capable of 24 knots, and was powered by a pair of Paxman 8YJCM 1,000 hp diesel engines. Two further Perkins diesel engines provided power for the generators and pumps and a smaller engine powered the fire pump. It had a steel hull and an aluminium superstructure, and was designed for an officer and eight crew. There were a large sickbay, a wheelhouse, a bridge, a radio room and innumerable electronic aids including sonar and search equipment and the latest navigational equipment.

Known as RTTL 4000 HMAFV *Spitfire*, this craft was under the command of Flight Lieutenant Cannock. She was immediately involved in mine recovery, the annual parachute drop of the Territorial Army in the Channel Islands and target towing operations in the North Sea. She had her first crash call on 17 August 1972. She was heading for Gorleston in rough seas and received word that there was a distressed vessel to the north of

Lowestoft. The vessel in question was a sailing yacht, the *Genapi Too*, its engine had broken down and the sea was pushing it towards a sandbank. There were six people on board, including two children. Despite the treacherous conditions HMAFV *Spitfire* managed to secure a towline and bring the yacht safely into Gorleston.

Although this rescue had been a complete success, there were major problems with the design of the vessel. She was shipping too much water over the bows and she would need a reshaped stern and other modifications. She therefore returned to her Brightlingsea boatyard in 1973 and had a new stem fitted and 5 ft (1.5 m) of flared bow added. The modifications were a great improvement and she went through extensive tests over the winter months of 1973 and 1974.

By 1973, with the wooden marine craft becoming increasingly unserviceable, there were still just the three long-range craft and a single Mark III rescue target towing launch. The second launch did not enter service until 2 April 1976, over five years after HMAFV *Spitfire*. She was known as RTTL 4001 HMAFV *Sunderland*. Many of the problems with HMAFV *Spitfire* had been dealt with, including the removal of the funnels, improvements to accommodation and an extended hull that was now 80 ft (24.4 m) long. HMAFV *Sunderland* was under the command of Flight Lieutenant Mike Tyrell and posted to 1102 MCU Gibraltar. She made RAF marine craft history when she became the first launch under 100 ft (30 m) to journey to Gibraltar under her own steam.

RTTL 4002 HMAFV *Stirling* was completed on 24 January 1977 and posted to 1104 MCU Bridlington. In April RTTL 4003 HMAFV *Halifax* was posted to the Marine Squadron at Mount Batten to work with HMAFV *Spitfire*. The next vessel in the series, RTTL 4004 HMAFV *Hampden*, was due to be delivered in December 1979, but problems with the engines, amongst other things, delayed her completion until June 1980. When she did enter service she replaced HMAFV *Sunderland* at Gibraltar, which then returned to the boatyard for a refit. Three more craft completed the series: RTTL 4005 HMAFV *Hurricane* became operational in September 1980, and RTTL 4006 HMAFV *Lancaster* and RTTL 4007 HMAFV *Wellington* in 1981.

In the new-look Marine Branch of the 1970s, which was

primarily equipped with LRRSCs as the long-range craft, the crew spent far longer on operations than had previously been the case. In March 1971, 1105 MCU Port Rush was closed and HMAFV *Seal* was sent to 1100 MCU Alness. Typical of the new conditions the men were working under, HMAFVs *Seal* and *Sea Otter* spent the bulk of the summer of 1971 on NATO exercises around the Shetland Islands. When HMAFV *Seal* spent six months out of service for refit, HMAFV *Seagull*, instead of operating from Mount Batten, operated from Alness. When *Sea Otter* returned to Mount Batten in the middle of 1971 she was almost immediately sent to Malta to replace IRV 5012.

In 1972 HMAFV *Seal* was involved in a bizarre incident in the North Sea. Working with Buccaneers based at RAF Honington she had been target towing at night. The exercises were just completed when news came that an aircraft had crashed in their immediate vicinity. A helicopter was scrambled to help with the search, and HMAFV *Seal* scoured the area, but could not find anything. Confirmation was sought as to the original position of the aircraft crash, and only then did it dawn on everyone that what had been seen were *Seal*'s own splash target and parachute flares.

In 1971 the RAF finally received a replacement for the marine tender. In effect a ferryboat, it was designated No. 2000. It was 24 ft (7.3 m) long and capable of 10 knots, powered by a Perkins 75hp engine. In truth it did not fit the bill and as a result innumerable modifications were required and it was not until 1977 that a new 27 ft (8. 2 m) version actually entered service.

HMAFV *Sea Otter* was involved in a search and rescue exercise in 1977. In force 9 gales, she went to the aid of a tug, the *Duke of Normandy 2*. Without the assistance of a standby lifeboat and helicopter she managed to tow in the tug and rescue the crew, bringing them safely to Campbeltown.

By the late 1970s the Marine Branch was under the command of Group Captain J. N. Burgess. It had contracted from a high of 5,000 personnel back in 1944 to what appeared to be a handful of men operating an ever smaller number of vessels. There had been innumerable redundancies in the early 1970s and by 1975 the branch was severely undermanned. There was a particular shortage of senior non-commissioned officers and junior officers. A recruitment drive swung into action, but the pay and conditions were in no way comparable to those in the merchant service. The direct entry officer drive netted eight new men, and commissions were offered to master coxswains. There was also a problem with the number of lower-ranked crew; it was therefore proposed that a quarter of the men in each unit would be locally based and that they would operate like civilians, not subject to overseas postings.

Group Captain J. E. Williams took over the branch in 1980 and quickly realised that there was also a shortage of qualified technicians in the branch. The post of chief technician was abolished and that of marine mechanic suspended. Men wishing to enter the engineering area of the branch would now have to attend a forty-six-week course at RAF St Athan. The rest of the training would take place on board after posting. In 1983 the trade of boatwright was abolished.

Group Captain J. S. Fosh was the last Director of Marine Craft. He received a directive from the Ministry of Defence on 4 May 1984 to begin the closure of the entire Marine Branch. By February 1986 most of the branch's support tasks were transferred to a ship management company. The remaining eleven seagoing craft and single harbour craft were passed over to civilian crews.

The Marine Branch was disbanded at 2400 hours on 31 March 1986. It marked the end of sixty-eight years of the RAF's association with the sea. The seaplanes, the flying boats and finally the marine craft had all passed into history, to be replaced by a mixture of helicopters, the RNLI, the Royal Navy and civilian vessels.

CHAPTER TEN

Life in the Service

T he following three accounts detail the experiences of three
men and their crewmates over the period 1925–49. They
provide valuable first-hand accounts of what it was like to
serve with the MCS and the ASR.

The first account covers the service record of C. W. Bullock,
who enlisted in the RAF on 5 August 1925 and left in 1949. He
then joined the Air Ministry Constabulary and had a further
fifteen years of service stationed in Norfolk, Cheshire, the Royal
Aircraft Establishment in Farnborough and finally Newmarket
in Cambridgeshire. By the time he eventually retired he had
worked for the Air Ministry for thirty-nine years.

After enlisting Bullock spent the following three months
training at Uxbridge. In November 1925 he was posted to 24
Communications Squadron, Kenley, where he was employed as
a fitter's mate on aircraft which included the Avro 504K, the
Bristol Fighter (which was used in the final stages of the First
World War) and the DHGA. He flew in the back seat of these
aircraft on morning test flights and reported back any problems.

In January 1927 he was posted, with his squadron, to RAF
Northolt. Six months later his application for training as motorboat crew was approved and he moved to the Marine Craft
Training School in Calshot for a three month course. This course
included tuition on elementary navigation, including the
construction of a marine compass, signalling with an Aldis
lamp, a thorough knowledge of semaphore and a working
knowledge of the international code of signals with flags. The
Aldis lamp and semaphore training were essential for signalling
between boats and from boat to shore, as no radios were available at that time. Instruction was also given in all types of knots

and splices, including wire splicing, the working and breaking strains of wire and various ropes, and rigging sheet legs. In addition a thorough knowledge was required of the buoyage systems in use around the British coastline, including the characteristics of lights on buoys, beacons and vessels. Models painted in the colours in use at the time were used for demonstration in the classroom. In addition an elementary knowledge of the international 'rules of the road' was needed for the prevention of collisions at sea. These rules contained thirty-nine articles and various subsections, and included lights displayed at night by vessels at sea and fog signals under all conditions. Instruction was also given in the repair of coir and canvas boat fenders, sewing using string, beeswax and palm, the construction of various types of marine craft, such as Carvel, diagonal and clinker boats, mixing and using paints and varnishes for marine craft, sailing ship recognition and basic first aid. Each trainee was issued with a copy of *The Admiralty Manual of Seamanship*, which, according to Bullock, was the instructor's 'Bible'.

Practical training sessions involved tuition on rowing and sculling dinghies, handling marine craft, including coming alongside jetty, securing to buoys and steering a compass course. Sailing instruction was given with a 27 ft (8.23 m) whaler and involved swinging the lead for soundings, making fast ropes for towing seaplanes, flying boats and marine craft and a demonstration of refuelling flying boats at their moorings and anchor drills.

During Bullock's time at Calshot (June 1927 to January 1930) he noted that a number of different craft were in use during the period. The 35 ft (10.7 m) general service Brooke motorboat, built by Brooke Marine of Lowestoft, had four crew; a coxswain (usually a corporal), an engineer and two deckhands. It had a covered foredeck, an open cockpit with a canvas windscreen for added protection for the coxswain and engineer and a stout, canvas canopy fixed over the stern sheets. This single-engined craft had a 65 hp petrol engine which was started by manual swinging – although it was later fitted with a self-starter – and had a speed of 12 knots. It was used primarily as a crash boat whilst flying was in progress. Aircraft were not permitted to fly or even to taxi without such a crash boat in attendance. It was also used for safety and patrol purposes, which involved taking buoys out to sea and mooring them to be used for bombing practice. In addition the craft was used for ferrying VIPs, postings and mail between coastal command stations and conveying patients to the military hospital at Netley, on the north shore of Southampton water. It was also often used as the standby craft for the RAF seaplane station at Lee-on-Solent. Signals from the craft to the Lee-on-Solent flying control were made using the Aldis lamp.

A 40 ft (12.2 m) Kelvin, which was constructed at Clydeside, was also briefly in use at Calshot during this period, although it soon became obsolete. It was also crewed by a coxswain, an engineer and two deckhands. The wheelhouse, engine room and cabin were completely built in. It was powered by a single paraffin 60 hp engine that was started by manual swinging and could achieve a speed of 10 knots. Bullock described the signals the coxswain used to instruct the engineer via a cord to a bell in the engine room. Two rings would indicate 'ahead', one ring 'stop' and three rings 'astern'.

The Kelvin was used as a safety craft during flying and for laying, lifting and inspecting marine craft and flying boat moorings, as well as changing buoys as necessary. It was also used for ferrying personnel to and from Lee-on-Solent and Gosport. In 1927 the buoys used for flying boat moorings were constructed of heavy layers of cork, covered by heavy canvas and painted. The MCS personnel were responsible for renewing the canvas when necessary; it had to be sewn on with sailmaker's needles. They also applied 'eyes' to the wire pendants used to secure the flying boats to their moorings. The cork buoys were subsequently replaced by spherical rubber buoys, which were inflated to 0.5 lb psi (0.03 bars) to maintain their shape.

Twice a day the Kelvins would be run to the Air Ministry pier at Warsash, on the Hamble River, to convey personnel and official mail to and from Group Headquarters at Lee-on-Solent. This route was over 30 miles (50 km) less than the road journey via Southampton. The boat crew were responsible for lighting warning lamps on the end of Warsash pier on the afternoon run and for extinguishing them on the morning run. Other types of craft were occasionally used for this run. The craft would also be used on a Sunday morning to convey Roman Catholic RAF personnel to Netley Hospital for a service in the chapel there.

There were also 50 ft (15.2 m) and 56 ft (17.1 m) single-engined, semi-diesel pinnaces in use. These craft had a primus cooking facility and canvas stretcher bunks, with a large brass steering wheel set amidships. The coxswain was protected from the spray by a stout canvas screen, but otherwise the crew was exposed to all weather conditions. The later craft of this type were fitted with a sturdier wheelhouse that afforded more protection. The spacious after cabin was ideal for conveying passengers. The 90 hp semi-diesel engine was a very heavy design with four large cylinders. The primitive method of starting the engine involved directing fixed blowlamps at the dome-shaped cylinder heads. The blowlamps were operated by compressed air and were ignited for ten to fifteen minutes until the cylinder domes became red hot. The fuel injection levers were then pulled over and once the engine had started the blowlamps were extinguished. The four-man crew communicated via the ship's telegraph system. The craft was fitted with an auxiliary engine, which was used to charge batteries and operate a compressor and a small but efficient searchlight, as well as a large four-bladed propeller.

The main functions of the craft were target towing for bombing practice, acting as a safety craft on the bombing range in a freshwater bay off the Isle of Wight, conveying personnel to Coastal Command stations, transferring patients to the military hospital at Netley, inspecting and maintaining moorings and towing flying boats to and from aircraft factories at Southampton and Cowes. In addition the craft was used to ferry flying boat crews to the aircraft factories and for practical instruction for Marine Craft Training School trainees.

This craft was very sturdily built and especially suitable for target towing owing to the comparatively slow-revving engine and the four-bladed propeller. A large towing hook was situated amidships, above the after cabin, which permitted the towrope to pass over the top of the cabin when the vessel was turning, causing the minimum obstruction to the tow. The craft was also fitted with very stout brass bollards fore and aft and a hand-operated winch to facilitate the raising of the anchor.

There were, however, some disadvantages to the semi-diesel pinnace. The large funnel-contained silencer chambers made the craft somewhat top-heavy, causing it to roll heavily in rough seas. In earlier versions this funnel had been situated in front of the steering position and had severely restricted the coxswain's visibility, particularly during the hours of darkness. Moreover the large amount of brass on the deck, including the steering wheel, bollards, cleats and various strips soon became tarnished by the seawater, which made cleaning very difficult.

The 35 ft (10.7 m) and 40 ft (12.2 m) refuelling craft which were used had a steel hull throughout and were powered by a single 50 hp engine, with a fuel tank capacity of 2,000 gall (9,000 litres). Later models incorporated two petrol engines and a 3,000 gall (13,600 litres) fuel tank.

In order to refuel the flying boats, their crew would first have to pay out the slack on their mooring cables to allow the flying boat to drop back from the buoy. The refuelling craft crew would then secure their craft to the flying boat mooring and put the craft's stern close to the nose of the flying boat using large rope fenders for protection. A heaving line was then attached to the fuel hoses, which were thrown to the flying boat crew, who were positioned on top of the plane, where the petrol tanks were situated. The petrol hoses were hauled up and inserted into the tanks, and the fuel was pumped up by the refuelling craft's auxiliary engine.

The 14 ft (4.3 m) rowing dinghy was also used during this period to ferry the crew of both the marine craft and the flying boats, as well as for rowing and sculling instruction for trainees. As their name suggests, these dinghies were originally rowed but were later powered by outboard engines. Finally, specifically designed dinghies were fitted with inboard engines.

Another craft in use at Calshot was the 27 ft sailing/rowing whaler. Station personnel used it mainly to instruct motorboat crew trainees in sailing and rowing, as well as for recreational purposes.

In 1931 two types of what came to be considered revolutionary boats were introduced into the service. The first was the armoured target boat and the second was the 37 ft 6 in (11.43 m) seaplane tender constructed by the British Power Boat Company at Hythe, Southampton. These seaplane tenders gradually took over the functions of the older boats and were fitted with two Meadows 100 hp engines. Later craft of this type had high-speed diesel engines, made by Perkins of Peterborough, situated right aft, and remotely controlled by the coxswain from the wheel-house right forward. Two control levers, about 4 inches (10 cm) in length, on the instrument panel acted as gear lever and throttle. When eased forward they operated the gear hydraulic-ally and the craft moved forward; when the lever was further advanced it opened the throttle and increased the speed. When one wanted to go astern the lever was eased back to beyond the neutral position. With one engine going ahead and the other astern manoeuvrability was improved in reasonable weather conditions. Initially the craft were fitted with the Hyland remote control, but this was later replaced by the Bendix. The speed of the boat was 24 knots. A small searchlight was fitted on top of the wheelhouse and a Kent clear-view windscreen disc installed to reduce the amount of heavy spray. This was a disc of glass driven by an electric motor, which was fitted in the windscreen and revolved at high speed.

Two hammock-type bunks were fitted in the cabin and the crew consisted of a corporal coxswain and two deckhands, with the addition of an engineer and a wireless operator for longer journeys.

This craft was used to tow a light splash target for bombing and torpedo dropping exercises. The target, shaped like a wheel-barrow, created a splash that was easily seen from the air.

Bullock was promoted to corporal in January 1930 and the following month he was posted from Calshot to Inverkeithing Bay, Fifeshire, for duty with RAF Station Donibristle, where two torpedo bomber squadrons, 36 and 100, were based. The main function of the MCS was to tow targets for torpedo practice, recover torpedoes and tow them to Inverkeithing, where they were lifted by steam crane onto railway trucks for transportation to Donibristle via the Air Ministry railway. The pilots were initially trained to drop torpedoes that were not fitted with engines, known as dummy torpedoes. These were dropped in the Firth of Forth about 5 miles (8 km) east of the Forth Bridge. Torpedoes fitted with engines and gyros were dropped in Kirkcaldy Bay, about 18 miles (29 km) east of Inverkeithing. For this exercise the torpedoes, which were set to run 800 yards, were dropped into the wind alongside a mark boat, from a height of approximately 30 ft (9 m), at a target being towed across wind. The mark boat would fly a red flag at a height of 30 ft (9 m) to assist the pilot. This invention was found to be particularly helpful to pilots in the Singapore area, owing to the prevalence of calm weather and the resulting 'glassy' effect on the surface of the sea, which made it difficult to determine the surface.

When a torpedo failed to surface because it had hit the seabed, the mark boat would drop a buoy to mark its position, and attempts would be made to recover it by sweeping. Two boats would tow wire and chain cable at a dead-slow speed in the same direction that the torpedo had been dropped. When a 'bite' was obtained they closed in on one another and a large shackle, attached to a light rope, was passed down the two legs of the sweeping gear. The boats would then increase their speed, trying to break the torpedo from the bottom of the sea. When it came clear it would surface. The crew had a maximum of forty-eight hours to recover a torpedo; once this time had passed it was written off. Later the torpedo racks were redesigned to carry the torpedo's nose at an angle of 12 degrees on the aircraft so that when released from a height of 30 ft (9 m) it would enter the water at the correct angle. The aircraft used for torpedo practice were Hawker Horsleys, which were single-engined and had three-seater open cockpits.

Whilst at Inverkeithing Bullock's other duties included attending flying boat squadrons that were moored at South Queensferry, near the Forth Bridge, on detachment from their stations for periodic exercises. The craft based at Inverkeithing during his stay (1930–32) included 35 ft (10.7 m) Brooke motor-boats. These were not considered powerful enough for the kind of work involved and were replaced by 56 ft (17.1 m) semi-diesel pinnaces in late 1931, as well as a 37 ft 6 in (11.43 m) seaplane tender and a 16 ft (4.9 m) rowing dinghy. From 1931 onwards an RAF auxiliary vessel, a Cawley, was based there. It was a former Humber pilot vessel manned by a civilian crew, with the exception of an RAF wireless operator. It was located on the torpedo range and after the torpedoes had been recovered it towed alongside and lifted them aboard for transport to Inverkeithing pier.

Bullock was posted to RAF Station Seletar, Singapore, in September 1932 and remained there until April 1935. His main duties involved torpedo exercises with No. 36 Squadron and later No. 100 Squadron, working with No. 205 Flying Boat Squadron on refuelling duties, towing aircraft as necessary and bombing range duties. A typical exercise, which was carried out by both day and night, consisted of torpedo attacks on Royal Navy vessels approaching Singapore on passage from Hong Kong. The vessel would be located about 20–30 miles (30–50 km) east of Singapore by flying boats, which radioed the base and, if it was dark, dropped parachute flares. The torpedo squadrons would then attack the vessels. When a torpedo hit a ship the nose would concertina but continue to float. The torpedoes were fitted with calcium flares to facilitate their location. The MCS crew would then tow them back to the base. During daylight attacks small buoys with flags attached were thrown overboard by the target vessels to indicate the number of direct hits scored.

Bullock was also involved in bombing and machine-gun practice on an isolated island called Pulo Suber, approximately 5 miles (8 km) west of Singapore harbour. Both torpedo and flying boat squadrons carried out this exercise. The MCS patrolled the bombing range in order to warn off any intruders, usually junks or fishing craft, and towed rowing boats close to the island to enable the range party to go ashore and check or change the targets. The island was not accessible by powered craft owing to the presence of a coral reef. To avoid making the daily 30 mile (50 km) journey from Seletar, the boats took their own moor ways in a towed barge and laid them close to Blackangmati Island, near Singapore harbour. When they were not working, the boat's were made fast to these moorings by the Malay deckhands and Chinese engineers that lived aboard. The RAF crew were accommodated with the Royal Artillery, who were stationed on Blackangmati Island. The exercises usually lasted for three to four weeks.

Live torpedo exercises also took place, particularly on an uninhabited island called Pulo Pisang approximately 70 miles (110 km) from Seletar. This island was selected as a target for a three-day exercise using live torpedoes during Bullock's time in Seletar. It rises sheer out of the sea and the torpedoes were aimed at its western side, exploding on impact. The MCS used two semi-diesel pinnaces, one 60 ft (18.3 m) launch fitted with two large petrol engines specially built by Thorneycroft of

Singapore for the RAF and one 16 ft (4.9 m) rowing boat. The main role of the crew was to patrol the large area of sea in the vicinity of the island and to warn off other craft. They also acted as a grandstand for spectators and as safety craft for those flying. There was a welcome addition to the food supply for those living on board the boat for the period of the exercise when large numbers of fish were killed and recovered as a result of the explosions. When not on duty the boats were anchored close to the island.

The pinnaces also towed barges from Seletar to an explosives anchorage approximately 35 miles (55 km) west of Singapore and loaded explosives from a ship then towed the barges back to Seletar. They were also used to convey personnel between the transit camp at RAF Changi and the RAF station at Seletar, as well as being used as a safety boat during practice bombing on a local range at Seletar that was moored about 1 mile (1.5 km) offshore.

Corporal Bullock was promoted to the rank of sergeant in November 1933. In April 1935 he left Singapore and was posted to the MCS at Haslar Creek, Portsmouth Harbour (formerly HMS *Hornet* Royal Navy Motor Torpedo Boat Base) for duty with the torpedo base at RAF Station Gosport. His main duties involved recovering dummy torpedoes dropped by Blackburn Baffin aircraft in Stokes Bay and towing them to Stokes Bay pier for return by road to RAF Station Gosport. They also towed targets in the Solent and off the Isle of Wight for runner torpedoes and conveyed them back to Stokes Bay pier. Day and night exercises were carried out in conjunction with the army and Royal Navy. At the time there were RAF personnel in the complement of the Royal Navy's aircraft carriers and marine craft crew were responsible for ferrying them to their carriers, which were anchored in Sandown Bay. They also conveyed both civilian and RAF maintenance parties to service radar installation on Nomansland Fort at Spithead.

During 1936 and 1937 a new type of pinnace came into service, the 60 ft (18.3 m) GS pinnace. It had two high-speed engines and could achieve a speed of approximately 14 knots, was completely enclosed and controlled by the Coxswain, with a large storage hold aft and racks for storing the torpedoes. It boasted a powered derrick for lifting torpedoes and other heavy equipment and was crewed by a sergeant or corporal coxswain, two deckhands, an engineer and a wireless operator on extended journeys. It was very seaworthy because of a particularly wide beam and during the Second World War one made the journey from Scotland to Iceland via the Faroes. Other craft based at Haslar included 56 ft (17.1 m) semi-diesel pinnaces and a 37 ft 6 in (11.43 m) seaplane tender.

The latter part of 1936 found Sergeant Bullock back at Calshot on a first class coxswain's course. Here he met his future wife and on return to Gosport arranged for a transfer back to Calshot, where he remained until May 1940. The duties at Calshot were many and varied, including the usual tasks with the new Sunderland flying boats and seaplane tenders and bombing range duties with moored targets in the Solent. He spent a period as coxswain in charge of a pinnace attached to the Marine Training School, as well as operating armoured target boats in Christchurch Bay between the Isle of Wight and Christchurch, and the usual ferrying between Calshot, Lee-on-Solent and Gosport.

In the spring of 1938 he became First Coxswain on the new high-speed launch (No. 103), the fourth to be constructed by the British Power Boat Company. Designed mainly for open sea rescue duties, but also used for other duties, including long-range exercises in conjunction with aircraft, this vessel was 63 ft (19.2 m) long and about 14 ft (4.3 m) across the beam. It was powered by three 500 hp Napier Sea Lion engines (twelve cylinder in three banks of four) and had a two-to-one reduction gear (propeller revolutions were half those of the engine). It had an auxiliary engine for charging batteries and pumping water from the bilges and could achieve a top speed of 40 knots, with a cruising speed of 30 knots. The five fuel tanks, situated under the wheelhouse, gave a total capacity of approximately 1,400 gall (6,400 litres). The range of the vessel was approximately 600 miles (970 km). The crew consisted of one officer, two coxswains, three deckhands, two engineers and a wireless operator. A medical orderly was occasionally carried on rescue duties. The crew's quarters were forward, and included double primus cooking facilities. They had canvas stretcher-type bunks and flotation cushions, full toilet facilities and a sleeping bag for each member of the crew. In the extensive wheelhouse there was a seat for the coxswain, an aircraft-type compass (P 3 or P 4) and two Kent clear-view windscreen discs, and the lookout position was directly accessible from the wheelhouse. The aft was fitted with stretchers and their fittings. In addition the sickbay was fitted with a comprehensive medical kit, including chloroform, ampoules of morphine, splints and assorted dressings. A gallon jar of rum was carried for use by crash survivors and for issue to crew during very inclement weather. In addition to the usual lifebuoys and lifejackets a light wooden dinghy was carried on the after deck. When it was under way, one engineer remained in the engine room and found it necessary to wear ear defenders, as the Napier engines were exceptionally noisy. The engineer operated the ahead and astern gears on signal from the coxswain by means of the ship's telegraph. The Coxswain operated the throttles as necessary.

Between 1938 and 1940 there was extensive exercises with aircraft. During one in particular, with the RAF School of Navigation, Thorney Island, the launch was instructed to proceed to a position about 30 miles (50 km) into the English Channel, south-west of the Isle of Wight. When the Anson aircraft containing the navigation trainees arrived, the launch would proceed on a set course for ten minutes, then alter course by at least 30 degrees every ten minutes and, at the same time either reduce or increase speed. The task for the navigation trainees was to estimate the vessel's course and speed at all times and to record it. An accurate record of the course and speeds was maintained in the launch's logbook and a copy was forwarded to Thorney Island for comparison with the trainees' estimates. Bullock was with HSL 103 on these exercises on numerous occasions in 1939 and early 1940, often detached to Poole harbour from Monday to Friday in order to save time and fuel consumption.

He was also involved in regional exercises. RAF bombers carried out extensive flights over the English Channel and the North Sea and the launches were usually detached to various bases to act as safety craft for the duration of these exercises. Amongst the bases used were Mount Batten, Calshot, Shoreham, Felixstowe and Grimsby. For the duration of the exercises, which usually lasted approximately one week, the crews lived and slept on board their launches. The old battleship HMS

Centurion had been adapted for use as a target by the RAF bombers; the deck had been specially reinforced and the ship was radio controlled from a destroyer. As well as being available for emergency purposes, HSL 103 took up position off Selsey Bill and maintained a radio listening watch throughout the exercise.

At the outbreak of war in 1939 HSL 103 was issued with six Ross .300 rifles, and the skipper and first coxswain received either a Colt automatic pistol or a Smith and Wesson revolver. Two Lewis machine guns and subsequently two twin Vickers in Anson Ford turrets soon replaced the rifles.

The marine craft based at Calshot from September 1937 to May 1940 included one 63 ft (19.2 m) high-speed launch, 60 ft (18.3 m) GS pinnaces, 37 ft 6 in (11.43 m) and 40 ft (12.2 m) petrol-engined seaplane tenders, armoured target boats, steel hull refuellers, powered dinghies, rowing/sailing whalers and steel hull bomb scows, which were specifically designed to carry bombs underneath the wing of a flying boat and secure them to the racks. The scows were necessarily of shallow design and contained lifting gear for the bombs.

In May 1940 Bullock was posted from Calshot to the ASRU at Grimsby, based at the Royal Dock Basin. He travelled there on HSL 103, stopping overnight at RAF Station Felixstowe. Grimsby was a two-launch station; there was one duty launch and one standby launch used exclusively for ASR duties. Most sorties took place at night in response to distress signals from bombers returning from raids on Germany and the occupied countries, and they usually necessitated long trips to the central North Sea between the Humber and the Dutch or German coasts. Many miles were clocked up, but most sorties at that time were unsuccessful because of the time taken to reach the estimated position of the ditched crew. In addition, the RAF rubber dinghies of that period were not of a very high standard and they tended to inflate prematurely. The duty crews lived in a hut close to the jetty and were connected to the RAF station at North Coates by a tie line telephone for emergency call-out. An extension was laid to the wheelhouse of the duty launch so that the duty engineer, who slept on board could be called and get the engine started for a quick get away.

One launch which was based at Grimsby, HSL 111, was believed to have been one of the first boats to explode an acoustic mine; this occurred in the Humber while it was on an engine test run. The mine exploded fairly close to the launch, which was operating at high speed, and although the crew were not seriously injured, the launch was written off. A large number of acoustic mines were parachuted by Heinkels into the Humber and its approaches. The comparatively shallow water was especially suitable for their use, with depths of 10 fathoms or less said to be the ideal. ASR crews were advised when entering or leaving the Humber to proceed either dead slow or flat out. A slow speed on one engine would not generate sufficient sound to activate the mine and if it was flat out it would probably explode the mine before the launch reached it.

In November 1940 it was decided to replace HSL 103 because of the mileage it had covered, often in rough weather. The vessel had deteriorated to such an extent that it was barely seaworthy. It was ferried to Calshot, where the crew collected their new launch, the HSL 142, from the British Power Boat works and returned to Grimsby.

On 1 January 1941 Bullock was promoted to the rank of warrant officer and posted, along with HSL 142, to Dover. He was on the way there, intending to stay overnight at Felixstowe, when, whilst cruising at about 30 knots in the vicinity of the Burnham buoy about 15 miles (25 km) north-east of Cromer, a mine exploded off the starboard quarter. It affected the launch to such an extent that the crew had to reduce speed considerably because of severe vibration. They were also making water.

An engineer onboard suffered severe bruising and Bullock, who was at the wheel, was thrown across the wheelhouse but suffered only slight bruising. He proceeded slowly to the ASRU at Gorleston, with a Spitfire escort, and was directed by Coastal Command to proceed to Brooke's Boat Yard at Oulton Broad the following day for repairs. The launch spent three weeks at the yard, where it was found that the engines had been forced out of alignment; the propellers and shafts had to be replaced and there was extensive hull damage. The crew were accommodated in private houses in the town whilst the repairs were carried out. The pilot of a Heinkel 111 seaplane had probably spotted the Burnham buoy and parachuted the mine where he assumed the channel to be. This route was extensively used by the inshore convoys and was quite close to the area known as

E-Boat Alley. Bullock and his crew were fortunate to have been travelling at a fairly high speed, otherwise they would have received the full force of the explosion.

Bullock therefore did not reach Dover until the end of February 1941. There he was joined by other launches to form a rescue base moored in the train ferry dock. For a few months, the crews were accommodated in the Lord Warden Hotel, which had been requisitioned by the Royal Navy to accommodate the crews of motor torpedo boats and patrol drifters and was known as HMS *Wasp*. During that period the Vice-Admiral Dover authorised the daily naval rum issue also to be given to the RAF crews and also gave them the privilege of duty-free tobacco. Later the RAF personnel took over and were accommodated in the Ferry House in Dover.

The main function of the launches was, of course, air sea rescue and occasionally a launch was detached to Ramsgate to supplement the launches based there. Dover was an extremely busy unit with fighter pilots operating by day and bomber crews at night. One well-known Belgian fighter pilot baled out of Spitfires twice in a few weeks and was picked up by launches from Dover on each occasion.

During June 1941 HSL 143 was attacked by an Me 109 whilst *en route* to pick up a German pilot in the mid-Channel. The launch caught fire and Flight Sergeant Squires was killed. The crew managed to launch the dinghy, but were picked up by an E-boat and taken prisoner. An RAF Lysander pilot saw them being landed at Boulogne.

A further duty for the Dover launches was a daily visit to specially designed survival craft that were moored at intervals in mid-Channel for ditched aircrew to get aboard.

Whilst they were with the Royal Navy the crews of the launches received naval emergency rations. These consisted of tinned sausages, tinned bacon, corned beef, tinned fruit and tea, sugar and milk, whereas RAF issues usually consisted of very hard biscuits, corned beef, tea and sugar. Moreover they firmly believed that the naval rations in the messes ashore were of a much higher standard than those of the RAF.

In April 1942 Bullock was posted to Ayr harbour, Scotland to take up the position of skipper of the yacht *Drusilla*. Formerly named *Beryl*, this craft was owned by Lord Inverclyde and had been requisitioned by the Royal Navy at the outbreak of war but later handed over to the RAF. She was 93 ft (28.3 m) in length, with two large paraffin engines and an auxiliary engine. The crew's quarters were forward and had a coal-fired cooking range and good sleeping accommodation. The quarters aft contained first-class sleeping accommodation, together with the original luxurious bedding, a full-sized slipper bath and various other furnishings. There was also a spacious wheelhouse with an excellent all-round view. The speed was 12 knots.

The crew consisted of a warrant officer skipper, a sergeant and an engineer, two deckhands, one cook, one wireless operator mechanic and one wireless operator. They lived on board and were issued with ration cards and a ration allowance to enable the cook to do the catering. Their function was to proceed to positions in the Firth of Clyde and the Irish Sea and transmit radio beams for aircrews under instruction from RAF Station Prestwick to home in on. They were required to maintain their position at least 7 miles (11 km) from the nearest point of land and transmit their position to Prestwick every hour. These positions were shown on a map grid superimposed on an Admiralty chart. The yacht was also available for ASR duties if required.

In September 1942 Bullock was posted to the MCS at Tayport, Fife. There were two separate units based there: the MCS and the No. 12 ASRMCU. This unit with two launches, was used exclusively for air sea rescue, but it was closed down in 1946. The main duties of the MCS, during the period 1942–45, were carried out with No. 333 Royal Norwegian Air Force Flying Boat Squadron, based at Woodhaven, 4 miles (6.5 km) from Tayport. The squadron was equipped with Catalina aircraft, which were often used to pick up and land personnel in the fjords of occupied Norway. Essentially the squadron was in two parts: the Catalinas were at Woodhaven and there were Mosquitoes at RAF Station Leuchars, which acted as a parent unit for Tayport.

Norwegian personnel manned all the aircraft, while the MCS crews carried out the usual flying boat liaison duties. Other duties included providing safety boat cover during day and night bombing practice in St Andrew's Bay, target towing for bombing and rocket missile practice in the North Sea and weekly visits to convey servicing parties to a radar beacon situated in St Andrew's Bay, about 4 miles (6.5 km) east of the control tower at RAF Station Leuchars and used by them for navigation.

Between 1943 and 1949 it was decided to carry out airborne lifeboat trials off the Fife coast. As we have seen, the boat was 24 ft (7.3 m) long and wooden secured to the bomb bay of a Lancaster bomber. It was fitted with two 8 hp Austin engines and a mast with its large sail painted red. This mast, when not in use, was securely lashed across the top of the boat. The Lancaster was directed to a suitable position by radio from the marine craft, usually a few miles from the coast and clear of the shipping lanes. On receipt of the 'go ahead' signal it released the lifeboat from 400 ft (120 m), and it floated down on four large parachutes attached to a single quick-release hook amidships. On impact an immersion switch completed a circuit, which fired a cartridge in the hook and released the parachutes, which floated clear of the lifeboat. At the same time four 100 ft (30 m) orange lines were fired from the lifeboat to enable people in the water to pull themselves to the boat. Once aboard, survivors could fix the rudder in position, start the engines and proceed. The sail could also be used and, by virtue of its colour, was visible from the air from a considerable distance. The marine craft on duty for this exercise would attempt to recover all four parachutes. Occasionally, however, the parachutes would spill air and lose buoyancy, and the weight of the shackles and wires would cause them to sink; several were lost during the trials. A member of the marine craft crew would start the lifeboat engines and ferry it to Tayport.

During 1946, whilst Bullock was warrant officer in charge, an incident occurred that created a degree of resentment amongst the MCS. It was decided that a small detachment of Royal Engineers and some German prisoners of war should use the accommodation vacated by No. 12 ASRMCU whilst they were carrying out bomb disposal duties in eastern Scotland. An army colonel arrived to inspect the quarters and informed Bullock that it was not up to standard for prisoners of war; considerable improvements would be necessary, including the installation of better heating facilities and additional cooking equipment. When Bullock informed the colonel, somewhat forcibly, that

RAF personnel had lived there for several years, he murmured something about the Geneva Convention.

Having left Liverpool at the end of June 1943 on the trooper *Rangitata* for Durban, South Africa, then the *Highland Brigade* bound for Bombay, India, then the *Cap Touranne* bound for Colombo, Ceylon, Ray Lancaster arrived there in October 1943 and was posted to 203 ASRU. The base was in a corner of the harbour in Colombo docks and Lancaster was billeted with an RAF balloon squadron unit. He was moved to various other billets during his stay, including the Bristol Hotel. At the base he became a member of the crew of HSL 164, one of the original 100 class Whalebacks. He stayed with her for eighteen months.

The crew's duty roster was twenty-four hours on and twenty-four hours off, life on board was a routine of cleaning, painting, refuelling and putting into practice what Lancaster had learned at Coursewall in Scotland during training. Refuelling was considered to be an irksome task; the boat was moored off the quayside on a buoy fore and aft, which meant that the 100 octane fuel, in 5 gall (23 litre) cans, had to be manhandled over the quayside into a dinghy below, can by can. It was then transported to the boat where it was all manhandled again and emptied into the fuel tanks. Then every can had to be taken back to the shore. This was particularly difficult in the high temperature, but the vessels had to be kept topped up, particularly after a trip. These trips were mostly practice runs, although often they would have visitors, and that involved some cleaning up after a rough sea trip.

HSL 164 had three crash calls whilst Lancaster was with her. The first involved a Fleet Air Arm kite that had ditched along the coast from the base. The crew had to leave the base in a hurry and as a consequence their medical officer was left behind. They discovered that some local fishermen had picked up the pilot and navigator of the kite, but the navigator was badly gashed on his head. With no medical officer on board the injury was cleaned with the contents of a bottle of rum.

The next crash call occurred on Lancaster's twenty-first birthday. He had been given the night off by the skipper, but during the evening they were informed that an Indian naval destroyer had reported sighting a body in the water. When the body was discovered it was so decomposed that it was left in the water.

The third call-out was a serious one. The crew was again off duty at the time and several of them had gone to the cinema. During the film a message was flashed on the screen asking them to report to base immediately. They rushed back to their billet in the YMCA and changed into their working gear, then ran to the base. It was approximately 2000 hours and getting dark, but the crew noticed that a pinnace nearby was manned and that they were preparing to follow HSL 164. The skipper informed the crew that a Liberator had gone missing and it was feared downed in the sea. It was later discovered that it was taking faulty depth charges out to sea to dump them, but they had blown up before they were disposed of.

The skipper set up a square search when they reached the last reported position of the aircraft, and the crew were all on watch in the hope of seeing some light from the crashed aircraft. They also stopped and listened for the sound of the whistles that aircrew carried, but they heard nothing. The search continued through the night. Then HSL 164 received a radio message that the other launch was returning to base because they were running low on fuel and eventually they had the same problem. As it was daylight by this time the skipper ordered a return to base. Whilst approaching the base they came alongside the pinnace, whose crew informed them that they had two survivors on board, but no medical officer or medical equipment. HSL 164's medical officer went on board the pinnace to deal with the men but it was apparent that they were in no fit state to be moved, so he remained with them until they reached the base. HSL 164 ran out of fuel just short of the base, but managed to drift in to the buoy. The crew had been out for eighteen hours but were very relieved that the two survivors would recover.

Lancaster did have two trips in other vessels, the first to take a pinnace from Colombo to Cochin in India. They had a scratch crew, with an officer skipper, a second coxswain, a fitter and three deckhands. They left Colombo at midnight in pouring rain and a howling gale, but it was not until they had cleared the harbour that they realised the full extent of the storm. The pinnace had a very broad, square stern, and there was a following sea. This meant that every time a wave caught up with the vessel from the rear the stern was lifted up and the bow pointed straight down. Slowly the wave passed under the boat and the bow came up again.

Lancaster's two-hour shift began at 0200 hours and the boat seemed to be doing everything but turn upside down, making it impossible for him even to make a cup of tea. The rest of the crew were all suffering severely from seasickness and when he began his watch Lancaster was alone in the wheelhouse, trying – with very little success – to keep the compass needle in place. At 0400, when his shift should have ended, his relief was too ill to take over and he had to do another two hours. At the end of that time the gale finally blew itself out and the sun began to shine.

The storm had blown them off course and they had to get directions to Cochin from some local fishermen. They arrived there just in time to catch their train back to Colombo.

Lancaster's second trip was to Trincomalee. Two American patrol boats had been delivered in Colombo and were required by the ASR in 'Trinco'. Lancaster volunteered to take one of them. By all accounts they were luxurious vessels, with hot and cold showers and refrigerators. During the night they saw a light flashing at them. Lancaster, who was adept with the Aldis lamp, signalled back, telling the other vessel who they were, where they were going and what they were doing. He never discovered whom he was giving this information to, as they did not meet the vessel again during the trip.

Shortly after this trip, Lancaster volunteered for an unspecified 'special job'. He boarded the SS *Manela*, an RAF depot ship, and there he found that he had been posted to 230 Squadron, Marine Craft Section. He would be stationed on his boat wherever it went to tend to Sunderland flying boats of 230 and 225 Squadron. They were told they were going across the Bay of Bengal; as they were heading towards Japanese territory, there was some concern about the possibility of encountering torpedoes.

When the *Manela* laid her moorings the MCS crew were told that they were in Burma and were to proceed up river to Akyab. The MCS vessels were lowered over the side. From an opening in the side of the ship a boom was rigged up, pointing outwards, with rope ladders and ropes hanging from it. The men moored the MCS vessels to the ropes on this boom. They had to slide out along the boom, climb down the rope ladder and whilst hanging on with one hand, pull the boat in towards them and then jump aboard, hoping that they did not jump too far. It was also imperative to remember to start the engine before the mooring line was untied, otherwise the men would be whisked away by the strong current.

The usual routine of a flying boat base was soon established, with the men running crews to their aircraft, refuelling and taking service crews to do repairs. The aircraft were moored up an inlet not far from the *Manela*. On one occasion Lancaster was on the marine tender, one of the smaller boats, and had just picked up two of the maintenance crew to take them back to the *Manela*. He had cleared the inlet and was out in the main river when the wind started to blow. Within a matter of seconds it had whipped the water into waves about 3 ft (1 m) high across the river. Knowing that it would be impossible to get straight to the *Manela* without turning over, Lancaster pushed the throttles wide open and headed out across the river. He had to do two sides of a triangle to get back to the *Manela*, then complete a full turn on the crest of a wave. He found out later that the wind had in fact been a typhoon.

He was also involved in night flying. Night flare paths on water were made up of very small dinghies with short masts in the centre. These mast's had mushroom-shaped structures at the top, with a bulb underneath lit by a battery. The dinghies' anchors were dropped over the side when they were in position in a straight line. When word was sent that the aircraft was due the MCS crew would return to the dinghies and switch on the lights. The lights then had to be switched off once the aircraft had landed and the dinghies retrieved.

Lancaster was awakened from his sleep one night by the sound of many aircraft engines. He went on deck and saw a mass of aircraft towing gliders; he later discovered that the army had taken Rangoon and that what he had seen had been some of the paratroopers going over. Shortly afterwards he was posted to Rangoon, to Syriam on the Pegu River. The MCS vessels were moored to a pontoon with a platform dock at the end. The buoys had already been laid for the aircraft and 230 Squadron's kites. The crew were billeted in tents and made their beds from floorboards and wire netting so that they did not have to sleep on the ground. Routine life soon got under way, with the regular duties of refuelling and ferrying crews and maintenance staff. On one occasion a Sunderland was tied to the pontoon whilst the fitters carried out a complete engine change.

There were problems on this river because of its 10 knot tide and a fluctuation in level of about 20 ft (6 m). The problem was particularly acute when they were towing Sunderlands. If the wind was blowing with the tide, the Sunderland would overtake the towing vessel. Similar situations arose when a refueller was going alongside a Sunderland, usually across the tide. If the wind was blowing then it was very difficult to get the refueller under the wing of the aircraft without knocking the float off.

Two incidents stand out in Lancaster's time in Syriam. The first was when a Catalina came into land and on hitting the water it broke its back, did a 90 degree turn and headed for other parked aircraft nearby. Fortunately it stopped in time, to the great relief of everyone, including those on the aircraft it was heading for. It was subsequently stripped and sunk.

The second incident occurred when Lancaster was detailed to take an air commodore from Syriam to Rangoon in the marine tender. They had travelled some way when the steering gave way and Lancaster thought he had lost a rudder. Slowly throttling down he turned and attempted to return to base, but with little success. The air commodore picked up one of the floorboards and hung it over the side. He told Lancaster to open up and he would steer, and that is how they returned to the base. On inspection it was discovered that the rudder had not been lost; the key of the shaft had sheered.

After Syriam, Lancaster was posted to Penang, off the coast of Malaya, to Glugor. It was a pre-war Imperial Airways staging post and the men were billeted in bungalows, each of which had its own shower and toilet. The base was used as a staging and refuelling post for the Sunderland flying boats travelling from Colombo to Singapore

Shortly after the war against Japan ended Lancaster returned home, via Singapore, on the *Empress of Australia*. The journey to the Far East had taken him three months, but the return home took only three weeks. He arrived back in August 1946 and after leave was posted to AMES at Felixstowe, where as duty crew he had to escort flying boats across to Harwich if the weather was too bad to leave them in open water. He also had the task of standing by when experiments were taking place with rocket-assisted take-offs with a Walrus flying boat. The idea was that if an aircraft ditched in stormy weather, the Walrus would use the rockets to blast it off the rough water.

The final account comes from a remarkable document dated 7 August 1944, written by Flying Officer Bromley, the Master of HSL 2692, addressed to the Area and Marine Officer, Headquarters No. 222 Group, RAF Ceylon, concerning his voyage from Trincomalee to Calcutta between 19 July and 3 August 1944.

> Upon receipt of 222 Group's signal, dated 14 July, preparation were at once put in hand for the ferrying of the launch to Chittagong. A test run was carried out, with satisfactory results. Fuel, water and provisions were laid in. Instructions regards w/t communications were obtained from RAF Station, China Bay. I visited Naval Headquarters, Trincomalee on 18 July and obtained shipping intelligence and recognition signals. On 19 July I was given a satisfactory meteorological report and having received your confirmation by signal left Trincomalee for Madras at 1608 hours.
>
> The passage to Madras was accomplished in moderate weather. The starboard engine failed through choked filters at 0610 hours on 20 July and was restarted at 0630 hours. On entering Madras harbour at dead slow speed at 0745 hours all three engines stopped, through faulty fuel supply.
>
> While at Madras July 20–22, the fuel system was thoroughly checked through, and filters cleaned. Launch was refuelled, and made ready for the next leg of the trip to Vizagapatan. I visited Naval Headquarters, Madras and sailing was arranged for 1700 hours, 22 July 1944. The launch cleared Madras harbour entrance at 1700 hours 22 July 1944 and arrived on ETA at Vizagapatan at 1100 hours next day. Somewhat heavy weather was experienced during the passage. At 1831 hours, the port engine centre branch pipe was found to be leaking, and a temporary

repair was carried out, the engine being serviceable again at 1919 hours. When entering Vizagapatan harbour, the centre engine failed through choked filters.

The fractured water pipe to the port engine was brazed at Vizagapatan and fuel filters cleaned out. Fuel tanks were filled to capacity, and water and food taken aboard. On arrival, I reported to XDO and saw him again on 24 July, to request permission to sail next day. He informed me that, in view of weather reports, he considered it inadvisable to do so. On 26 July, I visited XDO and arranged to sail on 27 July at 0600 hours. ETA Sandheads 1200 hours, 28 July.

At 0620 hours, 27 July, launch was underway and left Vizagapatan in calm weather. Speed was kept down to 1400 rpm in order to conserve fuel. At 1630 hours, I increased speed to 1800 rpm in order to obtain a departure from Purl before dark. A position was obtained 4 miles [6.5 km], 196 degrees Purl Pagodas at 1930 hours. Ten minutes later the centre engine stopped, and the fitter reported that the fuel pump to this engine was unserviceable. From this point, the launch proceeded on 2 engines at 1400 rpm.

On 28 July weather continued fair until the early hours when severe thunderstorms broke, and continued for about 3 hours until 0700 hours. Weather then cleared and sea and wind moderated. At 1245 hours, I signalled ASR Calcutta to inform them I was delayed owing to engine trouble. Engines stopped at 1300 hours and anchor dropped in 7 fathoms. A w/t fix obtained at this time was obviously erroneous, and I decided to move into 10 fathoms and wait until nightfall, when Western Channel Light Vessel should be visible. When heaving in the anchor, the cable snapped and anchor was lost, the tripping line failing to raise it. Launch ran south into 10 fathoms, and lay-to until 1930 hours when Western Channel Light Vessel was observed flashing to the westward. Course was set to west, south-west and the launch moved into the vicinity of the lightship. The pilot vessel was observed apparently steaming away to the southward, and attempts to contact her by Aldis lamp were unsuccessful. I decided to lie-to until morning, keeping the light vessel in sight. Starboard engine fuel pump had been giving trouble on the run towards the light vessel and had been kept going only by hand.

Between 0300 and 0400 hours, 29 July, weather closed in and obscured the light vessel. Wind increased to gale force from the east, backing north-east with heavy rain. At 0600 hours, attempts to start starboard engine were unsuccessful, and port engine only was put ahead. After running for an hour, course north-east, it was evident that wind and sea were too high, and I decided to lie-to until weather abated, in order not to waste fuel. Between 0800 and 1500 hours, I moved south and east for two periods of one hour each, to counteract some of the westerly set experienced, and to gain sea room. At 1540 hours, port engine could not be started, through faulty ignition, and though subsequently run for two periods of a few minutes, it was reported to me at 1920 hours that all three engines were unserviceable. Work was begun on removing the only serviceable fuel pump from the port engine, and fitting it to the centre. A sea anchor was run out, and lifelines rigged on deck. The launch lay quite safely to the drogue [canvas sea anchor] through the night, though wind increased and backed to west. The sea anchor rope chaffed through several times and had to be recast.

On 30 July at 0740 hours engine was started, but sea and wind being now very high, I decided to continue to ride it out until the weather moderated, and switched off. In view of the deteriorating weather, I signalled at 0815 hours for a vessel to be sent to stand by me. At 1345 hours, an A/SR aircraft was heard operating nearby on 500 kws, and an attempt was made to contact him, but without result. A bearing of 249 degrees was obtained by D/F Loop. A Wellington aircraft appeared on the scene at 1410 hours, and gave our position as 19 degrees 31 minutes north, 86 degrees 29 minutes east. Three Bircher containers were dropped, two of which came very well aimed. The third over-shot a few yards and could not be recovered. At 1645 hours, the weather closed in and increased in force and the aircraft flew off. Launch continued to ride satisfactorily until 0400 hours 31 July, when she was thrown on her beam-ends. It was afterwards discovered that the drogue had split and her head had been thrown off. Accumulators in the engine room broke from their racks and spilled oil over the engines, several drums of oil were upset and emptied into the bilges.

On 31 July at 0430 hours an attempt was made to start the centre engine, but it was found that water had affected the ignition, and that launch was now without hope of making harbour under her own steam. Air and sea aid were understood to be on the way from first light, and sea and wind were moderating, with rising barometer. A convoy was sighted, sailing north at about 1400 hours and by firing pyrotechnic signals, the attention of its escort vessel was attempted. The vessel T.268 came alongside and I asked to be taken in tow, but this was apparently considered to be impractical by her captain, and who steamed off to rejoin the convoy. At 1630 hours I signalled Calcutta, stating that I was adrift without engines and asking for a vessel to take me in tow. One of my crew LAC Shillitto was ill and his condition was giving anxiety. A position was obtained from w/t bearings of 19 degrees 47 minutes north, 87 degrees 30 minutes east at 1315 hours. On instructions from Calcutta, I displayed lights from 2300 hours, firing pyrotechnics at 20 minute intervals, and flashing the Aldis lamp around the horizon to the north and east every few minutes.

On 1 August a light was observed at 0430 hours away to the eastward, but my signals were not observed by the vessel carrying them. Nothing further was seen during the night. Weather continued to improve, and wind remained in the south-west. At 1230 hours a Liberator aircraft, flying north, passed across our bows at about 3000 ft [900 m] but the launch was not observed by her. I reported this fact at once to Calcutta and at 1350 hours a Liberator was again seen on the same course and again failing to see my signals. At 1500 hours however Liberator again came up and every available means of attracting her attention was employed. Strings of yellow and red international code flags had been hoisted, searchlight and Aldis lamp were flashed and pyrotechnics fired and this time the launch was observed and the aircraft began orbiting my position. A second

Liberator appeared at 1555 hours and took over patrol from the first which flew off. At 1705 hours a ship was sighted approaching from the eastward, and half an hour later HMIS *Khyber* came alongside. A line was fired to us, and a towing wire hauled aboard and made fast. After towing for 20 minutes the wire parted and was sent onboard again, breaking once more after two hours run. A heavy rope was then passed to the launch and with this attached to the bridle of the launch's cable no further trouble was experienced. A speed of 5 knots was maintained and WCIV was sighted at 1500 hours 2 August.

On 2 August the pilot was taken aboard the *Khyber* at 1600 hours and the vessel anchored at 2130 hours. Having no anchor the launch was warped alongside the *Khyber* and made fast. The crew of the launch were given a hot meal aboard the towing vessel which was very much appreciated.

3 August the tow was resumed next morning at 0537 hours and at 1110 hours launch was brought alongside *Khyber* for entry into the refuelling depot at Budgebudge. Here the launch was met by HSL 341 (Flight Lieutenant Dennis) of 229 ASRU and towed to RAF moorings in Garden Beach, Calcutta. On arrival, the crew were examined by the Senior Medical Officer, 231 Group and LAC Shillitto detained in sick quarters for the night.

W/t transmissions were maintained on 4575/3105 kws throughout the trip in accordance with instructions, and proved satisfactory. It is pointed out that I did not at any time consider my vessel was in sufficient peril to justify the use of the distress wave.

Slight damage was sustained to the port rubbing band and foot rail, through surging against the *Khyber* whilst at anchor. The forward clouts were both strained and are being replaced. The launch is now on the slipway at Garden Beach workshops and is being examined for damage by CNO.

Bromley's detailed log found its way to R. W. W. MacKay from Section Number 15, Headquarters Air Command, South-east Asia, who replied on 17 August.

I have just seen a copy of your voyage report and read it with great interest. You and your crew did a really good job of work and I would like to congratulate you all.

I can appreciate the discomfort and strain of the adventure better than most people, because I had a similar experience in HSL 104, a midwinter gale, and the North Sea in 1940.

I was pleased to note you did not use the distress frequency. Your experience bore out my own; that these hard chine jobs are practically unsinkable. The motion is terrific but the craft does not feel unstable and rides the most formidable wave like a duck. I take it the 68 ft [20.7 m] craft lies beam on and drives to leeward like a scalded cat – just as their predecessors did.

I would like a private note from you with the sort of particulars that don't go into an official report. Did your fw last – how did you manage about food – could you get a hot drink – who showed up best among your crew etc. Any ideas on these subjects would be welcome.

I hope you had a good rest after you got in and that your crew were all given good billets and were coddled for a few days. I found it took about a week to get over the reaction.

Good luck and please convey my congratulations to your crew.

CHAPTER ELEVEN

ASR and MCU Vessels 1918–86

THE BRITISH POWER BOAT COMPANY

Hubert Scott-Paine was born in Shoreham, Sussex in 1890 and from a very early age was fascinated by all matters relating to aviation. He spent considerable amounts of his time at the local aerodrome and was delighted to have the opportunity to talk to early aviators about their machines.

Together with Noel Pemberton Billing, he set up the Supermarine factory in Southampton in 1913 and together they won the Schneider Trophy in 1922. In the following year, however, Scott-Paine sold his interest in Supermarine. In 1927, he bought the Hythe Shipyard and established the British Power Boat Company. His first ventures were fast cabin cruisers and racing boats. One of the most famous was the *Miss England* that won the World Championship at Daytona Beach in 1929.

Scott-Paine quickly realised that there were military applications for the planing hulls he had been designing. The Royal Navy were not interested, but the RAF tested one of his cruisers to see if it would be suitable for duties as a seaplane tender. The tests were positive and the RAF ordered a prototype that would become known as the RAF 200. It was delivered to the RAF in 1931 and was extensively tested at Cattewater (later Mount Batten) by Aircraftman Shaw (Lawrence of Arabia). This signalled a long-standing collaboration between Scott-Paine and Lawrence and their developments even convinced the Royal Navy to place orders for a similar craft that would be used for torpedo recovery and as a flag barge.

Scott-Paine continued to develop a range of racing boats and cruisers, but his company also continued to develop military craft, principal amongst which was the 100 Class high-speed launch. New armoured target boats were also designed as well as 16 ft (4.9 m) and 18 ft (5.5 m) planing dinghies. Meanwhile, the Royal Navy were placing orders for fast motor boats, flag barges and 16 ft (4.9 m) dinghies.

In addition to producing a number of motor torpedo boats for the Royal Navy (both 64 ft (19.5 m) and 70 ft (21.3 m)), Scott-Paine struck up deals with ELCO in the United States, Canadian Vickers in Canada and the Cockatoo Boat Company in Australia to ensure increased production for all future craft. The arrangements with these companies worked well; The main British Power Boat Company factories in Hythe and Poole produced 478 motor torpedo boats, whilst the ELCO and Vickers Canada made another 476.

Whilst Scott-Paine ensured that the Royal Navy contracts were fulfilled, he was also concerned with the development and production of a variety of different craft for the RAF. He designed and produced 24 ft (7.3 m) marine tenders, seaplane tenders, 63 ft (19.2 m) high-speed launches and later the 68 ft (20.7 m) Hants & Dorset high-speed launch. Whilst doing this he designed and constructed 68 ft (20.7 m) high-speed target towing launches, 50 ft (15.2 m) general service launches and River Class fast launches for the army.

Throughout the war, the British Power Boat Company also dealt with damaged craft and continuously developed new craft, many of which never made it beyond the drawing board. Scott-Paine lived in the United States during the war years, but in 1946 he suffered a stroke and after a prolonged illness died in 1954.

The shipyard reduced its production in the post-war years and was closed down in 1956, the last launch being produced for the army (the Humber).

ST-200 SERIES – 37½ FT SEAPLANE TENDER MK I

Type:	200 class seaplane tender
Service:	Royal Air Force
Builders:	British Power Boat Company
Year Built:	1931
Number Built:	104 (RAF 200–299 & 300–303)
Displacement:	4.5 tons
Length:	37 ft 6 in (11.43 m)
Beam:	8 ft 6 in (2.59 m)
Draught:	2 ft 6 in (76 cm)
Hull:	Mahogany
Engines:	2 x 100 hp Power Meadows
Max. Speed:	29 knots

The British Power Boat Company at Hythe built this seaplane tender, also known as the 200 Class. The craft had been extensively tested by Lawrence of Arabia in his guise as Aircraftman Shaw. It had two engines, a V-shaped keel and was hard chined. It was designed for dealing with most weather conditions.

The craft's hull and skin was constructed of African mahogany whilst the stem, chine and gunwhale, hog-keel and other areas were made from Columbia pine. Canadian rock elm was used for the rubbers on the gunwhales and the chine. The craft sported a planked cabin roof, but later versions had three-ply wood with doped fabric stretched over the top.

A pair of Power Meadows engines powered the first of the 200 series; Meadows of Wolverhampton made these specifically for the British Power Boat Company. The 100 hp engines could maintain a maximum speed of some 29 knots for around half an hour, but realistically the operating speed was 24 knots, which meant that the vessel could cruise for around 140 miles (225 km) on the 65 gall (295 litres) of fuel it carried. Some of these vessels were ultimately converted into fire floats.

RSL – 43 ft Range Safety Launch

Type:	43 ft range safety launch
Service:	Royal Air Force
Builders:	Herbert Woods
Year Built:	1956
Number Built:	27
Displacement:	12 Tons
Length:	43 ft (13 m)
Beam:	13 ft (4 m)
Draught:	4 ft 6 in (1.37 m)
Hull:	Teak
Engines:	2 x Rolls-Royce C6.SFLM
Max. Speed:	20 knots

The RAF made the decision to switch over to craft powered by Rolls-Royce engines to replace the somewhat ageing converted 41 ft 6 in (12.65 m) seaplane tenders. The Air Ministry's Marine Craft Research and Development Department enlisted the support and expertise of Thorneycroft to come up with the new design. There were a number of key criteria for the new launch, specifically that it should be robust enough to cope with both Arctic and tropical conditions, be capable of maintaining a constant speed of around 20 knots and have a range of at least 200 miles (320 km). In addition to this the launch had to have a 2 ton tow hook, capacity to carry up to thirty passengers and be able to accommodate four stretchers. Both the passengers and crew also had to be under cover. As far as the crew requirements were concerned, the coxswain had to have good visibility from his position and a galley and a toilet were needed, as was a separate radio room.

The vessel that was created was originally considered to be a 43 ft (13.1 m) seaplane tender, but it became known as the Thorneycroft 43 ft range safety launch or simply the 43 ft range safety launch. It matched all the requirements in as much as it was indeed a robust craft which was ideal for seagoing activities including search and rescue as well as work on practice bombing ranges.

The first batch of the craft were designed and constructed at Hampton, with the Woolston yard dealing with the electrics and the Marine Engine Works at Reading handling the machinery. It was a big improvement on the 41 ft 6 in(12.65 m) range safety launch Mk I, much loved by crews because of comparative comfort, solid structure and endurance.

Although the craft was slightly slower than some of the earlier vessels (it used the same Rolls-Royce engines which had been fitted to the 63 ft general service pinnace), the craft was a far better all-round performer. The first batch came off the production line in 1953; further craft were ordered two years later being constructed by a variety of different builders to the same specification.

The vessel was given a hard chine wooden hull with diagonal side and bottom planking of double thickness. The deck planking, consisting of tongue and groove planks was laid longitudinally. The bulk of the deck superstructure was constructed of sheets of prefabricated aluminium. In recognition of the fact that it would be operating in areas where the docking facilities might be rather primitive, the keel was designed in such a way as to support itself if the craft had to be beached on a level slipway.

The hull comprised five separate bulkheads (the forepeak and the aft peak ones were water-tight up to deck level). The one which separated the wheelhouse from the galley was also water-tight up to the wheelhouse floor. The cabin was also fitted with an aluminium bulkhead that was watertight to the floor level.

The bottom and side planking was teak, each of the side planks, some ¹¹⁄₁₆ in (1.75 cm) in total, laid diagonally. The inner skin was ¾ in (1.9 cm) and the outer skin ⁷⁄₁₆ in (1.11 cm). The bottom planking was ¾ in (1.9 cm) (the inner ¼ in(0.63 cm) and the outer ½ in (1.27 cm)).

The entire superstructure, constructed of prefabricated aluminium, was both riveted and welded, encompassing the galley, wheelhouse, radio room and cabin. Port lights were fitted to the radio room; the galley and the toilet and standard windows were placed in the front, sides and rear of the main superstructure.

HSL 100 Type One – 64 ft High Speed Launch

Type:	100 class high-speed launch
Service:	Royal Air Force / Royal Navy
Builders:	British Power Boat Company
Year Built:	1936
Number Built:	22 (RAF 100–21)
Displacement:	19 tons
Length:	64 ft (19.5 m)
Beam:	14 ft (4.3 m)
Draught:	3 ft 6 in (1.07m)
Hull:	Mahogany
Engines:	3 x 500 hp Napier Sea Lion
Max. Speed:	39 knots

The 100 Class joined the RAF in 1937 in order to complement the existing 200 Class seaplane tenders. They were constructed by the British Power Boat Company, designed by Fred Cooper and built at Hythe.

In effect, the 100 Class was a stretched version of the existing 60 ft (18.3 m) motor torpedo boat and was designed specifically to RAF requirements for a high-speed launch. It had a range of 500 miles (800 km) and a top speed of 35 knots.

Three Power Napier Sea Lion engines powered the vessel, the port and starboard ones drove the outboard propeller shafts and the centre one powered the centre propeller. This meant that the craft could cruise using only the centre engine, but the arrangement of the engines and propellers also meant that it was extremely manoeuvrable.

The first 100 Class was launched in May 1936 and from the outset it outstripped all expectations and was seen to be ideal for a crew of eight. As a result of the successful trials, the Air Ministry ordered HSL 101–14 to be delivered in 1937. Two additional HSLs were ordered in 1938 and HSLs 117–132 were ordered in 1939. As it happened, the order was cancelled after the delivery of HSL 121 and the remaining eleven on order were transferred to the new British Power Boat Company's Whaleback design.

HSL 100 TYPE TWO – 63 FT HIGH SPEED LAUNCH

Type:	63 ft BPB high-speed launch
Service:	Royal Air Force
Builders:	British Power Boat Company
Year Built:	1941
Number Built:	69 (RAF 122–49, 156–90, 2546–51)
Displacement:	21.5 tons
Length:	63 ft (19.2 m)
Beam:	17 ft 6 in (5.33 m)
Draught:	3 ft 9 in (1.14 m)
Hull:	Mahogany
Engines:	3 x Napier Sea Lion 500 hp
Max. Speed :	39 knots

This high-speed launch is often known as the British Power Boat Company Type Two HSL. More commonly however, it is known as the Whaleback owing to its very distinctive humped cabin and curved hull.

As with the Type One, it was an adaptation of a successful design and production model that was being used by the Royal Navy as a motor anti-submarine boat. It used the same engines as the Type One, the Napier Sea Lions. From the outset it was armed, initially with a single Vickers .303 (or Lewis gun) in each of the turrets and later, with twin Vickers (on free mountings) either side of the wheelhouse and an Oerlikon 20 mm cannon on the foredeck. In some cases, the twin Vickers were replaced by Browning 0.5.

When the Whalebacks were brought into service in 1941, they were initially deployed in the North Sea and the English Channel. About eleven of these marine craft were lost to enemy action. Ultimately, the craft found itself in the Mediterranean and the Indian Ocean.

In all sixty-nine Whalebacks were delivered to the RAF between 1940 and 1942. The first production runs of HSLs 141–9 were built at Hythe. HSLs 122–40 had originally been earmarked for the South African Air Force, but these were actually handed over to the RAF. Most of the run of HSLs 156–90 were also built at Hythe but nine were constructed at Poole. The final batch of six was ordered in 1941.

After the craft had provided stirling service during the Second

World War, five were given to the Italian Air Force and it was proposed that a further ten would be converted into target towing launches – although this idea was later abandoned. The bulk of the Whalebacks were transferred to Royal Navy service and many were taken either to Dumbarton or to Calshot for final disposal. Nine were purchased by private buyers and became houseboats. HSL 168 was converted into a remote control target launch and was finally disposed of in 1950.

The Whaleback had a hard chine and the skin was constructed of a double layer of diagonally positioned Mahogany. The 4 in x ½ in (10 cm x 1.27 cm) planks had a layer of doped canvas between them and the planks themselves were fastened together by copper rivets and to the frame by brass screws. The frames were also made from mahogany, but had rock elm facings.

The wheelhouse and the cabin were constructed from plywood treated with a synthetic resin. The hull had six water-tight compartments separated by five bulkheads. Under the foredeck was the crew's mess, with bunks and a galley. Forward of the mess was a toilet and a washbasin.

Aft of the mess was a set of steps that led up to the wheel-house. Behind the wheelhouse, at deck level, was a chart room and a sickbay. The sickbay was designed to be able to cope with five stretcher cases. To starboard of the chart room was a small radio room and a double-berth cabin for the non-commissioned officers. To port of the chart room was a single cabin for the master.

The chart room also provided access to the forward turret. Underneath the sickbay was the engine room, and the sickbay provided access to the aft turret. There was also access to the engine via a small hatch behind the aft turret. There were three main engines, with an auxiliary engine to assist with battery charging, controls and powering the bilge pump. The two wing engines drove the propellers via direct gearboxes, whilst the centre engine drove the centre propeller. Levers controlled the engines and the engineer could communicate with the wheel-house by a visual display on the bulkhead of the forward engine.

Compared to many of the previous craft, this launch had a clear foredeck that proved invaluable for pick-ups. It was also equipped with an intercom linking the master with the coxswain, the gunners and the wireless operator.

The vessel was armed with two Boulton and Paul converted aircraft turrets, each housing a single Vickers .303 machine gun. Some also had twin Lewis machine guns on free standing mounts positioned either side of the wheelhouse. Others had a 20 mm Oerlikon fitted to the rear deck area. There was defensive anti-shrapnel padding on the sides of the wheelhouse, chart room, sick bay and radio room. There was also some armour plating behind the coxswain's and the engineer's position.

THORNEYCROFT WHALEBACK – 67 FT HIGH-SPEED LAUNCH

Type:	Whaleback high-speed launch
Service:	Royal Air Force
Builders:	John I Thorneycroft
Years Built:	1942–5
Number Built:	105 ##(191–9, 2500–14, 2563, 2583–92, 2607–18, 2632–41, 2651–76, 2717–37)
Displacement:	
Length:	67 ft (20.4 m)
Beam:	15 ft (4.6 m)
Draught:	
Hull:	
Engines:	2 x Thorneycroft RY/12 650 hp petrol engines or 3 x Power Napier Sea Lion 500 hp petrol engines
Max Speed:	25–26 knots

Thorneycroft was given the go-ahead to produce a high-speed launch after HSL 191 had been successfully tested. One hundred and five were delivered, most of them being constructed by Meakes of Marlo, at the Ranalgh Yacht Company on the Isle of Wight, or at the Walton Yacht Company.

This version of the Whaleback was used around the British Isles and in the Middle East, as well as the Indian Ocean. The armament varied, but in the early years it was usually fitted with three turrets containing .303 Vickers machine guns. In later models twin .303 Browning machine guns replaced the Vickers type. On some of the launches a 20 mm Oerlikon was fitted instead of the rear turret.

Hants & Dorset Type Three – 68 ft High-speed Launch

Type:	Hants & Dorset
Service:	Royal Air Force
Builders:	British Power Boat Company
Years Built:	1942–5
Number Built:	91 (2552–62, 2579–83, 2593–606, 2619–31, 2677–716, 2739–46)
Displacement:	
Length:	68 ft (20.7 m)
Beam:	17 ft (5.2 m)
Draught:	
Hull:	
Engines:	3 x Power Napier Sea Lion 500 hp petrol engines
Max. Speed:	28 knots

Initially the top-heavy look of this George Selman craft produced discouraging reactions. The large superstructure appeared awkward, but crews soon discovered that it was perhaps the best all-weather high-speed launch. Because the structure on the upper deck appeared so large, it was often referred to as a bus, hence its nickname, the Hants & Dorset, after a bus company operating along the south coast.

The size of the vessel allowed the crews to operate for extended periods of time away from base. It was an ideal choice, not only for the Mediterranean, but also for extended operations during and after Operation Overlord. Unlike many of the high-speed launches produced during the Second World War, the Hants & Dorset remained in service. It was converted into a rescue target towing launch, having had its armament removed. Normally it had three enclosed turrets, each with twin .303 Browning machine guns. In some cases the rear turret was replaced by a 20 mm Oerlikon cannon. Some of the craft that were used in the Mediterranean also had free-mounted Browning .5 machine guns.

MIAMI – 63 FT HIGH-SPEED LAUNCH

Type:	High-speed launch
Service:	Royal Air Force
Builders:	Miami Shipbuilding Corporation, Miami, Florida
Year Built:	
Number Built:	39 (2515–45, 2643–50)
Displacement:	
Length:	63 ft (19.2 m)
Beam:	14 ft (4.3 m)
Draught:	
Hull:	
Engines:	2 x Hall-Scott 650 hp petrol engines
Max. Speed:	33 knots

This craft, known simply as the Miami, was supplied to the RAF under the Lend-Lease Programme, in three different versions. The American version differed from the South African Air Force adaptation, and these two differed from the RAF type. The US version, for example, used Kermouth engines, producing 1,000 hp.

Unlike many of the other high-speed launches, the Miami was not used in and around the British Isles. It tended to be used in the Mediterranean, West Africa, and the Indian Ocean and around the Persian Gulf. It was this craft that was disguised as Greek caiques when HSLs 2516 and 2539 carried out clandestine operations out of Alexandria.

GROVES AND GUTTERIDGE – 60 FT GENERAL SERVICE
PINNACE

Type:	General service pinnace
Service:	Royal Air Force
Builders:	Groves and Gutteridge
Years Built:	1941–4
Number Built:	200 (1200–1399)
Displacement:	
Length:	60 ft (18.3 m)
Beam:	14 ft (4.3 m)
Draught:	
Hull:	
Engines:	3 x Gardner 6LW 102 hp diesel engines or 3 x Perkins S6M 130 hp diesel engines
Max. Speed:	13–17 knots

This 60 ft (18.3 m) hard chine pinnace was designed to replace the 56 ft (17.1 m) Admiralty version. Groves and Gutteridge at Cowes on the Isle of Wight constructed it, although Phillips of Dartmouth, as well as Herbert Woods, Ranalagh and J. S. White produced many of them under sub-contract.

There were several versions of this pinnace, including the specifically adapted ASR version and the special duty vessel that tended to be used as a hospital. Owing to its relatively slow speed and lack of armament, it tended not to be a front-line craft. Normally it was fitted with two enclosed turrets, each housing a single .303 Vickers machine gun. It was often used in conjunction with more heavily armed craft, particularly in the Mediterranean. When attached to more mobile ASR units it tended to be used either as a dormitory craft or as unit headquarters.

Vosper – 73 ft High-speed Launch

Type:	High-speed launch
Service:	Royal Air Force
Builders:	Vosper
Year Built:	1942
Number Built:	15 (2564–78)
Displacement:	
Length:	73 ft (22.3 m)
Beam:	16 ft (4.9 m)
Draught:	
Hull:	
Engines:	2 x Thorneycroft RY/12 650 hp petrol engines and 2 x 65 hp cruising engines on the wings
Max. Speed:	27 knots

Vosper Ltd of Portsmouth and Portchester were well known for producing motor torpedo boats for the Royal Navy. The Air Ministry placed a small order for 15 high-speed launches for delivery in 1942. The craft was essentially an adaptation of the D Class Fairmile, developed by Vosper's Chief Engineer, Peter du Cane. Its specific task was to deal with the hazardous conditions in the Western Approaches. It could run very well against the sea and take far less of a pounding than many other types of marine craft. It was not much loved by the RAF as it was considered to be slow and it gave the impression that it wallowed rather than sped across the water.

Fairmile – 115 ft Long-range Rescue Craft

Type:	Long-range rescue craft
Service:	Royal Air Force
Builders:	Fairmile Construction Company
Years Built:	1943–4
Number Built:	40 (001-040)
Displacement:	
Length:	115 ft (35.1 m)
Beam:	21 ft 6 in (6.55 m)
Draught:	
Hull:	
Engines:	4 x supercharged Packard 4M 1,250 hp petrol engines
Max. Speed:	33 knots

Built by Fairmile Construction Company of Cobham, Surrey, this craft was specifically designed for the Far East. It was based on the existing Royal Navy Fairmile D hull and the Royal Navy initially released twenty of these hulls for construction and modification. A further twenty hulls were ordered to complete the order. It was proposed that five flotillas, consisting of eight vessels each, would be created, and numbered 101, 102, 103, 104 and 105.

The first two flotillas were making their way to the Far East under their own steam via the Mediterranean and the Suez Canal when word arrived that the Japanese had surrendered. The Fairmiles were then used in the Mediterranean, primarily to provide search and rescue services on troop air lanes as men were being airlifted back to Britain at the end of the war. Many ended up being converted into officers' married quarters in Egypt, whilst one or two of the flotillas spent some time in Norway.

CANADIAN POWER BOAT – 70 FT HIGH-SPEED LAUNCH

Type:	High-speed launch
Service:	Royal Air Force
Builders:	Canadian Power Boat Company
Year Built:	1941
Number Built:	11 (332–342)
Displacement:	
Length:	70 ft (21.3 m)
Beam:	20 ft (6.1 m)
Draught:	
Hull:	
Engines:	2 x Packard Marine 4M supercharged 1,250 hp petrol engines
Max. Speed:	42 knots

Possibly nine of the ten Canadian Power Boat Company high-speed launches actually reached the MCU. They had been built in Montreal, Canada, and were almost identical to a 70 ft (21.3 m) high-speed launch that was being produced for the Royal Canadian Air Force. It was broadly based on Scott-Paine's 70 ft (21.3 m) motor torpedo boat hull. At least nine of the vessels, which were armed with 20 mm Oerlikon cannons, were shipped and bound for Bombay onboard merchant vessels. They were to equip Nos 231, 232 and 233 ASRUs, based respectively at Karachi, Cochin and Trombay, but it is believed that they did not arrive before the Japanese surrender.

British Power Boat – 41.5 ft Seaplane Tender

Type:	Seaplane tender
Service:	Royal Air Force
Builders:	British Power Boat Company
Years Built:	1941–4
Number Built:	67 (357–366, 441–445, 1500–1519, 1592–1609, 1612–1625)
Displacement:	
Length:	41 ft 6 in (12.6 m)
Beam:	11 ft 9 in (3.6 m)
Draught:	
Hull:	
Engines:	2 x Perkins S6M 130 hp diesel engines
Max. Speed:	23 knots

This was, perhaps, the most common ASR seaplane tender. It was widely used around the British Isles, notably by 11 ASRU Montrose, 29 ASRU Littlehampton, 31 ASRU Sheerness, 37 ASRU Lyme Regis and 46 ASRU Porthcawl.

Arguably the most accomplished seaplane tender was 1515, which operated out of Lyme Regis. On D-Day alone it picked up twenty-six paratroopers in Lyme Bay. On the same day ST 441 collected the whole crew of a Flying Fortress and ST 444 the crew of a Lancaster. This seaplane tender was designed by George Selman and was perfectly capable of coping with most sea conditions.

RTTL MK II – 68 FT RESCUE AND TARGET TOWING LAUNCH

Type:	Rescue and target towing launch
Service:	Royal Air Force
Builders:	Vosper
Year Built:	1956
Number Built:	
Displacement:	34 tons
Length:	68 ft (20.7 m)
Beam:	19 ft (5.8 m)
Draught:	
Hull:	Hard chine double diagonal planks
Engines:	2 x Rolls-Royce Sea Griffon Mk101 1700 hp engines
Max. Speed:	

An example of this launch, RTTL 2757, can be seen at the Royal Air Force Museum at Hendon. It arrived at Calshot in 1958 and served with 1100 MCU Alness between January 1958 and August 1965. It was then sent to RAF Mount Batten, where it remained until the summer of 1966, when it was transferred to the MCU at Port Rush, remaining there until the unit closed in 1971. It was then returned to Mount Batten and she was given to the museum the same year.

Vosper of Portsmouth designed the launch in 1956 to tow splash targets for aircraft gunnery purposes and had a sickbay on hand for casualties. It was also used for fire-fighting and several of the vessels made timely rescues from aircraft and from merchant shipping.

CHAPTER TWELVE

ASR Aircraft 1918–86

BLACKBURN IRIS

This large flying boat entered service with the RAF in the mid-1920s. It was powered by three 504kw/675 hp Rolls-Royce Condor engines and had a wingspan of some 95 ft (30 m). It was certainly one of the largest flying boats of its period and it was easily identified by its large biplane tail units.

The Iris had a crew of five. The two pilots sat alongside one another in a large cockpit in the bow. Aft of it was a single cockpit housing the navigator. It had guns positioned in front of the pilots, amidships and aft of the wings.

In 1927, accompanied by a Valkyrie and a Southampton, an Iris flew the Secretary of State for Air, Sir Samuel Hoare, 9,400 miles (15,100 km) around the Baltic, acting as a 'flagship' for the visit. In the following year one flew all the way to India and back, covering a staggering 16,800 miles (27,000 km).

In 1929 an improved version, the Iris III, was developed, with improved accommodation for the crew but most importantly cooking facilities, sleeping berths and space to carry out repair work.

CONSOLIDATED CATALINA FLYING BOAT

The PBY or Catalina was arguably the most famous of all flying boats. It made its maiden flight in 1935. The original aircraft had two Pratt and Whitney Twin Wasp engines and the prototype XP3Y-1 managed to achieve a speed of 184 mph (296 kph).

Its principal feature, however, was not its speed, which was quite respectable for a flying boat, but its range of 3,100 miles

(5,000 km). This meant that in any theatre, in any part of the world, it would be able to operate effectively, which was to prove to be decisive when it was deployed in the Pacific.

The Consolidated Catalina became the backbone of the United States Navy's flying boats, but compared to the Sunderland it was very poorly armed. It had two hand-operated machine guns in large observation blisters, constructed of Perspex, on either side of the hull, aft of the main cabin.

The aircraft proved an instant hit with the United States military. From the prototype alone some sixty craft were ordered. Production got under way in San Diego, California, and within a decade over 4,000 were ordered.

The first overseas purchaser was the Soviet Union, which quickly began production of their own version. In 1939, the Royal Air Force bought a PBY, and quickly followed up with further large orders. It was the RAF who dubbed the craft Catalina. The name stuck and by 1942 even the Americans were calling it by this name.

In December 1939 the new PBY-5A, with a retractable landing gear, was developed. (It was later named the Canso by the Royal Canadian Air Force). The Canadians, through Vickers and Boeing Canada, went on to build many hundreds of both the boat and amphibian versions. Other variants, such as the PBY-6A (built in New Orleans) and the PBN-10 (Naval Aircraft Factory, Philadelphia) had heightened tailfins.

In its early years with the RAF, it was used as a maritime patrol craft, for anti-submarine warfare, for torpedo attacks on surface vessels and for rescuing downed aircrew and crew that had abandoned ship. It soon established a sound combat record, being used extensively against U-boats. Perhaps more famously, it was Catalinas that located the German battleship *Bismarck* after it had evaded the Royal Navy.

The Catalina had a crew of seven, a service ceiling of 18,200 ft (5,500 m) and an average range (cruising at 100 mph (160 kph)) of 3,100 miles (5,000 km). Fully loaded it weighed 34,000 lb (15,400 kg) and had a wingspan of 104 ft (31.7 m) and length of 63 ft 11 in (19.48 m).

The aircraft excelled on long-range search, rescue and reconnaissance missions. In the Pacific in December 1941 a Catalina found and sank a Japanese submarine lurking near Pearl

Harbor; the pilot feared that he had despatched one of his own vessels when he landed at Kaneohe. In the subsequent Japanese attack on Pearl Harbor and other installations, the Catalina base was severely hit and all except three of the thirty-six aircraft were destroyed; the three remaining were airborne at the time of the attack.

As far as the RAF was concerned, the Catalina was a vital addition to its armoury. It remained a firm favourite with MCS crews who looked after the flying boats, coming second only to the much-loved Sunderland.

Martin Mariner

The Martin Mariner was the second most used American flying boat after the Consolidated Catalina. The first prototype flew in February 1939. The company had already produced some good flying boats and they were being widely used as passenger aircraft by Pan American.

The Mariner was designed primarily as a patrol bomber and since the development of the Catalina in 1935 the engines had much improved. As a result there was a significant improvement in overall performance. The aircraft was fitted with a pair of Wright Cyclone (1,500 hp) engines.

Distinctive 'gull wings' were fitted to lift the engines and the propellers away from the bow wave and spray in bad conditions. The twin fins and rudder also had a distinctive inward tilt upwards. The production model was planned to have a 0.30 gun in the nose and tail, a pair of 0.50 guns in the dorsal turret and a single 0.50 gun either side of the aircraft, housed in transparent 'blisters'.

The addition of equipment did impair the prototype's performance, and it was decided to opt for the Double Wasp engines (2,100 hp), which meant that with a full load of 8,000 lb (3,600 kg) it could cover some 2,700 miles (4,300 km). The top speed was now 215 mph (346 kph). The main reason for the upgrading of the engines was the fact that the Mariner now sported no less than eight 0.50 guns (three turrets and two waist hatches). Over 1,400 aircraft were built.

Its role as a search and rescue as well as an attack aircraft cannot be underestimated. In 1942 a Mariner picked up nine survivors from the torpedoed tanker *Arcadco* in terrible weather and under the noses of German U-boats. In 1943 when the *Cape San Juan* was about to sink, a Mariner plucked forty-eight survivors out of the sea. Mariners were also employed directly against U-boats, particularly in the Atlantic.

SARO CLOUD

The Saro Cloud had a very limited life from its first flight in 1931 to the last delivery of the sixteen ordered in June 1935. It was an amphibian and was used essentially as a 'flying classroom' to train pilots in how to fly the flying boats. It had a fully enclosed cockpit, which was a novelty for that period, and its large cabin space was ideal for the role it adopted.

SAUNDERS-ROE LERWICK

Only twenty-one of these aircraft (L7248–L7268) were built. They entered service with No. 209 Squadron (Oban, Scotland), despite the fact that there were several unresolved problems with it, notably handling difficulties.

Despite modifications there was little improvement in the aircraft's overall performance and reliability and after a few short months of operational service, it was removed from active duties in December 1941. It was just no match for the champion all-round performer, the Catalina.

SAUNDERS-ROE A27 LONDON

The London attempted to fill the role of a twin-engined coastal reconnaissance flying boat. It was a robust, simple aircraft, well known for its low maintenance needs.

A pair of Bristol Pegasus III 750 hp engines powered the prototype. The maiden flight took place in 1934 and it went into production the following year. After the prototype and the first ten production models the aircraft was remodelled as the Mark II, with Pegasus X engines (the major visual difference being the circular engine cowlings, which replaced the angled ones in the prototype and Mark I versions).

The Mark Is entered service with RAF Coastal Command in

April 1936. Only ten were built, in addition to the prototype and these were converted to Mark IIs. In all some forty-nine Londons were constructed, and it was withdrawn from service in June 1941.

The Mark II had a wingspan of 80 ft (24.4 m), was 50 ft 6 in (17.22 m) long and 18 ft 9 in (5.72 m) high. Its maximum take-off weight was 18,400 lb (8,350 kg). It had a maximum speed of 155 mph (250 kph) at a height of 6,590 ft (2,000 m), a ceiling of 19,900 ft (6,060 m) and a range of 1,740 miles (2,800 km).

Short Singapore

The Short Singapore prototype was produced in 1926, the first all-metal flying boat. The aircraft won early fame as a result of a mammoth flight around Africa by Sir Alan Cobham – a total of 20,000 miles (32,000 km).

This remarkable trip nearly began with disaster. Because of adverse weather conditions Cobham put into St Paul's Bay, Malta. Early the following day he flew on to Cala Frana, the nearby RAF base. Just as the aircraft was being towed into shelter, a large wave tore off the starboard wing tip float and it lurched to one side. It was only saved when the crew scrambled out onto the wing and kept it stable. All the time large waves threatened to wash them into the sea and in the end 200 lb (90 kg) of sandbags replaced the men.

When the bad weather had subsided the Singapore was towed ashore for repairs. Once again a terrific storm hit the base; the other wing float was lost and the port wing sank into the sea. The MCS towed it inland, but still it was battered by large waves. It was dragged over the sea wall and the port wing was smashed.

When the weather finally did clear it appeared that the aircraft was a write-off. But the RAF ground crew replaced the port wing, added new floats and generally made it airworthy once more. If nothing else, it had proved that it was indeed a sturdy and robust aircraft.

The Singapore I used by Cobham was powered by twin Rolls-Royce Condor engines (650 hp). It had a wingspan of 93 ft (28.3 m). It was, however, one of a kind, as an improved Singapore II was developed in 1930. By this time the aircraft was powered by four Rolls-Royce Kestrel engines (525 hp). The power was doubled and the hull was streamlined to prevent drag.

By 1934 the Singapore III had arrived; it was the last of Short's biplane flying boats. It was powered by four upgraded Rolls-Royce Kestrel engines (730 hp) giving it a maximum speed of 145 mph (233 kph), a range of 1,000 miles (1,600 km) and a crew of six.

The Singapore III was used out of Malta in 1937 during the Spanish Civil War, to protect British shipping. Elsewhere it was used in the Mediterranean and in the Far East. Very few were left in active service by the outbreak of the Second World War, but three were based in the Fiji Islands in 1941, being the only air cover for the islands.

SHORT SUNDERLAND

In 1937 the first all-metal monoplane flying boat, the Sunderland, showed the way forward and spelt the doom of the biplane as a flying boat.

It was powered by four Bristol Pegasus 1,110 hp engines and the huge hull was divided into two distinct sections. On the lower deck were the crew restrooms, a galley and the mooring compartment. The upper deck, apart from accommodating the flying crew (two pilots, flight engineer, navigator and wireless operator), held the huge bomb bay. The aircraft was capable of carrying up to 2,000 lb (900 kg) of bombs. These were run out on rails through hinged panels in the side of the aircraft. They were then locked into place in their dropping position under the wings.

Initially the prototype had two power-operated gun turrets (one in the bow with a .303 machine gun and a stern turret with four .303 machine guns). It was decided, however, to improve the defensive capabilities of the aircraft by adding single machine guns to the port and starboard upper beam.

When war broke out the RAF could call upon four squadrons of Sunderlands. In the early years of the war they operated out of bases in Cornwall, Devon, the Shetlands and Wales, and were the first point of defence against German U-boats. They engaged U-boats up to 360 miles (580 km) offshore. This capability,

Broadbeam Seaplane Tender 364 at Calshot in 1947. *Courtesy of John Sutherland*

A General Service
Dinghy alongside
HMAFV *Bridport*
1948.
Courtesy of John Sutherland

HMAFV *Bridport*'s Bell being handed to Corporal Coxswain John Sutherland by the mayor of Bridport, Dorset in 1948. *Courtesy of John Sutherland*

Corporal Coxswain John Sutherland on duty watch onboard HMAFV *Bridport* in Plymouth, 1950.
Courtesy of John Sutherland

Marine Tender 3129 at Mount Batten 1951. *Courtesy of Owen Newlands*

RAF Fire float at Mount Batten in 1951. *Courtesy of Owen Newlands*

MCS crew at the Lytham St Anne's transit camp, awaiting embarkation to the Far East in October 1952. Corporal Coxswain Owen Newlands is second right. *Courtesy of Owen Newlands*

HMAFV *Bridport* at Gosport in 1951. *Courtesy of Owen Newlands*

2753 pictured either 1958 or 1959. This was the last launch to serve at Gorleston.
Courtesy of Rick Mortby.

The Isle of Sheppey, Sheerness, 1957. RSL 1668, a 43ft Vosper Thorneycroft.
Courtesy of Rick Mortby

Pembroke Dock 1950-1953, showing seaplane tenders 1510 and 1511 and Hants & Dorset 2743 and 2740. *Courtesy of Rick Mortby*

Crew reclining outside of the huts at Gorleston in the 1950s. *Courtesy of Rick Mortby*

Crew of 2579, 1956-7. *Courtesy of Rick Mortby*

A post-war shot of Hants & Dorset 2556, with a cradle fitted ready to be hauled ashore at Calshot. *Courtesy of Ted Shute*

Hants & Dorset 2743 at Pembroke Dock in 1950. *Courtesy of Rick Mortby*

RSL 1668 in the Port of London during Battle of Britain Week, 1957 or 1958.
Courtesy of Rick Mortby

2748 in London 1957-8. *Courtesy of Rick Mortby*

James and Stone of Brightlingsea. This is an early 1960s RTTL Mk III, probably on acceptance trials with the RAF. *Courtesy of Rick Mortby.*

Hants & Dorset 2586 awaiting disposal at Fenara. *Courtesy of John Sutherland*

Alongside at Fenara in 1946, showing Miami HSL 2542, Pinnace 91 and Whalebacks 129 and 142. *Courtesy of John Sutherland*

1660 and 1659 at Mount Batten in 1956. *Courtesy of Rick Mortby*

Pinnace 1386 in Bridlington harbour. 1386 was probably lost off Bridlington in 1965 with the loss of two crew members. *Courtesy of Don Thurston*

Rick Mortby and Roy Smith at Sheerness, 1957-8. *Courtesy of Rick Mortby*

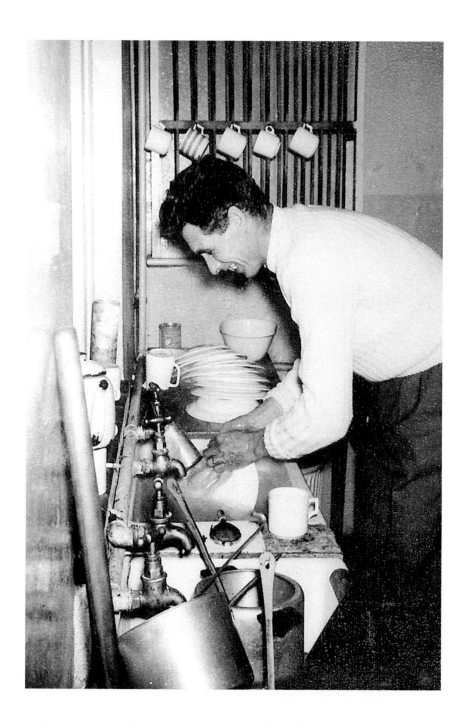

Jock Thompson at Garrison Point in the galley, Christmas 1957-8. *Courtesy of Rick Mortby*

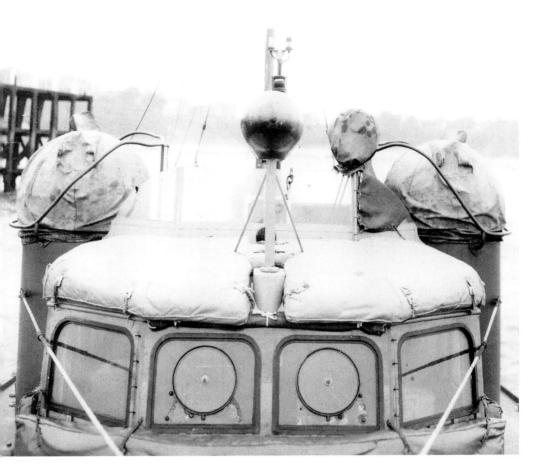

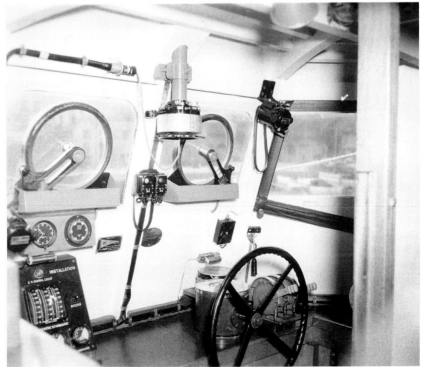

The cockpit and wheel-house of a Thorneycroft launch.
Courtesy of Ted Shute

Pinnace at Gorleston, visiting for aircrew training during the late 1970s or early 1980s. Note the privately-owned HSL on the right. *Courtesy of Rick Mortby*

together with the efforts of Coastal Command and their aircraft, kept the U-boats away from their prey close to the British ports. Gradually the effectiveness of the Sunderlands meant that the U-boats had to hunt for their prey further and further out into the Atlantic. Sunderlands were later deployed in Iceland and along the African coast in this role and proved to be a great deterrent. In its hunter-killer role the Sunderland had an endurance of around sixteen hours, compared to the Catalina's twenty-seven.

Perhaps the most remarkable feat of a Sunderland crew was a seven-day mission led by future Air Commodore Kelly Barnes. Barnes patrolled in his Sunderland for a time without seeing a single U-boat, so he put down on the water and waited, then resumed his patrol. In this way he conserved his fuel and his patrolling capability for an extended period of time, but still without spotting a U-boat.

Sunderlands were also used on rescue missions to pick up aircraft crew and ships' companies that had been forced to abandon their craft. They also engaged in mine laying.

A good example of the cooperation between services involving Sunderlands was an incident that took place on 24 June 1943. Flight Lieutenant David Hornell of the Royal Canadian Air Force's No. 162 Squadron, operating out of Reykjavik, Iceland, was aloft in a Canso. He attacked and sank U-boat 1225, but was shot down and he and his crew clambered aboard two dinghies. Two died from their injuries and exposure. Hornell had not had the chance to send off an SOS as his aerial had been shot away, but purely by chance Carl Crafft, piloting a Catalina from No. 333 Squadron, spotted the survivors of both the Canso and the U-boat. He radioed in and circled until his fuel ran dangerously low. The following day a Warwick dropped an airborne lifeboat, but Hornell and his crew could not reach it. Meanwhile an ASR launch had been despatched. A Sunderland, piloted by Ole Evensen of No. 330 Squadron, rendezvoused with the launch in the early afternoon and gave it the survivors' exact position. Evensen then flew to the spot and circled until the ASR launch arrived. Finally, shortly after 1500 hours the survivors were picked up. Unfortunately Hornell died shortly after being picked up and was buried in Lerwick.

SUPERMARINE SEAGULL (WALRUS)

The prototype of the Supermarine Seagull, better known as the Walrus, was built in 1933. It was designed by R. J. Mitchell, and was the latest amphibian aircraft in a long line of success stories.

The Walrus was originally designed to be catapulted from warships. It was very rugged, and needed to be. It was powered by a Pegasus 635 hp engine. In order to reduce drag the wheels were retractable. The pilot sat in an enclosed cockpit and there were two gun positions set in the bows and to the aft of the wings.

It became the Royal Navy's spotter aircraft, and was fitted to all catapult-equipped vessels in the fleet, but it was in its amphibian role that it won its greatest fame on air sea rescue duties.

The initial order for the Walrus came from the Royal Australian Air Force; they knew it as the Seagull IV. It had a metal hull and initially Supermarine itself constructed it. However, when they needed to step up production of the Spitfire, manufacture was transferred to Saunders Roe Ltd.

The vast majority of Walruses that were used in an air sea rescue role were wooden hulled, and were known as the Mark II. The wooden hull was an adaptation undertaken by Saunders Roe, and helped to improve the aircraft's ability to take off and land on water.

Some 746 Walruses were built, 461 of them by Saro, by the time production was finally stopped in January 1944.

SUPERMARINE SOUTHAMPTON

The Supermarine Southampton prototype was built, tested and delivered to the Air Ministry in just over seven months. It was designed to replace the F-5 in a coastal defence and Royal Navy cooperation role.

It had a crew of five (two pilots sitting together in open cockpits, a wireless operator/gunner in an amidships cabin, a bomb aimer/gunner in the bows and another gunner in a cockpit aft of the wings). The crew had facilities such as cooking and sleeping cabins in the wooden hull.

The aircraft was somewhat distinctive with its cantilever tailplane (with three fins and rudders) and the W-shaped centre interplane wing struts. It was powered by two 470 hp Napier Lion engines and streets ahead of the flying boats of its period. It had a range of some 770 miles (1,240 km), a service ceiling of 14,000 ft (4,270 m) and a top speed of around 108 mph (174 kph).

It was reliable and robust; in the summer of 1925 one flew from Britain to Egypt and Cyprus, covering a remarkable 7,000 miles (11,300 km). These were the first trials to test to see how independent and self-sustaining the aircraft could be as far as running repairs were concerned. Later, in October 1927, four Southamptons made the 27,000 miles (43,400 km) trip to Australia and Hong Kong. In early 1928 they headed out from Hong Kong to Nicobar and the Andamans, covering 19,000 miles (30,500 km).

SUPERMARINE STRANRAER

The Stranraer was a coastal reconnaissance flying boat designed by R. J. Mitchell. It was to be the last biplane flying boat. The RAF turned down the initial design, but Supermarine continued its development and it became known as the Southampton V. Eventually the improved design led to approval for a prototype to be built in 1933; powered by a Bristol Pegasus III M engine. At this point the Southampton V became the Stranraer.

The aircraft made its maiden flight in July 1934 and the prototype was delivered to the RAF the following October. In August 1935 the RAF placed an initial order for seventeen aircraft, with the production version being fitted with the Pegasus X 920 hp engine. This production model first flew in December 1936 and the first aircraft joined No. 228 Squadron, stationed at Pembroke Dock, in early 1937. An additional order for six was placed in 1936, but was later cancelled. The Stranraer was withdrawn from operational duties in March 1941, but they were still being used for training purposes until October 1942.

It was the Royal Canadian Air Force that championed the Stranraer and had longer-term faith in the aircraft. In Canada, Vickers undertook the production and the first Canadian-built Stranraer was tested in October 1938 after an initial order of three. This order was later increased to forty, but it was not until December 1941 that the full order was fulfilled. As a consequence of the slow production, only eight were in service with the Royal Canadian Air Force when war broke out. They were used for sea patrols in the Atlantic and Pacific Oceans, and were not pensioned off until February 1945.

The growing numbers of Catalinas and Cansos finally replaced the Stranraer, but the last aircraft did not leave Canadian service until January 1946. The Canadian aircraft only differed from the British version in that they had landing lights fitted to the wings. The first seventeen had Pegasus X engines and the remaining twenty-three were fitted with Pegasus XXIIs.

The Stranraer had a wingspan of 85 ft (25.9 m), a length of 54 ft 10 in (16.71 m) and a height of 21 ft 9 in (6.63 m). It had a maximum speed of 165 mph (265 kph) at 6,000 ft (1,800 m). The operational ceiling was 18,500 ft (5,600 m) and a range of 1,000 miles (1,600 m).

VICKERS WARWICK

Although the Vickers Warwick was initially designed as a light bomber, design and production delays meant that by the time it entered service in 1943 its role had been reappraised. It was used as a transport and anti-submarine patrol craft but it is, perhaps, for its air-sea rescue role that it is best known as it was capabe of carrying an airborne lifeboat. Although originally designed to replace the Wellington bomber, the prototype orders were cancelled in 1936 when the decision was made to standardise 4-engine bombers. Vickers, however, persisted with the development of the aircraft, initially deciding to use Rolls-Royce Vulture water-cooled engines. But due to production difficulties air-cooled Pratt and Witney engines replaced these. Vickers' persistence paid off and some 219 Warwick Is were built.

Coastal Command began using them in an anti-submarine role, but from 1943 they were deployed in an air-sea rescue role, loaded with the MkIa lifeboat. The Warwick could drop the lifeboat to ditched aircrew from a height of around 700 ft.

The Warwick II was designed to carry both bombs and torpedoes and 132 were built. The Warwick III was primarily used as a transport. It was unarmed and some 100 were built. The Warwick V was heavily protected by 7 machine guns and also carried mines and depth charges. Although 210 of this model were built they did not see active service in World War Two.

Westland Lysander

Although it was not a flying boat, the Westland Lysander was much used in an air sea rescue role from 1940 onwards. It saw extended service in the English Channel and the North Sea. It was used to spot downed airmen in the sea and to radio surface vessels with instructions for picking them up. It also carried a dinghy and other lifesaving equipment, including food and medical supplies, which were dropped from the wings.

Originally Lysanders was designed for close cooperation with the army; they became known for their ability to land and take off in extremely small fields, and were widely used to transport agents to, and pick them up from, enemy occupied Europe.

At the outbreak of war there were four Lysander squadrons operating in France, 170 aircraft in total. By the time of Dunkirk, after being heavily committed in spotting roles and other duties, the aircraft began to take heavy casualties. By the time they returned from France, some 120 had been lost.

They continued to patrol the skies after the fall of mainland Europe in the role of anti-invasion reconnaissance. Had the Germans launched Operation Sealion (the proposed invasion of Britain), the Lysander was earmarked for use in machine-gun and bombing attacks on German troops on the beachheads.

CHAPTER THIRTEEN

Bases and Operations 1918–86

Many of the pre-war MCS bases have already been mentioned in the first two chapters of this book. Also of interest in this respect is the account of the service of C. W. Bullock in Chapter 10. The main focus of this chapter is the war and post-war years. Particular attention is given to the key bases during the history of the MCS and later the ASR and the MCUs.

SUMMARY OF AIR SEA RESCUE UNITS DURING THE SECOND WORLD WAR

Number	Location
1	Lerwick
2	Shapinsay
3	Thurso
4	Wick
5	Meike Ferry
6	Invergordon
7	Burghead
8	Buckie
9	Fraserburgh
10	Aberdeen
11	Montrose
12	Tayport

13	Methil
14	Berwick-upon-Tweed
15	Blyth
16	Hartlepool
17	Scalloway
21	Bridlington
22	Grimsby
23	Wells-on-Sea
24	Gorleston-on-Sea
25	Lowestoft
26	Felixstowe
27	Dover
28	Newhaven
29	Littlehampton
30	Cowes and Gosport
31	Sheerness
32	Calshot/Ostend
33	Calshot/Norway
36	Poole
37	Lyme Regis
38	Exmouth
39	Torquay
40	Portland/Weymouth
41	Salcombe
42	Newlyn
43	Mount Batten (Plymouth)
44	Padstow
45	Barry
46	Porthcawl
47	Aberystwyth
48	Tenby
49	Fishguard

50	Swansea
51	Pwllheli
52	Holyhead
53	Fleetwood
54	Douglas (and Peel and Ramsey)
55	Kirkcudbright
56	Porta Ferry
57	Donaghadee
58	Larne
59	Stranraer
60	Lough Foyle
61	Campbeltown
62	Lock Boisdale
63	Menia Bridge
64	Drummore
65	Oban
66	Stornaway
67	Port Ellen
70	Iceland
71	Gibraltar
101	Calshot/Malta
102	Calshot/Fraserburgh
103	Calshot
104	Calshot
105	Calshot
201	Freetown/Aberdeen
202	Bathurst
203	Colombo
204	Kalafrana
207	Aden
208	Alexandria
214	Masirah (detachment at Ras-El-Hadd)

215	Hedjuff. In March 1945 215 ASRU was at Mesirah with Miami HSLs 2538, 2649, 2650, 2738.
216	Aden. In January 1945 216 ASRU was at Aden with Miami HSLs 2515 and 2536.
217	Banana. The unit was Banana in April 1944 with Miami HSL 2644 and Pinnace 1300.
218	Port Etienne. The unit was at Port Etienne, Dakar, in July 1943 with Miamis 2648 and 2545.
219	Mombasa. In January 1944 the unit had Miami HSLs 2643 and 2645. It was in Basra in February 1945 with HSLs 2517, 2527, 2531 and 2535.
220	Hordio. The unit is posted as being at Benda Alula, Aden, in March 1945 with HSLs 2646 and 2650.
223	Bone.
224	Phillipeville. The unit was created in Algiers in September 1942 with HSLs 139, 171, 179 and 2546. HSL 139 was scrapped at Port Said in 1945, and 171, 179 and 2546 were given to the Italian Air Force. ASRU 254 loaned HSL 2600 to ASRU 224 in July 1943. It too was given to the Italian Air Force. In February 1944 the unit comprised HSLs 133, 139, 171, 179, 182, 2546 and 2606.
225	Algiers. Created at Algiers in November 1942 with HSLs 174, 175, 176 and 182. HSL 182 was detached to 223 ASRU Bone in March 1943. 172 was sent to Bari in November 1943 to replace HSL 176. In December 1943 HSL 172 was posted to ASRU 253 and HSL 174 was similarly transferred in January 1944.
226	Calcutta
227	Maiskal Island
228	Chittagong
229	Calcutta
230	Vinzagapatan
231	Madras

232	Cochin
233	Bombay
234	Trombay
235	China Bay/Trincomalee
236	Khulna/Kayts
237	Galle
238	Cochin
239	Chittagong
240	Vizagapatan
241	Jiwani
242	Bombay
243	Colombo
249	Takoradi
250	Nassau
251	Bone. Formed at Bone in January 1943 and took delivery of Pinnace 1245 in February 1943 and Pinnaces 1221 and 1217 in March 1943. Allocated HSLs 2593 and 2581, which left for Malta for routing to 207 ASRU Aden in October 1945. All personnel transferred to 253 ASRU in January 1946.
252	Ischia. Formed at Algiers January 1943 with Pinnaces 1222, 1238 and 1263. ASRU 223 and 224 were merged in February 1944 to create ASRU 252 Western Italy. In April 1944 HSLs 2606 and 139 were at Anzio, 133 and 179 at Ischia and 171 and 187 at Ponza. Most of the unit was transferred to ASRU 254 at St Tropez in June 1945. HSL 2599 of ASRU 253 and 2699 of ASRU 254 arrived in Piraeus in November 1944. This created the new 252 ASRU, to which would be added Pinnace 1246 and 1267 and in October 1945, from 204 ASRU Kalafrana, Pinnaces 1263 and 1266. HSL 2599 was handed over to the Royal Hellenic Air Force in August 1945. In November 1945 252 ASRU was disbanded with

	the remaining personnel posted to 253 ASRU Bari.
253	Bari (detachment Ancona). Unit formed in June 1943 with two crews from Dover and two from Gorleston. In July 1943 the unit had HSLs 2581, 2598, 2593 and 2599 in Malta and in late July moved to Syracuse. In November 1943 2598 was attacked; one crew killed, one wounded and the launch sunk. In March 1946 253 ASRU disbanded.
254	Ajaccio (detachment St Tropez). Created in West Kirkby June 1943. June and July 1943 it assembled at Algiers, with HSLs 2580, 2582, 2595, 2596, 2597, 2600, 2601, 2699 and Pinnaces 1266 and 1267. 254 ASRU closed in November 1945.
255	Khulna

AIR SEA RESCUE CONTROL UNITS (ASRCU)

There were three ASRCU, 300 at Palermo, 301 at Bastia and 302 at San Maria Di Leuca.

MARINE CRAFT TRAINING SCHOOLS (MCTS)

Number 1 MCTS	Calshot, then Corsewall
Number 2 MCTS	Kipevu
Number 3 MCTS	Fanara

Maintenance Units for Marine Craft (MU)

62 MU	Dumbarton
84 MU	Calshot
85 MU	Felixstowe
97 MU	Ferryside
213 MU	Dumbarton
238 MU	Tewkesbury

Marine Craft Units (MCUs) during the Second World War

Abidjan	Aboukir	Addu Atoll	Akureyn
Akyab	Alexandria	Alness	Apapa
Arzeu	Bahrain	Bally	Banana
Basrah	Batavia	Bathurst	Beaumaris
Bermuda	Bizerta	Bowmore	Budareyi
Calshot	Castle Archdale	Changi	China Bay
Cochin	Cononada	Cocos Islands	Colombo
Congella	Dakar	Dar-Es-Salaam	Diego Garcia
Diego Suariz	Dumbarton	Falmouth (Mount Batten in support)	
Fanara	Felixstowe	Fisherman's Lake	
Fornebu	Fourah Bay	Freemantle	Gibraltar
Grasnaya	Habbaniya	Half Die	Hamworthy
Hedjuff	Helensborough	Invergordon	Ischia
Iwakuni	Jessone	Jiwani	Jui
Kai Tak	Kalafrana	Kelia	Kemajuran
Killadeas	Kipevu	Kisumn	Koggala
Korangi Creek	Lake Indawgyi	Lake Timsah	Langebaan
Largs	Lawrenny Ferry (Pembroke Dock in support)		
Libreville	Lindi	Lough Erne	Lough Neagh
Manfredon	Masirah	Mauritius	Mount Batten
Naples	Oban	Oesthaven	Palermo
Pamanzi	Pembroke Dock	Penang	Pointe Noire

Poole	Port Etienne	Port Reitz	Port Said
Port Suiz	Port Victoria	Rangoon	Redhills Lake
Reykjavik	Scaramanga	St Lucia	Seletar
Seychelles	Socota	Soerabaya	Stranraer
Stavanger	Sullum Voe	Tayport	Thorney Island
Tjilitjap	Trincomalee	Trombay	Tulear
Wig Bay	Windermere Lake		Woodhaven

POST-WAR MARINE CRAFT UNITS (MCU)

1100 MCU	Invergordon/Alness
1101 MCU	Fowey
1102 MCU	Falmouth
1103 MCU	Felixstowe (with detachments at Gorleston and Sheerness)
1104 MCU	Bridlington
1105 MCU	Porthcawl/Portrush
1106 MCU	Drummore
1107 MCU	Newhaven and Thorney Island
1108 MCU	Blyth
1109 MCU	Boston
1110 MCU	Immingham
1111 MCU	Lyme Regis
1112 MCU	Tayport
1113 MCU	Holyhead
1114 MCU	Ramsey
1124 MCU	Seletar
1125 MCU	Glugor
1151 MCU	Marsaxlokk
1152 MCU	Khormaksar/Masirah
1153 MCU	Fanara/Limmassol

CALSHOT

Between 1918 and 1961, RAF Calshot was home to the School of Air Sea Rescue, No. 1 Marine Craft Training School, No. 103 ASRMCU, No. 84 MU, No. 32 ASRMCU, No. 102 ASRMCU, No. 33 ASRMCU, No. 104 ASRMCU, No. 105 ASRMCU, No. 10 ASRMCU, No. 1102 MCU and No. 238 MU.

In October 1912 the Admiralty had decided to set up a chain of air stations to help defend the coastal waters. On 29 March 1913, with Lieutenant D. A. Spenser Grey (RN) in command, Calshot came into existence. Initially it was unimpressive, with a handful of Coastguard's cottages and three sheds to house twelve aircraft.

From the outset it became one of the primary bases to test the seaplanes that would be used by the Naval Wing of the Royal Flying Corps. On 20 January 1914 Squadron Commander A. M. Longmore took command of Calshot. With war looming, the Castle Yacht Club's clubhouse became the officers' mess and with an influx of personnel Calshot became an integral part of the coastal defences. It was primarily involved in anti-submarine warfare, convoy protection and training. In 1916 aircraft from the base flew nearly 3,500 hours, with the loss of only five officers and men. On 30 November 1916 Flight Sub-Lieutenant Ross helped sink the German submarine UB 19 off Portland.

Calshot and its two sub-stations at Portland and Bern Bridge were amalgamated in January 1917 and called the Portsmouth Group. Wing Commander A. W. Bigsworth was the commander. From May to July 1917, Newhaven (seaplane station), Cherbour and Polegate (airship station) became part of the group. Another submarine kill was recorded on 18 August 1917 when Flight Sub-Lieutenant C. S. Mossop, in a Wight seaplane, sank UB 32.

During 1917, another 3,500 hours of flying was carried out by the Calshot (Portsmouth Group) pilots using Short seaplanes, Felixstowe flying boats and Curtiss H 12s.

On 1 April 1918 Calshot became part of the RAF, and was now officially known as RAF Calshot. It was in this guise that innumerable ASR and MCU personnel would know the place. Calshot had three flights, two of flying boats (345 and 346) and one of seaplanes (410). The three were merged in August 1918 as 240 Squadron, commanded by Captain C. L. Scott.

After the First World War, Calshot became the School of Naval Cooperation and Aerial Navigation. It was now the home of training for maritime air and boat crew in the RAF. In 1922, No. 480 (Coastal Reconnaissance) Flight took the base over and it officially became the RAF Base, Calshot. In February it became the home of the Marine Craft Training Section (MCTS) and over the next few years this grew, becoming the centre not only for motorboat crew training, but also for marine engine fitting and boat-building.

In 1927, Calshot was visited by the RAF High-speed Flight (see chapter 1). It returned in 1929 to defend its Schneider Trophy title. According to C. W. Bullock, who as motorboat crew at Calshot witnessed the two Schneider Trophy races on the Solent in 1929 and 1931, there was a large fleet of RAF vessels present. He estimated that around fifty craft of various types were there for the 1931 race. The duties of the crew of course involved 'standby flying' at selected positions around the course during the practice sessions and the race itself. They also towed racing seaplanes and ferried visitors to and from Lee-on-Solent, Portsmouth and Southampton. On the race day they ferried visitors to the aircraft carrier *Argus,* which was at anchor off Ryde and operated as a floating grandstand. Visiting marine craft were on station at Calshot for around two weeks.

Before the 1929 race a Royal Navy control motorboat was transferred to the RAF and used as a safety boat at Felixstowe, which was then the permanent base of the Schneider Trophy team, and they moved to Calshot before the race. A number of 22 ft (6.7 m) Sea Cars, made by Brooke Marine of Lowestoft, were used with the High-speed Flight, powered by 100 hp engines; they were withdrawn from service shortly after the races.

Aircraftman Shaw (Lawrence of Arabia) was a frequent visitor to Calshot in the 1930s. Together with Wing Commander S. W. Smith, he tested and reported on a number of RAF marine craft during this period, including the 200 Class.

Work continued at Calshot throughout the 1930s. Empire Air Days were held at the base, notably in 1935 when 1,000 people watched the five hours of flying. With the outbreak of war in 1939 the base reconfigured itself for possible attacks, adding 3 in (7.5 cm) anti-aircraft guns and barrage balloons. There was a growing commitment to the training of marine boat crews, who would be much needed during the looming hostilities. Five of Calshot's seaplane tenders left for Dunkirk on 31 May 1940. Two were lost, but the others managed to evacuate around 500 men. Another was lost when they tried to drop off a naval landing party (see chapter 3).

Calshot was mercifully saved from the worst of the bombing offensive in 1940, but on 24 September one of the anti-aircraft guns claimed a Heinkel bomber.

On 31 March 1941 the first conversion course to train fitter 11Es to become marine fitters got underway. There were forty-five men on the course and by the end of the year some 600 had been through the training.

On 21 May 1942 the Marine Training School transferred to Corsewall, Galloway, but Calshot continued to run and repair marine craft. Many of the ASRUs created during the war started at Calshot and this trend continued, with the base operating as a 'way station' for crews and craft.

After the war, Calshot became the home of Nos. 230 and 201 Squadrons in 1946 and the following year No. 4 (Coastal) OTU was transferred there from Pembroke Dock. It became No. 235 OCU, flying Sunderland flying boats. During Operation Plain Fare, the Berlin Airlift in 1948, Sunderlands out of Calshot flew 1,000 sorties, taking in supplies and evacuating over 1,000 children.

The OCU returned to Calshot in December 1948, but were almost immediately transferred to Pembroke Dock. In October 1953 Coastal Command lost Calshot and it became part of Maintenance Command and the home of No. 238 Maintenance Unit.

The base soldiered on through the 1950s, becoming the home of the Bomb Disposal Flight and the Equipment, Explosive and Fuels Training Unit in 1956. In 1957 it was home to the Maintenance Command Ground Defence School. It was finally closed on 1 April 1961, after forty-eight years of service to the RAF.

LYME REGIS

The RNLI left Lyme Regis in 1932, because it was felt that the lifeboats operating out of Torbay and Weymouth were adequate to cover this stretch of the coast. It was, however, subsequently found to be an ideal site for an RAF MCU; the coastal waters around Lyme Bay were being used for bombing and firing practice. The first of the RAF personnel began to arrive in 1937.

The MCU initially comprised armoured target boats and range safety launches. They were at hand in case an aircraft was forced to ditch in the sea. Many of the personnel had to cover both Lyme Regis and the bombing and machine-gun ranges at Chickerell and Chesil beaches. It was at first issued with two 30–31 ft (9.1–9.4 m) seaplane tenders. A further craft was later added. The basic duties included patrolling the bombing and machine-gun ranges, keeping other craft out of the area and, of course, responding to aircraft crashes.

The unit became known as 37 RAF MCU, under the command of Warrant Officer Biff Turner, who was later posted to Malta and survived the siege, but was mugged in Alexandria whilst on leave. He was pushed under a tram and lost an arm, but returned to ASR duties.

In 1938 there was an incident when a new craft nearly did not arrive at Lyme Regis. Coming by road, it got stuck against a tree partway down a hill leading to the base.

An incident in August 1939 saw the unit out searching for two boys who were lost in a dinghy. After a box search from Charmouth to Seaton the boys were found. Also in 1939 an armoured deck craft arrived to be used as a target for bombing practice. The crew were paid an extra 1s (5p) per day as danger money.

When war broke out in September 1939, Lyme Regis was given its own not very impressive defences. A single First World War vintage Lewis gun, in a sandbagged emplacement, was placed in front of the old cement works. The RAF crew were allowed limited practice with a handful of rounds against a floating drum in the sea.

One of the MCU craft was attacked soon after, whilst undergoing engine tests off Monmouth beach. Luckily there were no injuries and RAF fighters scrambled from Exeter shot down the

German aircraft. Around this time it was decided that the MCU craft should be armed and gun-mounting rings were fitted in preparation for the arrival of Browning machine guns.

The first ASR call-out took place in the summer of 1940. A Heinkel bomber of KG 27 was intercepted by 213 Squadron's Hurricanes. Pilot Officer H. D. Atkinson shot it down and the crew of five baled out. The MCU duty craft hunted the seas and managed to rescue one of them; another was captured, two bodies were washed up on the coast and the body of the fifth was never found. During the 1950s the bodies of the two men were exhumed from Lyme Regis and buried with full military honours at the German cemetery at Cannock Chase, Staffordshire.

In January 1942, 37 ASR/MCS Lyme Regis was formed. It came under the command of nearby RAF Warmwell. At that time the seaplane tenders (304, 305 and 480) were set aside for ASR duties. In addition the unit had a 16 ft (4.9 m) inboard dinghy and a pair of dumb dinghies. The Royal Navy air sea rescue boat *Ministre Lippens* supported the unit.

On 3 February 1942, Flying Officer Sir Algernon Guinness took command of 37 ASR/MCS. His first crash call was on 15 April when an RAF Halifax, flying back to its base at No. 10 Squadron, Leeming, Yorkshire, was hit and lost height about 8 miles (13 km) out of Lyme Regis. It was too low for the crew to bale out and they had to ditch. ST 480 easily picked them up.

On 11 May 1942 the unit took possession of ST 1506 from the British Power Boat Company, after tests at Calshot. Then on 30 July the *Ministre Lippens* picked up the crew of a Beaufighter. The biggest operation that year, however was the rescue of refugees fleeing from Guernsey after the Germans occupied the island.

October saw the arrival of ST 1515 to replace the ageing ST 480, which was sent to Mount Batten. In fact the unit received ST 480 back in January 1943 after ST 304 sank in force ten gales in the harbour on 12 November 1942.

On 31 August 1943, ST 480 managed to save a Mosquito pilot of No. 151 Squadron (Middle Wallop), but throughout September the unit was largely confined to harbour by the poor weather conditions. An armoured target boat arrived on 21 October, and the last action of the year took place on 5 December, when ST 1506 picked up a crew off Abbotsbury.

In 1944, 18 March proved to be a busy day for the unit. The seaplane tender towed a Sea Otter into the harbour, as the aircraft had been unable to take off. Later the unit heard that a Ju 88 had crashed into the sea off the coast at Honiton. ST 1515 was despatched to find the crew, but it later transpired that they had baled out over the land and had been arrested by the Honiton police.

In April 1944 the unit was busy covering the American landing exercises at Slapton Sands. The exercise, Operation Tiger, was designed to simulate the landings on the Normandy beaches. The whole area was evacuated and there was, in theory, a strict cordon around the sea approaches. Somehow, however, on 28 April, several German E-boats slipped through the net and created havoc; some 750 American soldiers were killed when their landing crafts were sunk. The entire episode was kept under wraps and the soldiers were buried in mass graves. The full truth of the disaster was not made public for forty years.

There was intense activity in the region in May 1944, when the unit received official warning of the D-Day landings on 6 June. The unit saw vast numbers of Typhoons and other fighters on exercises in the area. One of the unit's craft, ST 1515, was posted off Portland Bill on D-Day itself; all the other craft were put on station all day, the men watching the vast airborne armada passing over their heads. Fortunately the only crash in the area was dealt with by local fishermen, but two days later a Warwick went down 6 miles (9.5 km) off Seatown. ST 305 picked up the crew and ST 1506 salvaged what they could from the wreckage. On the same day, 8 June , ST 1506 was sent to pick up the crew and passengers of a Horsa glider that had gone down 10 miles (16 km) off the Normandy coast. The crew of ST 1506 had to smash holes in the fuselage to get the men out but they were all brought safely back to Lyme Regis.

On the 24 June, with most of Calshot's vessels operating out of the Mulberry harbours off the Normandy coast, ST 1515 and ST 480 were detached and sent to Calshot for a month. On 25 June the crew of ST 1506 managed to pick up the crew of a ditched B 17 Flying Fortress that had gone down 10 miles (16 km) to the south of Lyme Bay.

On 13 July 1944 the unit made another rescue around 20 miles (32 km) south-west of Lyme Regis. The rest of the year was dogged by poor weather and by the turn of the year, the war in Europe had progressed well away from the shores of England. On 15 February the unit hunted for survivors from two landing craft off Exmouth, but nothing was found. The following month saw an inspection by the Air Ministry and the arrival of RSL 2546. The war in Europe was drawing to a close; it was an ominous sign for the unit.

On 11 August 1945 an aircraft went down off Wyke Regis and ST 1506 and HSL 2509 (out of Weymouth) headed off to find them, but local fishermen had found them first.

On 6 November the unit became the responsibility of RAF Exeter and by early 1946 it had been reduced to just ST 1506; the other craft were sent back to Calshot. By 30 January the Lyme Regis unit had become non-operational. A handful of men were retained and as late as 1951 there were still thirty officers and men there. On 24 January of that year Air Chief Marshall Sir Hugh Saunders inspected the unit and ST/RSL 1509 was posted there.

The Royal Navy and the RAF constantly used the waters close to Lyme Regis for live bombing practice. This clearly upset the local fishermen, who were barred from the area on live bombing days. What irked them even more was the lucrative trade being carried out by the unit. The RAF launches, which were faster than the fishermen's boats and already knew where the bombs would be dropped, hastened to the scene and scooped up the dead fish. They then sold them to local hotels and fishmongers, much to the chagrin of the fishermen. After complaints, a suitable accommodation was made.

On 9 September 1952 a Meteor F8 (226 OCU) crashed 50 miles (80 km) south of Bridport. The unit's craft went out to investigate over two days, but found nothing (the pilot was actually picked up by the Royal Navy).

There was a disaster on 22 October when ST 1594 broke from her moorings and was washed ashore in the early hours of the morning, and was very badly beaten up. Then on 31 October a Hawker Sea Fury of 738 Fleet Air Arm Squadron crashed into the sea 3 miles (5 km) off Charmouth. The unit's launch managed to rescue the pilot, Lieutenant Dru Montagu, and the crew managed to keep the aircraft afloat long enough for a Royal Navy salvage unit to recover it.

In 1952 the unit's strength stood at thirty-six airmen and two civilians. During this period (and up to 1955) various exercises were carried out to test the efficiency of helicopters and their ability to pick up ditched crew.

In 1959 there were no less than three helicopter crashes in the Portland area. They were all HAR 3 Whirlwinds (two from 815 FAA Squadron on 21 and 29 April and one from 737 FAA Squadron on 29 September), and all failed as a result of difficulties with the rotor gearbox. Despite these problems, the MCU knew that it was only a matter of time before helicopters replaced their craft.

In 1960 the MCU had an establishment of twenty-six airmen and five civilians. An accident that year to RSL 1660 led to an inquiry by Flight Lieutenant Twibill (1107 RAF MCU Newhaven), but no action was taken. Repairs were undertaken, but it was a quiet period for the unit.

The bombing ranges were still being used by a variety of aircraft, including Canberras, Scimitars, Hunters, Sea Vixens, Meteors and Shackletons. On 15 August 1960 the unit's RSL 1664 towed in a yacht that had got into trouble off Burton Bradstock. Then in September it towed in another yacht that was in difficulties in heavy seas off Beer Head; a fishing boat picked up the yacht's crew. October saw a series of 'wet jumps' by 1 Parachute Training School, Abingdon, on the first occasion twenty-seven troops were picked up by the unit and later 200 more.

The end of the unit seemed imminent by the close of 1960, there were fewer calls, lower establishment figures and the ever-present helicopters. However, increases in flying operations in the area caused the decision to be delayed until 1964. On 24 July 1964 the end finally came and the launches were repainted for the occasion. Many of the crews were posted to other ASR bases. Several of the men settled locally and when the RNLI re-established itself at Lyme Regis in June 1967 they were amongst the first to volunteer as crews. Officially, 1111 MCU was no more.

MOUNT BATTEN (CATTEWATER)

No. 39 ASRU Torquay, which began operations in July 1942, was officially placed under the command of Mount Batten from

February to September 1944. The unit initially had one high-speed launch, but this was later increased to four.

No. 41 ASRU Salcombe which was established in April 1942 was also under the command of Mount Batten. The unit had two pinnaces, working with No. 276 Squadron's Walruses. After a time, four high-speed launches were attached to it, and it continued operations until it was disbanded in July 1945.

No. 43 ASRU Mount Batten existed for only a short time in 1944. It covered the D-Day landings with six high-speed launches. It was formed on 20 April and disbanded on 9 September.

No. 1101 MCS Fowey was originally established in June 1942 with a pinnace converted into a target-towing vessel transferred from Mount Batten. RAF Fowey was officially created in September 1942, becoming operational in the September. In April 1945 the Fowey unit was redesignated as No. 1101 MCU. It remained at Fowey until March 1958, when it was transferred to Mount Batten.

Mount Batten, or Cattewater as it was then known, was a Royal Naval Air Service (RNAS) station from 1913–18. In 1913 seaplane trials were carried out there, but the site was not developed until 1916. It was operational by 1917, primarily as a base for the fourteen Short 184 seaplanes that carried out patrols in the coastal waters.

Cattewater became RAF Mount Batten after the RNAS joined the RAF. Initially the new base was run down, largely because the Air Ministry did not wholly own the land. This all changed with the purchase of the land in 1923 and over the next eight years enormous building work was undertaken. Quarters and sheltered hangars were built. RAF Mount Batten went operational in early 1929 with the arrival of No. 203 Squadron, equipped with Supermarine Southamptons. Later, in January 1930, No. 209 Squadron, flying Blackburn Iris and Blackburn Perth flying boats, was stationed there until May 1935.

In 1930 Aircraftman 'Shaw' (the pseudonym of Lawrence of Arabia) also arrived. He was to play a huge role in the development of high-speed launches and pinnaces, and spent three years at Mount Batten.

In 1936, No. 204 Squadron, which had been at Mount Batten briefly in 1929, returned, flying Saro London Mark II flying boats.

When war broke out in 1939, the squadron converted to Short Sunderlands, although only six were operational at that time.

By the middle of 1940 Mount Batten had administrative control of ASRUs 39 Torquay, 41 Salcombe and 43 Fowey. In August 1940 a detachment of No. 10 Squadron, with four Sunderlands, arrived. No. 204 Squadron was posted north and then to West Africa.

On the night of 27–28 November Mount Batten was heavily bombed, but perhaps an incident in June of that year was more significant as far as the long-term use of the base was concerned. On the 18th a Walrus, flown by Flight Lieutenant J. Napier Bell and Sergeant Harris of the Royal Australian Air Force and Corporal Novell of the RAF, took off for Brittany. Their mission was to pick up the wife and children of General Charles de Gaulle. Unfortunately, after taking off just before 0300 hours, there was no further contact from the aircraft. It was foggy on the Brittany coast and the aircraft crashed, with no survivors, near Keranou.

The men of No. 10 Squadron were Royal Australian Air Force personnel, and the RAAF were stationed at Mount Batten for the duration of the war. They played a major role in the Battle of the Atlantic in 1943; No. 10 Squadron accounted for three U-boats and lost eight aircraft. Another eight were lost in 1944.

Throughout this period the MCU was busy dealing with the needs of the flying boats, using Pinnaces 15 and 17, seaplane tenders, refuellers such as 1197 and bomb scows. In addition, of course, there were the ever-present ASRUs with their high-speed launches. Even after hostilities ended in Europe, No. 10 Squadron remained at Mount Batten. There were several German U-boats to round up as they had returned to the waters off the south-west of England towards the end of the war. Having flown over 3,100 operations and covered over 4.5 million miles (7.2 million km), they finally returned to Australia in October 1945.

Mount Batten now became the base for No. 238 MU, which remained there until September 1953. It was then taken over by the Marine Craft Training School, which had a thirty-year association with Mount Batten. Interestingly, for much of that time the personnel attending the training school were taught their skills on wartime craft.

By 1961 Mount Batten had become the main station of the RAF Marine Branch. The existing hangar and slipways were improved to assist the training of the crews. For the most part the personnel were engaged in air sea rescue and target towing, although the former was gradually being phased out as a result of the introduction of helicopters.

Many of the newly trained crews found themselves posted overseas from Mount Batten, whilst others were transferred to home stations. During the 1960s the base was also the home to the School of Survival. All aircrews were required to take a course there; the facilities at the base were ideal, particularly with the presence of the Marine Branch. The other users of Mount Batten were the Engineering Branch, who were charged with the responsibility of servicing vessels and transports.

By the mid-1950s the RAF had helicopters, which meant that the ASR role of the Marine Branch was less important. None the less, at Mount Batten and elsewhere, there were instances when helicopters were not suitable for pick-ups and marine craft were still deployed in the traditional ASR role. As with many of the RAF bases that were home to the Marine Branch, however, the demise of the flying boat inevitably spelt the end of a long association. Gradually at Mount Batten, as with other stations worldwide, the marine craft and personnel were first scaled down and then disbanded.

The Marine Branch, as a separate entity, closed in January 1986.

Index